THE ROAD HE TRAVELLED

The Revealing Biography of
M. SCOTT PECK

ARTHUR JONES

London • Sydney • Auckland • Johannesburg

First published in 2007 by Rider,
an imprint of Ebury Publishing, Random House,
20 Vauxhall Bridge Road, London SW1V 2SA

Random House Australia (Pty) Limited
20 Alfred Street, Milsons Point, Sydney,
New South Wales 2061, Australia

Random House New Zealand Limited
18 Poland Road, Glenfield,
Auckland 10, New Zealand

Random House South Africa (Pty) Limited
Isle of Houghton, Corner Boundary Road & Carse O'Gowrie,
Houghton 2198, South Africa

Random House Publishers India Private Limited
301 World Trade Tower, Hotel Intercontinental Grand Complex,
Barakhamba Lane, New Delhi 110 001, India

The Random House Group Limited Reg. No. 954009

The Random House Group Limited makes every effort to ensure that the papers
used in our books are made from trees that have been legally sourced from well-
managed and credibly certified forests. Our paper procurement policy can be
found on www.randomhouse.co.uk

Typeset by SX Composing DTP, Rayleigh, Essex
Printed and bound in Great Britain by Clays Ltd, St Ives plc

A CIP catalogue record for this book
is available from the British Library

Hardback ISBN 978-1-84-413576-9
Trade Paperback ISBN 978-1-84-604079-5

Dear God

I ain't what I wanna be,
And I ain't what I'm gonna be,
And I sure ain't what I ought to be.
But thank God I ain't what I used to be!

Gert Behanna

For Meg Stewart, and Leslie and Marilyn Jones,
my sister, brother and sister-in-law.

CONTENTS

INTRODUCTION

Life is difficult.

> The opening sentence in
> *The Road Less Travelled*
> M. Scott Peck, MD

Mention *The Road Less Travelled,* and back like an echo comes the name M. Scott Peck. Three decades ago, Peck, an American psychiatrist, literally trailblazed his book of that name across the United States, and then around the world, to create a new genre of personal development coupled to spiritual self-exploration. He had created one of the most successful commercial books in history. It sold more than seven million copies in the United States and a further three million worldwide. Peck became an entry in the *Guinness Book of Records* as the living author who'd spent the longest period with one book on the *New York Times* bestseller list.

But it was not Peck's impact on publishing, rather his effect on his readers' lives, that warrants an assessment. On the strength alone of correspondence to Peck, judged from the thousands of letters the book generated because he included his home address, *The Road Less Travelled* liberated people from the emotional, traumatic or abusive spectres of their past.

Six months after his death in 2005, and forty years after he decided to write *The Road Less Travelled,* the post for 'Dr Peck' was still arriving at the house on Bliss Road, New Preston, Connecticut. In March 2006, a reader in Bargara, Queensland, who had only recently discovered the book and, unaware Peck was deceased, wrote, 'I want you to know it has given me courage and hope and has helped, in part, to clear the mists of confusion and doubt more than anything else anyone has written or said to me. You have been as a Prophet to me by speaking my own language, by being a translator, a conduit, a transmitter, a conductor – I am now allowing myself to accept the Grace that is offered to me. It is hard to take, but I cannot throw it back any more.'

Peck knew the book's origins. 'It was my own journey,' he said, 'and I was even working out my journey as I wrote it.' But it became much more. An American college dean of students in Maryland, Paula Matuskey, said she believes *The Road Less Travelled* 'began a movement of writing that looks to spiritual journeys – something we Baby Boomers seem to dwell upon. I'm just glad I read it when I did.' Another college dean, who wrote to Peck from the American South, revealed what Peck's book triggered as people read it, 'a very difficult although important synthesis of psychology and religion. Your writings have done much to help crystallise some of my thoughts and to raise other far-reaching questions.'

There are hundreds of such letters in Peck's archives covering the three decades since *The Road* appeared. Pathos abounds in some. One man wrote, 'I finished reading your chapter on dependency and I can't do anything until I find help for my problem in that area. I want to live so badly and yet I am not living now. I am numb and empty and helpless to change.'

A woman 'in the middle of reading your book,' liked it because 'you so honestly say what is wrong, as in facing problems. I have never heard anyone speak so honestly. I want to thank you for that. I also want to solve my problems. I want to try to escape suffering. I want to feel the pain inside. I want to help myself grow emotionally. I want some mental health. I need these things.'

His readers felt they knew Peck, they later came in their hundreds to his workshops and talks, as he brought them out of isolation into a community of readers who realised they were not alone in their emotional upheavals. 'I can't tell you how wonderful it feels that I am not alone,' wrote a doctoral student who said she felt 'alone, outside the group of others who seem so certain about God and what life is all about. Now I feel that I'm not just a misfit who couldn't accept the religion I grew up with, to leave a marriage looked upon by friends and family as perfect, but which felt empty to me. As I read your book I knew certainly and instantly why I had to leave.'

Psychotherapist M. Scott Peck, in part a wounded healer, became far more. He was dubbed, 'the nation's shrink'. Through *The Road Less Travelled* millions of Americans adopted him as their therapist and guide on their own psycho-spiritual journey out of personal woundedness and familial or social uncertainty, unpleasantness or pain. Dr James Guy, then dean of Fuller Theological Seminary's Graduate School of Psychology, called Peck 'a prophet to the seventies'. It's a comment to return to. *The Road* addressed, in Peck's later words, 'a lack of rigour' in the society of the seventies. If he was a damaged man examining a damaged generation he was also, in *The Road* and later books, placing first a generation, and then the nation on the couch he normally reserved for individuals in his psychotherapy sessions.

Americans in the 1960s, said Peck, were numbed and confused by the traumas of presidential crime (Richard M. Nixon and the 'Watergate' burglary), soaring prices, Cambodian bombings, the National Guard shootings at Kent State, the assassinations of innocent Vietnamese at My Lai, the brutal Manson murders, the police riots at the Chicago Democratic Convention, the assassinations of two Kennedys (John F. and Robert F.), of Martin Luther King and Malcolm X. By contrast and comparison, Americans in the 1950s, when Peck was an adolescent and then collegian, were regarded as staid and conformist. It was something of a mirage. Those who grew up in the 1950s (Peck's generation), knew about the tumultuous undercurrents and understood them because many of them were generating a questioning turmoil themselves by decade's end. It was the late 1940s of Peck's parents in their prime, when things were truly staid and conformist.

The 1950s' young Americans broke through the chains, the 1960s' generation picked up their new freedoms and ran with them this way and that. By the 1970s, Americans of the troubled 1960s were already trying to resolve their anguish, come to terms with the anything-goes society and hedonistic values that roiled what was otherwise a current of genuine concern for society and its needed transformation. Young America had locked on to the anti-War movement, the Free Speech movement, and the Hippie Movement. Peck's later take was that hippie-dom in its first flowering – despite the hippies' extremely vocal detractors down to the present – in fact initially did give hope to millions of young people. But the Hippie Movement fizzled, a fizzling that left many of those same Americans more bereft than before. They joined the millions of others not caught up in the social movements and hippie-dom, who were nonetheless similarly uncertain and disillusioned. They, too, sought certainty amid doubt. The 1960s decade of legitimate protest, serious rhetoric and social debate had deteriorated from genuine cause to personal narcissism and hubris. It was hard to sift out the sense from the blather.

Many Americans were troubled, they were in therapy. Others were drinking too much, they were in AA. Some were abusing drugs too freely and frying their brains. A generation engaging too widely and wildly in Free Love could not identify true love or learn to settle down. Some bailed out, others looked on. It was among those struggling out of this maelstrom, and those who had been standing around its perimeter looking on with a mix of awe and fear, who provided the many millions of readers who found a new, definable, understandable, graspable handhold in *The Road Less Travelled*. Peck became their guide out of their personal and social wilderness, as he provided a psychotherapeutic commonsense along with the particular hope found in spiritual direction. These were the people who, in the 1980s and 1990s, came annually by the thousands to Peck's lectures and workshops. Seekers. And questioners.

The US socio-religious mixing bowl of the 1960s and 1970s was further stirred by new currents of religious thought and questioning. The immutable Roman Catholic Church had held the Second Vatican Council (1962–1965) and turned the inward church outward. Catholics are a quarter of the US population. There was enthusiastic talk of ecumenism and inter-faith dialogue. There was a new mood in many branches of religion for inquiry, for a cautious setting aside of built-in prejudices. In the United States, certainly, individuals were nearly always wondering about God in their lives. The wave Peck caught was well described in 1975 with the question 'Are We a Nation of Mystics?' posed by National Opinion Research Center sociologists Andrew M. Greeley and William C. McCready. (Peck later commented, 'God, don't I wish.')

It was the statistics that said America was a nation of mystics, and the trend continued. In 2003 sociological researcher Jeffrey Levin and his colleagues noted that the majority of Americans reported some mystical experience in their lifetimes. Plus, the prevalence of mystical experiences was increasing. Some 67 per cent of Americans reported incidents of déjà vu, and 65 per cent instances of extra-sensory perception (ESP). Americans, as usual, were wondering what was going on in their lives and minds. Peck, with *The Road*, was on hand to tell.

The plethora of self-help books and seminars – soon to be jolted out of favour into obscurity by *The Road Less Travelled* – existed at a time of burgeoning of retreat centres and houses of prayer, along with a widening variety of twelve-step programmes. The Western trek to the mystical East was well under way, popularised not least by the Beatles' journey to the ashrams and their consorting with gurus. Peck, through reading, had made that Eastern trek in the 1950s, when it was still considered weird. At age twenty he described himself as a Zen Buddhist, a declaration that would cause an uproar with his future in-laws. By the 1980s, the United States had added an academic edge to the spiritual searching. American universities, institutions that previously had offered only 'theology', now opened Departments of Religious Studies.

The book's title was conflated in short form from two lines in a poem by Robert Frost and 'The Road Less Travelled' quickly entered common usage and endless adaptation. Travel writers frequently use 'The Road Less Travelled' as a headline highlighting little known vacation venues. Sports headline writers love the phrase, modified to 'the road least travelled' when unlikely teams make it to the finals. In *Men's Health* magazine, the car talk column by 'Crankshaft Don' is 'The Road Less Troubled'. And on it goes.

Peck was a healer, a man whose door, in his son's words, was always open to the psychologically wounded and emotionally damaged. In person, or through the printed page, psychotherapist Peck had a reputation for reaching into the depths of people's agony to find the words, the knowing description, the spiritual message, delivered with a firmness of purpose, that would assuage their pain. It was an incredible feat. He wrote what he felt, and what he felt was pain. He wrote about what they needed, and he needed unconditional love. He wrote about what held everything in life together, about love, and a sense of the spiritual. He had a dark side. To paraphrase the Australian author and critic Clive James (writing about the poet Philip Larkin), Peck may have done and said noxious things, but he didn't do them or say them in his books. On the printed page Peck won attention, and eventual fame, by revealing what psychological self-exploration meant, as he explained how to move forward from emotional pain with a spirituality-based contemplation.

He created a standard for writing about achieving or regaining psycho-spiritual stability after an emotional trauma, or a traumatic start to life. When he died in September 2005, widely editorialised though less frequently eulogised in obituaries in the major publications and on the radio, despite his dozen other titles, it was Peck of *The Road Less Travelled* who received the plaudits. In the obituaries, his second book, *People of the Lie*, often received favourable mention, but beyond that, like the books and the man himself, the story seemed to matter less and less. His work was labelled 'self-help'. Many he helped would regard that categorising as a debasement of his strenuous accomplishments. Much of his later work was short-changed. But as his reputation slipped into the shadows, he was also spared an expanded public lambasting for some of his behaviour had the writers and critics gone investigating.

His nephew, the Rev. David Peck III, an Anglican priest, summarised that Scott Peck's 'deepest contribution to the Church and psychiatric and therapeutic communities was his apologia of the faith of Christ and the place of grace in the world, in communities and individual lives, however marred by sin and selfishness. His defence of the faith was probably the most effective in popular culture in his generation. He was a great teacher and evangelist in the American Protestant self-help tradition.'

In the three decades since *The Road Less Travelled* first appeared (in 1978), initially nationally unnoted and unloved, Peck lived much of his inner life, and a modicum of his personal life, in public. As book followed book, and talk followed talk, Peck, in print and person, increasingly spoke of his struggles through his life, acknowledged sins and failings, yet steadfastly refused to cease his Christian searching, questioning, and his need to teach, all the while providing his readership and listeners with the best answers he had for every step of the way. On the printed page, the answers were frequently – though not always – written in short, sharp, succinct sentences, or meaningfully told through well crafted cameos. He was a worldwide phenomenon. His work was translated into more than a dozen languages, including Korean and Arabic, Serbo-Croatian and Japanese, Italian and Russian.

At Peck's memorial service in New York's Christ Church on Manhattan's Park Avenue, the country music producer Kyle Lehning said that despite Peck's own views to the contrary, M. Scott Peck was 'ninety per cent artist and ten per cent scientist.' And that parallels the perception of this biography, which is offered as a writer's tale of a writer's tale.

Peck never became the writer he'd early hoped to be. He was a good genre writer, but never a great one. He was, however, a great healer through the printed word. It was an impressive achievement and if not always art, there was a certain artistry that created a fresh literary medium, the fusion of science and spirituality in popular form. On the road, on the platform, usually seated because of a bad back, he was warm, witty, likeable and encouraging – an engaging and enduring teacher. People loved him as a teacher. But he loved his students only up to a point. He didn't want them to get too close, though he did love them in return, and many who came to know him in the two decades following the 1978 publication of *The Road Less Travelled*, in overwhelming number speak and write of him with a deep affection, even love.

In December 2003, when the interviews and research for this book began, Peck was sixty-seven. He was still on a spiritual quest but had other companions on the road last travelled. One was Parkinson's disease. It had begun to make steady inroads into most aspects of his daily living and threatened, in time, to dominate the external man. His Parkinson's disease was officially diagnosed in 1999, but Peck suspected he'd already been battling it for quite a few years beforehand without acknowledging its presence. More likely, he was denying its presence.

On that December day, four years after the Parkinson's diagnosis, Peck glanced out of his front window. On the other side of the narrow road, Peck could see Lake Waramaug partly frozen. He explained there was a one-dollar bet, a lottery with his staff, on the precise date the lake would freeze over completely. It was an annual ritual. The betting originated early, when Peck and his wife Lily first moved into the house, in early winter 1972. He could bet with Lily no more. Earlier that year, Lily, his wife of forty-three years, had walked out of the house and filed for divorce. Lily, a friend said, 'had left the marriage long before she left the house.' Lily and Scott had two daughters and a son. Peck was estranged from one of his daughters and had a strained relationship with the other two children.

Peck was alone in his large eighteenth-century-origin lakeside home in rural western Connecticut, except for a staff of two. During the week he was writing songs, planning a musical, completing his book on exorcism, urging the establishment of a third political party, drafting discussion starters on democracy and, within limits, entertaining a flow of guests. He'd never had much interest in society's social ills. 'I will admit to having a contrarian streak,' he said. He didn't see the 'light of Christ' among the poor, he said, 'precisely because I'm told to see it there.'

In his New Preston home, Peck made his way to the sunroom. Even though Parkinson's was causing him to stoop, Peck was still almost six feet tall. His fair hair had thinned; behind the circular glasses that were a trademark his eyes were bright. He moved carefully, he'd added weight since his slender years on the speaker's circuit. His sonorous speaking voice was beautifully modulated, his vocabulary range that of the well-educated, his ability to present clearly complex concepts undamaged by Parkinson's, though his memory for names would occasionally fail. A recent CD of his song 'Free Will' was circulating among friends. He called its message 'anti-secularist'. The phrase 'secular humanist' was a nasty epithet in Peck's lexicon. Around the house he whistled as he walked, walked sometimes steadily, sometimes unsteadily. 'Parkinson's changes from one minute to the next,' he said.

Through the side windows the bright red of the two barns stood warm sentinel against the chill of a snow-covered countryside. He settled down into a cushioned rattan chair with his Camel cigarettes, a six-decade addiction. He was also a gin drinker. When on the lecture circuit he invariably had a bottle of the local brand, Lake Waramaug Gin, in his luggage; that and several cartons of the Camel cigarettes he still smoked at the rate of more than a pack a day.

The tape recorder was on, the face-to-face conversations began. He wanted it immediately known that he hated journalists, didn't trust them, never had. Over the next two years of interviews, if Peck could think of some incident or scene to better express his dislike of journalists he never hesitated to make the most of it. He had reason to be afraid of their questioning. His occasional blistering attack on reporters was no more severe, however, than some of his asides and scorn dropped on preachers, publishing house editors or US presidents. He had his opinions and was pleased to air them to any who would listen.

At no time was Peck bowing to his winters, or to his Parkinson's disease. He was working on his next book. He might walk with death, his own dying, but he wanted to talk and – as he had for decades – to continue to capture his experiences as teaching moments. In our interviews he was candid almost to a fault, whether describing his discovery of sex as a teenager, his loss of his libido in his fifties, his spirituality, or his Parkinson's disease.

He was like the zinnia stalks in his winter garden, a bit bent and battered by life's changing season, and by his Parkinson's disease. Like the zinnias, though, he was nonetheless still erect, still defying the season much of the time. He could be moody, even depressed. In company he was determined to keep talking, moving on, moving forward.

Those who know Peck's public story will recall that Peck's Christianity was non-denominational, and not lifetime. He was not baptised as a child but in 1980 at age forty-three, in the chapel of an Episcopal convent by a southern Methodist minister. He belonged to no particular church, attended several, and until Parkinson's ended his driving regularly took the Eucharist. Now it had to be celebrated at the house. Sometimes he celebrated his own 'rogue eucharists'. Was he afraid of death? Peck replied, 'Less than I used to be, but yes, still afraid.'

As a writer, in his best snatches he was a fine stylist, tight and to the point, with an understated humour. On the road, with practice, Peck became a polished performer at the lectern, with a particularly winning, low-key style. He was a convincing homilist in the pulpit, and could be a hands-off leader in a workshop.

In 2003, Peck in those unsteady days rode his stairlift up to his bedroom at night, took rare excursions outside the house reliant on canes and the company of others. Scientist, psychotherapist, physician, preacher or prophet, he was still tapping into people, as challenging as ever. His psychotherapeutic secret, to the extent it was a secret, was that he knew what people yearned for, even when they didn't quite know themselves, because he yearned for it, too. His skill was his ability to convey his understanding of their yearning in words that helped.

In September 2004, he gave his 800-page manuscript for his final book to his agent. It was overdue and over-long. He had good reason for being late. But it was done. It's about the Devil, the two exorcisms he led, a tale of two women possessed, and Evil. Capital D for Devil, capital E for Evil. He'd wanted to call it *Glimpses of Satan*, instead *Glimpses of the Devil* appeared in 2005 to mixed reviews as he and his new wife, Kathy Yeates Peck, sailed off on a fifty-eight-day cruise around Latin America, and successfully avoided two months of media interviews.

In an introduction Peck wrote for *A Thomas Merton Reader*, he described Merton as 'an extraordinarily complex and complicated man, multifaceted, diverse and variable.' If that is writer-psychotherapist Peck introducing himself, it will, for the moment, do quite nicely indeed.

BIOGRAPHER'S NOTE

M. Scott Peck wanted a 'warts and all' biography. He did not object to, or hide, much of the darker side of his personality and behaviour. Equally, he was determined that people around him not be further hurt. He agreed in advance, in writing, that he would not see this manuscript or any draft of it prior to publication, and yet would co-operate. His specific no-go areas were that I not approach his children for interviews, though if they chose to approach me that was up to them. And that though he would not discuss their divorce, I was free to contact his ex-wife, Lily. I wrote to Mrs Peck. She did not reply. After Scott Peck's death, Mrs Kathy Peck, Scott's second wife, in a move not prompted by me, arranged matters so that indeed I did interview Christopher Peck, Scott and Lily's third child and only son.

It must be said that during our sixty or seventy hours of interviews and telephone chats, a majority of them tape recorded, Peck's decision to stay with the truth on difficult topics was generally steadfast. I also had full access to twenty hours of interviews with Peck conducted in the late 1990s by the psychologist Dr James Guy of Pasadena. Guy had thought at one point of attempting a Peck biography. The tapes were transcribed and remained in Peck's keeping. Peck made them available to me. I am grateful to the generosity of both men. Because Peck gave many of the same answers to Guy's and my similar questions – occasionally word-for-word identical answers – Guy's interviews are woven in with my own (begun half-a-decade later), except where otherwise indicated.

Peck was a performer, many of his answers were a verbatim repetition of paragraphs in his books, or anecdotes or jokes he'd regularly told, or replies given repeatedly during interviews or during question-and-answer sessions following his talks. His recall of what he'd written or said was uncanny.

Elements of the Jones–Peck writer–subject relationship as it developed in the course of our interviews are discussed in a closing Appendix.

ACKNOWLEDGEMENTS

Scott Peck's public saga began with reviewer Phyllis Theroux's landmark assessment of *The Road Less Travelled* in *Book World*, the *Washington Post*, 27 September 1978. For permission to use it in its entirety over chapters seven and eight I am particularly grateful. Thank you, Phyllis.

This book opens with the phrase, 'Life is difficult' (epigraph to the Introduction), from *The Road Less Travelled*, by M. Scott Peck, MD. Copyright © 1978 by M. Scott Peck, MD. Reprinted with the permission of Simon and Schuster Adult Publishing Group.

Jonathan Dolger of Jonathan Dolger Literary Agency, New York, as Peck's literary executor, kindly gave permission to excerpt the material regarding the Rev. Malachi Martin from the closing chapters of *Glimpses of the Devil: a Psychiatrist's Personal Accounts of Possession, Exorcism and Redemption* (2005).

The material reprinted from *The Hartford Courant* (23 February, 1986), specifically from its *Northeast* magazine article, 'On the Road with M. Scott Peck', by Gary Dorsey, is 'Copyright, 1986, Hartford Courant. Reprinted with permission'.

My thanks to Ben Yagoda for permission to quote at will from his on the road with Dr Peck article in *Connecticut Magazine*.

Quotations from *Aurora* magazine's interview with Dr Peck are used 'With Permission of Athabasca University's *Aurora*.'

I talked about Dr Peck with Dr Gerald May, and acknowledge the now late Dr May's permission to quote from his review of Peck's book in the *National Catholic Reporter*. My thanks to the *Reporter*'s editor, Tom Roberts, for permission to quote extensively from May's review, from my Peck essay, and other kindnesses. Similarly, I am grateful to the Rev. Richard Woods, OP, for permission to quote from his review of *Glimpses of the Devil* in the same publication.

The Rev. John W. Donohue, SJ, kindly gave permission to quote from his article on Dr Peck in *America* magazine.

I acknowledge the quotation in chapter two regarding Sullivan & Cromwell is from *Dulles: A biography of Eleanor, Allen and John Foster Dulles and their Family Network*, by Leonard Mosley (Dial Press/James Wade), and I am grateful to Sullivan & Cromwell partner John L. Warden for providing a copy of Judge David W. Peck Senior's contribution to the firm's *Centennial Book*, for details regarding the firm's early Jewish partners, and other information.

I acknowledge two one-line quotations, by Eleanor Roosevelt and US Senator Joseph McCarthy, from William Manchester's *The Arms of Krupp* (Little, Brown & Co.), also in chapter two.

The antepenultimate and penultimate paragraphs of chapter fifteen are from *The Door* magazine. To Harry Guetzlaff and all those in times past associated with *The Wittenburg Door* and *The Door*, I am grateful for permission to quote those and other items. (I'm particularly grateful to them for the opportunity to finally use the word 'antepenultimate' in print.) Dr Peck's quotation regarding Thomas Merton is taken from Peck's Introduction to *A Thomas Merton Reader*, by Thomas P. McDonnell (Random House).

I acknowledge quotations regarding Peck from the *Watchman Expositor* (Rick Branch) and H. Wayne House's article M. Scott Peck, 'Travelling Down the Wrong Road' (Christian Research Institute), and the line quoted from Roy H. Smith's article in *Pastoral Psychology* (Volume 40 (3), January 1992, 179–187. My thanks also to Dr Hendrika Vande Kempe for permission to quote from her chapter, 'Historical perspectives: Religion and Clinical Psychology in America', in *Religion and the Clinical Practice of Psychology* (1995). To Cindy Lollar for an interview and permission to quote her article in *Campus Voice*, my thanks.

My thanks to Dr Melissa Jones for permission to quote from her research into the religious revival of the 1960s and 1970s. My thanks to Jonathan Yardley of the *Washington Post* for permission to quote from one of his columns (*Book World*, 10 January 1988) a remark concerning the writings of John P. Marquand. Similarly, Michael Dirda kindly allowed me to quote from his 13 February 2003 essay in the *Washington Post* 'Book World'. And while I did not quote from *Marquand: An American Life*, by Millicent Bell (Atlantic Monthly/Little, Brown & Co.), I did read it for the period Peck was close to Marquand.

Andrew Billen of *The Times* of London gave permission to quote from his interview with Peck, Peck's final interview of any length in a newspaper.

I suppose I could write a book without the assistance of Jean Blake, my aide-de-camp for three decades, but it would be a sorry thing and I wouldn't want to attempt it. Once again, thank you, Jean.

Genuinely appreciated is the generosity of Dr James D Guy, executive director of the Headington Institute in Pasadena, California, a psychologist and friend of M. Scott Peck, in making his interviews with Peck available. And while in Pasadena, my thanks to Michael Murray of Fuller Theological Library and the archives there, whose staff gave me every assistance in researching the Peck material in 2003 and 2006.

Alas, I could not trace the successor to Vineyard Books, Inc. for permission to use the closing prayer (from *Celtic Invocations* by Alexander Carmichael, Vineyard Books, 1972). However, as Vineyard had kindly given me permission years earlier to use similar material in one of my books, I trust they would have done the same for this.

If, at gatherings or on airplanes, someone asked me what I do and I admitted I was an author, this book-in-progress was always a conversation starter. Not since my biography of *Malcolm Forbes* (Harper and Row, 1978) had I been engaged on a biography whose subject was almost universally known among the glass-of-wine-in-hand or airline-travelling Westerners. The reactions to *The Road Less Travelled* (I never, in passing, met anyone who'd read more than three of Peck's books) were almost invariably an endorsement of Peck's skill in reaching them.

These casual conversations added immeasurably to my understanding of Peck's impact. I thank my momentary travelling companions, and those, too, who responded to the 'Author's Queries' in the American daily newspapers.

In the same vein, among colleagues called on for insights, I thank Joe Feuerherd, Tom Fox, Lewis Wolfson, James Flanigan, Geoffrey Smith and James Srodes. I happily acknowledge the bubbling enthusiasm of Johann and Addy Griesser at our meeting in San Diego, plus insights from *The Road Less Travelled* readers and writing enthusiasts who included relatives – Terri Griesser, many O'Briens and the Glatzes – and neighbours: Joanne Duffy and Dan Saffer,

Cheryl and Jeff Bubier, Suzie and Al Coven, Heather and Bill Brach, Yvonne and Glenn Treslar, Felicia Parker, Linda Hawkins, Kathy Rogers, Barbara and Richard Sirudy, Mary Jean Davis, Pat and Neil, et al.

One's agent is in at the start of the process, one's editor in at the conclusion.

Following the death of my agent, Robert Ivo Ducas, who was in at the book's beginnings, Tom Wallace of New York's T.C. Wallace Agency scooped up Robert's bequest, the as-yet unsold Peck manuscript, and through the English agent Laura Morris, saw its sale to Random House/Rider UK. Thank you, Tom and Laura.

I salute Robert's memory and thank his wife, Louise Chinn, for her continuing interest in the project.

At our initial meeting in London, Judith Kendra, Random House/ Rider Editorial Director, and I quickly found ourselves on the same wavelength. Judith handled the editing, my queries and changes by email with dispatch. She fine-tuned an upright piano of a manuscript into something approaching concert grade. It was a pleasure to work with you, Judith. Thank you.

To my children and daughter-in-law, Chris, Ian, and Mike and Kim, my apologies for beginning every conversation with 'Peck's progress' for the last several years.

As ever, I am grateful to my wife Margie for her steadfast refusal to read a word I write before it is published (and sometimes not even after it is published). And for her refusal to touch even a single piece of carelessly strewn paper in my chaotic study. On such considerations and kindnesses are built long-lasting love and marital harmony. Love ya, kid.

CHAPTER 1

THE PECKS OF PARK AVENUE

U ntil he was eight, life for M. (for Morgan) Scott Peck was, essentially, reassuringly pleasant. The household on New York's prestigious Park Avenue was dominated by two ambitious and sports-minded macho males – Scott's father, David Warner Peck, Senior, an extremely successful young lawyer, and his brother, David, Junior, almost four years older than 'Scotty'.

David was an outgoing, highly energetic, physically brave and strong, and oft-times bullying, older brother. He was a stark contrast to Scott Peck's own introspective, weakling temperament. Fortunately, 'Aunt Sally' Hooten in the kitchen, the housekeeper who came in daily from Harlem, was good at drying tears, for unfortunately, Scott Peck frequently needed his eyes wiped. He was a bright lad, eager to please, happy to enjoy the world around him, but he cried easily. However, one day when Scott Peck was eight, the tears dried up. With a couple of minor exceptions, M. Scott Peck did not cry again for almost thirty years, by which time he was a thirty-six-year-old Lieutenant Colonel in the US Army and a practising psychiatrist.

Two incidents in one week induced the no-crying trauma. Scott and David were attending a private middle school in Manhattan when, for reasons undisclosed to history, David, age twelve, was asked to leave. The Peck parents placed David and Scott in a another exclusive boys' school, St Bernard's, but, again for reasons never explained, Scott Peck skipped a grade and, instead of going into third grade, entered fourth grade. St Bernard's 'was a decidedly British-style private grammar school with a fairly harsh regimen,' he said. It possibly needed a harsh regimen to cope with David. Scott was a different child.

On his first day in class he was no sooner seated than the teacher, a Mr Spicer, began to slowly read the story of Robert the Bruce and the spider. The tale deals with how, under the watchful eye of the Scottish king, the spider continually tried yet failed to start its web. The story describes how the spider tried and tried again until it was successful. Because the spider did not give up, Robert decided he must not either, but must return to battle and regain his rightful throne. Scott Peck was fascinated, and enjoyed the tale. He had noticed his classmates taking notes. When Mr Spicer finished, they were 'still scribbling frantically,' he recalled. 'I looked over at the little red-haired boy to the left of me to try to figure out why. When he finished, he saw me peering at his paper, raised his hand, and exclaimed in a loud voice, "Mr Spicer, sir, the new boy next to me is cheating."' The teacher arrived from his desk at Peck's, snatched up the paper and said, 'Why, this paper is empty.' They stared at each other, 'he with astonishment, me with dawning horror. "There isn't anything on it." It had been a dictation class,' said Peck. 'I began to cry, which was hardly the thing for a boy to do on his first day in fourth grade in a new school.' (The humiliation associated with his snickering classmates and his own despair burned itself into Peck's psyche. Sixty-one years after the incident, the medicated and dying Peck was in tears as he recalled yet again the oft-told tale of his humiliation.)

Scott's parents did not deal with the incident kindly. An evening or two later, Mr and Mrs Peck were walking near Times Square when they saw a novelty store that printed mock front pages of newspapers. The next day they presented a newspaper to Scott. The headline stated: 'Scott Peck Hired by Circus as World's Greatest Crybaby.' So stung was he by this parental prank that Scott Peck vowed to never cry again. (Thirty years later his own three children were so tired of hearing the story that they had another front page mock-up made with the same headline and stuffed it into Peck's Christmas stocking.)

Until that moment, for young Morgan Scott Peck life wasn't difficult, it was comfortable. He was a Depression-era baby but never experienced the effects of financial hardship. In the early 1940s, the Peck apartment at 863 Park Avenue, the first one he remembered, was spacious, one in a twenty-two-unit condominium building at 65th Street, where apartments today go for between $5 million and $6 million. Father, David Warner Peck, Senior, who'd graduated from Harvard Law School at twenty-two – two years ahead of his age group – had already worked for the US Attorney

General in New York, next with an international cartel arbitration team in London, and was then brought into New York's Sullivan & Cromwell, Wall Street's most prestigious international firm, to build its litigation department.

Mother, Elizabeth Saville Peck, easily handled cocktail hours and dinners for guests such as the brothers Dulles, John Foster and Allen, Tom Dewey, and their ladies. John Foster Dulles was not only Sullivan & Cromwell's senior partner, he became President Eisenhower's Secretary of State, a position at that time regarded as the second most powerful in a US administration. Allen Dulles, also an S&C partner, had been an Office of Strategic Services (OSS) operative in Switzerland during the Second World War, and, when the Central Intelligence Agency (CIA) was formed, was in time its chief. Thomas Dewey was an organised-crime-busting district attorney, later New York governor. As an unsuccessful presidential candidate against President Harry Truman, Dewey was famed as the man in a *Chicago Tribune* headline that declared, the morning after the voting closed, 'Dewey Wins', though in fact Dewey lost.

Evidently a fledging social scientist and anthropologist, Scott early understood the isolation which life at 863 Park Avenue represented. 'There were two apartments to a floor, separated by a small foyer and an elevator. As there were eleven storeys above the first, this building was the compact home for twenty-two families. I knew the last names of the family across the foyer. I never knew the first names of their children. I knew the last names of two other families in the building; I could not even address the remaining eighteen. I did address most of the elevatormen and the doormen by their first names; I never knew any of their last names.'

David Peck and Elizabeth Saville Templeton very likely met in 1928 on a New York-bound ocean liner out of Southampton during the period Peck Senior worked in London. They were married in 1929, just after the Wall Street Crash, herald of the Great Depression. Scott Peck believes one of the reasons his father may have married Elizabeth, in addition to the fact she was very beautiful, was that she was a very beautiful WASP, a White Anglo-Saxon Protestant, and his father much prized WASP status and style. Three years after they were wed, their first child, David Warner Peck, Junior, was born. And three years and ten months after David, on 22 May, 1936, came Morgan Scott Peck. The Morgan, for his paternal grandfather, was early dropped in favour of 'Scotty'.

There was not only a profusion of Pecks, but a confusion of David Pecks – three Davids across three generations. And as they emerge and merge together in the story to follow, it is probably fair to tag them now for easy identification. Scott's father is referred to as 'Peck Senior' until the point he is named a judge; thereafter he is 'Judge Peck'. Scott's brother David is 'brother David', even though the term sounds slightly monastic. And Scotty's nephew, brother David's son, the Rev. David W. Peck, III, known to the family as 'Tertius', is – after his initial introduction – referred to as 'nephew David'.

Scott Peck's forebears trace back, as do those of practically all New England Pecks, to two brothers who arrived in the American colonies in the mid-seventeenth century. A genealogy compiled by a distant relative traces Scott Peck's branch back to Deacon Paul Peck, who arrived in 1635 on the ship *Resolution*, to settle in Hartford, Connecticut. Deacon Paul's brother, Joseph, arrived three years later and settled in Milford, Connecticut. New England offered only rocky soil farming and when, in the nineteenth-century, better lands opened up in the Midwest, Scott Peck's great-grandfather, Egbert Peck, was apparently among those who left Vermont and elsewhere in New England for richer soil in Indiana. He settled in Goodland, Indiana and married Gertrude Morgan. She and Egbert appear to have had only one child, Dumont Morgan Peck ('Pecky', Scott's grandfather), who attended Wabash College in Crawfordsville, Indiana. Dumont remained in the town after graduating, and became partner in a haberdashery with a man called Warner. Either before or after establishing that partnership, Dumont married Warner's daughter, Juliet, Scott Peck's grandmother. They also had one son, David, Scott Peck's father, later to become Judge Peck.

Dumont Peck loved his son David and showed it by teaching him two things: how to drive and how to play golf. Dumont Peck owned one of the first automobiles in Indiana, and as there were no driver's licences in those days, David was permitted to drive the family car at about the age he could first see over the steering wheel. Family trips were not always a joy, and for the times, became extensive voyages. On rough roads, regularly stopping to fix flat tires, Dumont, Juliet and David annually drove the thousand miles from Indianapolis to visit the Morgan family homestead in Vermont. There was always a side trip to Buffalo, to visit Juliet's relatives.

The Peck generations, from grandfather Dumont to Scott, also represented three generations of golfers. Though Scott played on occasion with his father, he never was on the links with his grand-father. 'Pecky was good fun,' said Peck, whereas 'my grandmother, a tiny woman, was very smart. She was kind of tart-tongued and she and my grandfather would argue about bridge hands they'd played thirty years earlier. She was also a bit of a disciplinarian. I never felt she liked children much.' At age eleven Peck, who suffered from eye infections, was sent to Florida to his grandparents because his parents thought the change of climate might be good for his eyes. The elderly couple had moved from Indiana to a small apartment on New York's Lower East Side, and they wintered in Florida. When his visit was over, but before he was put on the train to return home, Scott stole a block of hard maple rock sugar from the sugar box, still common in homes of the time, to munch on the train. 'And thereafter, boy did my grandmother give me holy hell, which I deserved.' By contrast, 'My grandfather, who never seemed to be a very smart man, was extraordinarily loving.'

Scott Peck adored his grandfather and there were two ways Dumont and his grandson, Scott, spent much private time together, in the toilet and at the movies. 'My grandfather would spend at least three hours on the toilet every day. He claimed it was constipation. My surmise is that it was the best way of getting away from his wife and her arguing. He used to unlock the door and let me in. And so while he was sitting on the toilet, with nothing happening really, me sitting on the edge of the bathtub, we'd have these three-hour conver-sations.' The movie marathons occurred once a month, from the time Scott was eight until he was about thirteen. He'd take the subway downtown on a Saturday morning, have lunch in his grandparents' cramped little apartment – 'always good food, my grandmother was famous for it – and then my grandfather would take me to a Saturday matinee double feature movie. Then we'd come back and have dinner, and he'd take me to my second double feature, then we'd come home and sleep it off. Sunday mornings, in deference to God, the movies were closed. But Sunday afternoon he'd take me to my third double feature before sending me home. That's love.' Scott had had six hours of films; Dumont had six hours away from Juliet with a good excuse into the bargain.

Walking to and from the cinema, however, was not always an unbridled pleasure for Scott. 'My grandfather was a kind of *species Americanus*,' he said. 'A conventional thinker, he was filled with clichés and proverbs. On our walks he had all these corny proverbs, "all work and no play makes Jack a dull boy", "don't put all your eggs in one basket", "if wishes were horses beggars would ride", "all that glitters is not gold", "spoonful of sugar makes the medicine go down". He gave me a lot of sugar along with the proverbs.'

Elizabeth Saville Templeton Peck, born in 1902, was from a decidedly WASP family that had known wealth. Her mother was Lavinia Saville; her father died when Elizabeth was six months old. Some time after Elizabeth's father's death, Lavinia married a man called Getty, who owned a fleet of tugboats in New York harbour. Scott's mother would call herself Elizabeth Getty at times, rather than Elizabeth Saville, so she could wittily say she was 'Betty Getty'. She grew up in Little Silver, New Jersey, just across the Hudson River from New York City, with her mother and stepfather, and her brother, George. There's a poem about George, 'Uncle George's Visit', in Scott Peck's *Golf* book. 'George married Madeline, dumpy and unattractive, though George was very, very attractive. The family, eyeing Madeline, always referred to him as "poor Uncle George,"' said Peck. He considered his uncle far smarter than people thought.

There was no Saville family genealogy on record, but Elizabeth's background was American and English, the latter connected to a Baron Saville, whose antecedents in turn would have been French. Scott Peck's maternal grandmother, Lavinia Saville Templeton, had a brother, Herbert, a lifelong bachelor, and a sister, Victoria 'who married a Brooklyn banker, Al Taber, a strange sort of guy, cigar-chomping, squat. Vickie and Al. Al was as ugly as Vickie was beautiful. I used to visit them, and liked them very much,' said Peck, 'but Uncle Herbie was my favourite. He was elegant. Mother was a very beautiful woman as well as a very loving one. She was not particularly bright in terms of IQ, when compared to my father. She had a conventional kind of mind, and though she was a great storyteller she never talked much about Getty. The Getty relatives were never close. She'd tell about the wonderful adventures she'd get into as a girl with two of her friends who remained friends for life, Edie Hazard and Dorothy McClave. Mr Hazard was the first househusband I ever came across. He kept the home and she worked as a secretary at Riverside Church.' Edie corresponded with Scott Peck until her death, for she read all his books. Edie was a very religious woman, who had no children. Dorothy never married.

'Mother was very patient. When I was ill, which was frequently, she would sit with me for hours on end. She was mildly obsessive compulsive when it came to child-raising. She was obsessed about my bowels and one of my unfortunate memories of my childhood was rather frequent enemas. But she could get angry.' The attention he received when he was sick may have exaggerated a lifelong tendency towards hypochondria. At boarding school he was frequently in the infirmary with coughs and colds, writing home about sleeping twelve and fourteen hours a day. 'Don't be worried . . . I have a little chest cough.' Or again, 'Well, I had a feeling I would land in the infirmary . . .' And he did.

When Scott Peck was about four his mother collected him from a kind of summer day camp and as she drove home, 'She bawled me out for peeing on a toilet seat at camp, so angry she drove the car off the road and had to get a farmer to tow it out of the field. She had strange ideas about what kinds of food were good for children, particularly for the bowels. We were always in a battle over food.' Scott's favourite was chocolate cake and when quite young he'd wake up early to climb on to the kitchen counters before anyone else was up to search through cupboards to find some.

Baby Scott Peck was not baptised. The senior Pecks attended Christ Church on Park Avenue several times a year, 'for appearances' sake,' said Scott Peck, a remark that could be interpreted as both accurate and snide. There were no Peck family religious observances. God, family prayers, nominal Christianity were never mentioned in the home. In his mother's old age he learned she was in fact a 'crypto-Presbyterian', and had been all her life.

Toddler Scott Peck's early Park Avenue world was not limited to his immediate family. His parents were great travellers, and had no objection to leaving their young children behind when they sailed for Europe. Young Peck had a vivid imagination that included a phobia as a child about being lost, not in the sense of being deliberately abandoned but of being accidentally left alone. From such a period very early in his childhood, perhaps when he was three or four, Peck retained hazy though fond memories of an Irish Catholic nanny with whom he attended Catholic weddings or church services. Were she typical of the influx of Irish nannies into New York in the 1920s and 1930s, the nanny would have talked fairly constantly to Scott about God and Jesus, the Virgin Mary and angels watching over him, and taught him some rudimentary night prayers. Of those possibilities Peck had no recollection whatsoever, though he did say that from the Irish nanny he received 'the Catholic corpuscles' in his spiritual bloodstream.

Irish nannies were so prevalent in Manhattan in the first half of the twentieth-century they even gave their name to a room, the 'biddy' room. 'Biddy' made it into song as the diminutive for 'Bridget', a common Irish name, and in popular parlance a 'biddy' meant a domestic servant. New Yorkers understood perfectly when Rodgers and Hart, in *The Girlfriend* of 1926, wrote a verse for 'The Blue Room' that included, '. . . here's the kiddies' room, here's the biddy's room'. In the Peck apartment at 863, there were two biddy rooms off the spacious kitchen. Generally, they were only ever occupied overnight as a last-minute bedroom for guests.

Scott had other troubles at St Bernard's. In skipping third grade, there were fourth-grade level skills he had not yet acquired. One was the ability to tie his own necktie, a social gaffe and quite a dilemma in a boys' school where ties frequently came undone during horseplay. And an undone necktie was an offence against school decorum. Scott had to suffer through the embarrassment of being shown in a crowded hallway by a teacher how to loop it back together again. 'That symbolised the whole of that first year,' Peck said. 'The second year at St Bernard's, I would have been in fifth grade, was wonderful. I did well in school, well academically, and enjoyed the school. We had a weekly theme to write. Had to write it over the weekend as homework and hand it in on Monday. I got a lot of experience starting at a very early age of writing and I enjoyed writing themes. I think I got praised for some of them. I don't remember. People were always saying, even then, that I thought too much. I'm a Gemini. And it seems a terribly fitting sign that I'm always seeing at least two sides of everything. I'm totally enamoured with paradox. I'm paradox in motion.'

Sixth grade, however, was as bad as fourth grade. 'A new kid, we'll leave off his name, precocious and way ahead of himself, he was shaving already. One of an adopted pair of twins, a boy and a girl, raised with incredible pressure to excel. He was a superb athlete, absolutely brilliant and he and I became almost instant friends for about six weeks. Suddenly the entire class, including him, turned against me. This guy remained the leader of the school, a captain of every team, star pupil and whatnot. It wasn't until years afterwards that I realised what had happened. It was a battle for leadership and I threatened his being Number One, so he turned them against me. Even back then – looking at things now – I realised I was in fact the leader but I didn't think of myself that way.'

In the summers of the early years, the family went out to East Hampton, Long Island for vacations. The 1770 House in East Hampton was operated by a Mr and Mrs John F. Williams, and on a piece of 1770 House notepaper is an early note from Scott to his mother. In a penmanship that alternates between block capitals and cursive, Peck, possibly eight years old, writes: 'Dear Mom, I'm out to supper. Will be back for 90 cents at 6.40. If not in leave with Williams. I still love you and I hope that my manner hasn't changed so much that you don't love me. Much love Scotty.'

During the years Scott was three to five, they summered also in a rented 'magical house', Hooper House, near Sharon, in rolling western Connecticut. When many years later the time came for Scott Peck, a married man with three children, to settle down, it was in rural Connecticut he and his wife found their home, not thirty miles from his boyhood summer home. 'The Hooper House was magical, for there were sheep in a pasture beyond the gate. There was an ice house in the back.' A half century later, when he and his wife, Lily, drove there to see it, 'it was just as magical. She thought so, too. It's all changed now. I would say I have a hundred memories of the Hooper House. When we discussed it, years later, my brother couldn't remember anything about the place. It was the only time my father ever lived in a valley. Otherwise he always lived on mountaintops, as befitted his image of himself.' The year Scott was five, Peck Senior built Windland, his 'mountaintop' house on a hill in Sharon, and they spent their first summer in it the following year. Many years later, the senior Pecks had a final summer home in western Connecticut, The Schloss, in Quaker Hill.

Among early memories, Peck recalled as a three-year-old being awakened by his mother and being carried outside to see the Northern Lights 'dancing in the sky'. The impression was so vivid that as an adult he checked with his mother to see whether it had happened. She remembered it as September, 1939. Europe was already at war. A year later he stood at the top of the stairs in Hooper House in his pyjamas and watched his mother and a group of neighbour women knitting 'Bundles for Britain,' warm clothes for the war-torn British. As a seven-year-old, Scott's deepest desire was to become a Boy Scout. He was too young. He came across a Boy Scout handbook, was entranced by its advertisement for the official

Scout hatchet, received a similar one for Christmas, cut his knee with it the first time he tried to chop down a tree, and was given stitches without an anaesthetic. His father took away the hatchet. Sixty years later Peck was willing to talk about the pain of those stitches and to hitch up his trouser leg to reveal the site of the minute scar.

A self-proclaimed 'New York tunnel rat – children not adults were mugged in New York then, by other kids, for their school money', Peck nonetheless liked to think of himself as a country boy. And he did what young country boys do – roam. As a ten-year-old he roamed in a field behind his parents' house until he saw in a new light the farmer's hayrake that was parked there. It was, he decided, no more than a giant Meccano or Erector set put together with nuts and bolts. Armed with a supply of wrenches, and accompanied by a summer pal his age, Scott methodically dismantled the hayrake into its more than a hundred component parts and left them scattered across a dozen acres. A half century later Peck mulled over the 'wanton destructiveness that seemed like great fun at the time'.

When Scott was ten, life became more difficult still. That summer of 1946, his parents had 'fierce quarrels' and his mother talked about getting a divorce, though not in front of her sons. Scott was eavesdropping, listening from an adjoining window. 'I knew the issue had to do with my father's morality and integrity and I was definitely on Mother's side in these arguments from the sidelines. I didn't really know anything about what divorce meant at the age of ten, but I don't think a woman in her mid-thirties with two children could have divorced a wealthy, successful lawyer. What happened after that summer, after that period of arguing, was that my mother totally capitulated for the rest of her life. She just sort of gave up the ghost of her individuality, with the exception of a few rare moments of courage.'

Peck referred periodically in conversation to his father's 'lack of integrity'. He gave an instance of it the summer he was eleven and David was fifteen. The family went out to a dude ranch in Montana for a two-month vacation. The parents didn't like it, it was too rough-and-ready for them. But David, at fifteen, thoroughly enjoyed the experience and wanted to return the following year. Judge Peck agreed, provided David earned half the cost of $400 by working on a farm near the family's summer home. David agreed. In Sharon, Connecticut, the Pecks belonged to 'a very WASP country club with the customary golf course and tennis court,' as Peck described it. There was an annual Labor Day tennis tournament for which partners were drawn out of a hat. David and Scott were 'fairly good tennis players, as good as the average adult, but there was a kid by the name of Donny Green, who also always played in the tournament.' Peck said Donny was 'a terrible tennis player'.

Two years earlier, when tournament partners were drawn from the hat that year, David was paired with Donny Green. A year later on Labor Day, Scott Peck ended up with Donny as a partner. Then the third year when the drawing was made – the year of the dude ranch trip – once again David was paired with Donny Green. When David saw the result he said the tournament draw, given there were more than a hundred participants, was obviously rigged. Clearly no-one wanted to play with Donny Green so he was palmed off on the other children. David decided to make a formal complaint to the tournament committee. His father was appalled and said, 'If you don't complain I will release you from the remainder of your debt.' David had worked off $100 for his return trip to Montana.

'David said, "That's a bribe",' said Peck, 'and I sat there and said, "Certainly seems like a bribe to me."' David did complain to the tournament committee and the tournament match-up was re-drawn. For Scott, however, the lesson was elsewhere: 'It was a very powerful experience for me to see my father, a powerful judge, who had this huge reputation for honesty and probity, make a bribe. It was my father's desire not to make any waves when he was in WASP heaven.'

A lifelong friend of Peck's with a home in the area was Elizabeth Peale (later Elizabeth Allen), whose father was Dr Norman Vincent Peale, the famous author of *The Power of Positive Thinking*. Elizabeth Peale would be a couple of years ahead of Peck at high school in New York where both attended Friends Seminary. It was a region of luminaries, many from the media world.

It was a period when being a broadcaster was the height of fame. Two neighbours were broadcast personalities, Edward R. Murrow, and Lowell Thomas. Murrow was famed as the radio war correspondent who brought the Blitz to American audiences, with his broadcasts during the attacks on the British capital that began with the words, 'This – is London.' Later, during the heightened anti-communist fervour of the early Cold War in the United States, Murrow was the television interviewer who exposed the 'witch-

hunting' Senator Joseph McCarthy to the American public for
blacklisting people through guilt-by-association. This segment of
Murrow life's was made into the 2005 film *Good Night and Good
Luck*. Lowell Thomas was a globe-trotting radio broadcaster who
also made documentary movies, one of which, shot during and after
the First World War, introduced 'Lawrence of Arabia' to Americans.

There were other Peck memories from the trip to the Montana
ranch. 'It was on the Montana trip I remember my mother flirting
with someone and I swear to God in my memory it was with Roy
Cohen. [Cohen was a lawyer involved with US Senator Joseph
McCarthy during the US 'Red scare witchhunts' and blacklisting.]
But it could be a false memory and that she was flirting with some-
one else.' The second incident was that on the journey out West,
Scott had a last clinging to boyhood. 'I don't think I ever had a
Oedipus complex but during that trip I had practically an uncon-
trollable very intense desire and need to cuddle with my mother.
She allowed this. I sat for significant periods during that trip on my
mother's lap, cuddling her. My brother teased me like crazy about it.
But that was what I wanted to do and my mother seemed accepting
of it. That was the only time I remember that, but I remember by
the time I was twelve I no longer had that need or desire. I never
consciously had any sexual thoughts about my mother.'

The next year he became a smoker. 'I was thirteen and on
vacation with my parents on Fire Island (off New York's Long
Island), long before it became a gay community. Some little fifteen-
year-old bastard taught me to inhale. He smoked Camels.' Peck
stopped smoking a couple of times, once, in his forties, for two days,
in a convent. 'David smoked and drank like I did. He was a great
believer in [the organisation] Smoke-enders, which he went to twice.
He said he was the only member of his group that didn't quit. My
father, though not frequently, smoked cigars, which he loved. He
always chided my mother rather nastily for smoking cigarettes.'

Sexual knowledge and awakening came a little late to Scott, but
he caught up quickly. He'd fallen in love when he was six and again
when he was eight or nine, that time with a young woman, a
neighbour ten years his senior. Her name was Cynthia, he said, and
she always seemed pretty oblivious to him except one night she
telephoned, and said, 'I just wanted to let you know, Scotty, I'm
getting married tomorrow.' She didn't invite him to the wedding. 'I
was relatively late in learning the facts of life, which I learned riding

our bikes back from the tennis club from that guy, Donny Green. I was just horrified at the thought you would take your penis and put it inside a woman's bottom. I thought, I'm never going to have sex.'

Scott, as a pubescent, emerges less as a case of precociousness than as a child with a capacity for directness. In Sharon, he made friends with a couple of children, last name Piel, whose father was his father's protégé, a litigation specialist in Sullivan & Cromwell. 'Mrs Piel was one of the few people who would take some time out when I was ten years old to rally with me in tennis. And she gave me the most important point in playing tennis that I ever got. She'd say, "You're rushing the ball. Just remember you've got plenty of time to hit the ball." I started saying to myself, every shot, remember to take the time and my game suddenly, dramatically improved.'

Years later, he and Lily met the youngest of the Piel children, Tom, a Green Beret, and invited him to dinner. Tom Piel mentioned it to his mother and asked her if she remembered Scott Peck from Sharon days. 'This was before I'd written *The Road Less Travelled*,' said Peck. And she said, 'Oh, yes, he was the little boy who was always talking about the kind of things that people shouldn't talk about.' Commented Peck, 'It was an echo from my childhood: an affirming kind of comment.'

In Peck, his adult directness of manner was present in the child, in the bluntness that came from saying precisely what he thought, felt, observed. These characteristics would have been entertaining to some adults, disconcerting to others. Yet he also was deeply introspective and observant at an early age, and gives an example in one of his poems. Peck wrote a great deal of poetry, some of it quite acceptable, all of it revealing of some aspect of his character, his despairs, his faith, his hopes. The first few lines of 'A Star in the East' offer an insight into his introspective childhood:

Two nights before Christmas
In the year of Our Lord nineteen hundred and forty-three,
My earthly Father and I drove to the train station
Through bitter cold and darkness to meet my two great
Uncles and one great aunt.
I looked through one of the windows,
Frosty with our combined breaths,
And saw the hugest star I had ever seen.
None of the adults seemed to notice.

I checked to be sure;
There was no doubt,
The star was definitely in the East.
My roaring inclination was to scream, 'Look there's
The star in the East!'
But in that moment, I took a step out of innocence.
Somehow I knew that their response would be, 'Oh,
Isn't he cute?'
So with my new-found wisdom,
For perhaps the first time in my seven years,
I held my tongue.

His new-found wisdom about holding his tongue didn't last long. At age eight he attended a wedding in Lakeville, Connecticut with his mother. He had a glass of champagne. He 'called across three people – not realising that one was the bride's mother [and yelled] "Hey Mom, it's a lousy wine, isn't it?"' His mother, extremely embarrassed, quickly silenced him. In the car later, she more soundly rebuked him. 'She gave me hell.' Scott continued to insist that the wine was of poor quality. They went round and around on the incident, and finally his mother admitted, 'Yes, it was a rather poor wine.'

There are several ways to consider this incident, one to do with his mother, the others with Scott. His mother expressed no concern that Scotty was drinking wine at age eight, only that he had transgressed the social code. Young Scott spoke out, as do many young children, occasionally inadvertently or inappropriately. His wedding outburst could be regarded as childishness or foolhardiness. Its aftermath could also be a first indicator of his courage in taking a stand (however ill-advised) based on an opinion he had formed and refused to relinquish. It was especially satisfying to him on this occasion when he discovered by sticking to his guns that his impression was correct. Contrarily, there is always the possibility, of course, he was simply behaving like a spoiled brat, or, that like many another eight-year-old boy, he'd learned that getting a rise out of adults is, despite the risks, one of the finer forms of childhood entertainment. For the moment, it is simply worth noting that the maturing Scott Peck would always have the courage of his convictions. Sticking to his guns forecast trouble for his teenage years. He would pay a heavy emotional price when he decided he must take a stand against his father's wishes, indeed, against the social code that was his father's lodestar.

CHAPTER 2

LIFE WITH FATHER

At least Scott's mother listened when young Peck issued his declarative opinions, for that he was grateful. His father, in the son's view, rarely considered any opinions other than his own. He expected obedience, not argument or challenges. On the positive side, Peck described his father as 'an affectionate man in his way', if controlling. 'At age eight or so I climbed up on his knee and asked him, "Dad, what do you want me to be when I grow up?" And he said, "Well, whatever do you want to be, Scotty my boy." And I said, "Well, I'd like to be a doctor." And he said, "Well, I would prefer it if you study law." His affection had that sort of quality to it. He was a good man in a number of ways. He was playful. He liked to be teased.'

While theirs was not a religious household, said Peck: 'My father purported to have had in his teenage years some kind of "altar call" experience [an open admission of being a follower of Christ]. It never rang quite true with me. He was probably the most secular person in the world. My father, despite being a judge of repute, had very little understanding of ethics.' He had, said Peck, 'a brilliant capacity to find holes in other people's arguments and absolutely none to find any in his own. He was a very powerful man, in bearing, appearance and manner.' Peck told his psychologist friend Dr James Guy, 'My father had a capacity to block out the stuff that he wanted to block out.'

Another facet of his father dawned on Peck years later when he and Lily were vacationing in Florida with Christopher. Peck had received two manuscripts to review from publishers, hoping for favourable comments from him. 'Both manuscripts were about Dr Jekyll and Mr Hyde, Jungian books about the Shadow, and whatnot. And I said to Christopher, he was seventeen, "I just realised my father is the closest thing to Dr Jekyll and Mr Hyde that I've ever

met." And Christopher said, "You just realised that?"' Again, the
only example Peck could give of this Jekyll and Hyde-ism was never
knowing his father's mood when he returned home for dinner of an
evening.

Despite these ambivalent feelings towards his parent, Peck
needed the security of his father's caring. As a boy, Scott had a fear
of being separated, he said. 'On certain drives, as soon as we were in
unfamiliar territory, I would really practically cry and scream,
"We're lost! We're getting lost! I know, I know we're getting lost."'
His parents did not respond to this chink in their son's psychological
make-up particularly wisely, for Peck gave as 'one example of
sadism on both my parents' parts, was when we were in New York
City walking through Chinatown. This was when I was six, and
there was a metal stairway in the sidewalk going down to a kind of
cubbyhole. And my parents said, "Wouldn't it be fun to walk down
there and then he won't be able to find us."' Again and again in *The
Road Less Travelled*, Peck writes from the perspective of the injured,
hurting, or overlooked child.

On occasion, Peck could take a detached view of the judge's
'controllingness', as he called it, as at the lunch one day when he
asked his father what he was going to do that afternoon. The judge
replied he was going to talk to a young lawyer who wanted his career
advice. Peck said he left the table thinking, '"Jesus Christ! Why on
earth would any young lawyer go to my father for advice? My father
doesn't give advice. My father will tell you what to do." And then I
suddenly realised my father was not necessarily the same with young
lawyers as he was with my brother and me, and perhaps wasn't controlling at all. My brother experienced him as extremely controlling.'

Scott Peck's formative years, dominated by his father, deteriorated into a father–son rupture when Peck was twenty-three. It was
a brief but severe rupture, the culmination of a growing stand-off
between a father and a boy, soon a young man, desperately trying to
go his own way. Peck escaped his father's presence, but never fully
his father's shadow. In many a conversation Peck would raise some
point of conflict he'd had with his father, or he would use his father
as an object of criticism or a point of comparison. Then, realising he
had again raised the parent as a spectre, he would search for
phrasing that might moderate or explain his criticism.

This father–son competitive spirit could surface in an instant on
almost any topic. For example, when the work on this biography

began, Peck pointedly noted that no one had ever written a biography of his father. That was true enough, though Judge Peck himself, in a brief memoir, noted it first: 'If my biography were ever written, which thankfully will not happen . . .' Scott, perhaps aware he was slighting his parent again, as if in recompense gave his father's two books, *The Greer Case: A True Court Drama* (Simon and Schuster, 1955), and *Decision at Law* (Dodd, 1961) high marks. The competitive father could have engaged in a brisk one-upmanship with Scott, too, by remarking that no one had ever made a movie of one of Scott Peck's books, whereas, Judge Peck's *The Greer Case* was a 1957 made-for-television movie starring Raymond Burr and Zsa Zsa Gabor.

It was not simply that Judge Peck hovered over the Park Avenue Pecks' dinner table: so did his law firm, Sullivan & Cromwell. The mighty S&C was the family's social arbiter. 'In some ways it governed our life,' Peck admitted. The family's standards were set by, and Scott Peck grew up as a child of, Sullivan & Cromwell, and the power behind its throne, John Foster Dulles. If Scott Peck neither forgot, and possibly never fully forgave his father, his comments about Sullivan & Cromwell could be equally searing – for the manners and mores of the law firm represented one cause of the fissures between father and son.

David W. Peck, Senior, as he grew into his high school years, was after bigger things than his father's haberdashery. He was a handsome young man, well-tailored, slender, of medium height, quite broad-browed, with a pointed nose and penetrating eyes. In later years he wore glasses with circular frames. In a short memoir written in 1979 for Sullivan & Cromwell's centenary, Judge Peck wrote that when his mother tried to force him to take violin lessons, his counter-offer was he would take elocution lessons instead. His ploy worked, he wrote, 'and led in natural progression to oratory and debate in high school and college, and thence to law school.' He also clerked in his father's store during his undergraduate years, he said, and wrote its advertising: 'both being by nature advocacy.'

Where David was concerned, Juliet was the ambitious mother with one son. He was undoubtedly fuelled as much by her ambition as his own. She knew the cultured East Coast, experienced it in her Buffalo, New York family milieu and could undoubtedly compare life there to the narrow confines of small-town life on the Indiana farmlands. In their later years, when the Peck grandparents sold the haberdashery business, Juliet was likely the one who insisted they move back East, to New York City, to retire. If the future Judge Peck was an equal product of his parents, his drive came from his mother, and his affability from his father, Dumont, Scott Peck's 'Grandfather Pecky'. Peck Senior was a phenomenon, a man's man, a lawyer's lawyer who, as a pastime, could completely redraft the New York State Constitution (though his version was never adopted) while maintaining a gruelling pace at his practice, and writing books. Were there strong traces in Scott Peck of his father's, and perhaps his grandmother's, determination?

Like his son, Scott, years later, Peck Senior early had a confrontational mind of his own. Crawfordsville High's principal was a Miss Anna, very popular with the students. Said Peck, 'For some reason they fired her. My father, at sixteen, was already ahead of himself and beginning his senior year in high school. He quit in protest at Miss Anna's firing.' Dumont Peck had gone to Wabash College. David, at sixteen, followed suit. The college accepted him even though he'd left high school before graduation. David graduated from Wabash at nineteen with honours and went straight to Harvard Law School. There he helped support himself by tutoring.

Peck Senior's trajectory after Harvard Law School was that he joined the United States Attorney General's office in New York City as a twenty-two-year-old assistant prosecutor, under reform-minded US Attorney General Emory R. Buckner. In his 1978 memoir, Judge Peck wrote that Buckner had 'cleaned house and appointed a lot of young assistants, mostly just out of law school, to replace political hacks, attracting them through the promise of valuable experience, thus procuring ability that could not be procured in experienced lawyers with the stingy salaries permitted.' Peck Senior, one of a group 'known more or less disdainfully as Buckner's Bright Young Men', became president of the Young Republican Club when future presidential candidate Tom Dewey was chairman. According to the *New York Times'* (Judge Peck obituary, 24 August 1990), these were 'liberal Republicans who began modernising the Republican Party in New York County.'

In 1928, Peck Senior left the Attorney General's office for corporate and international work at the International Telephone and Telegraph Company. Long before Scott's birth, he spent several months living and working in London on 'an important arbitration over breach of a cartel agreement'. It was not the only occasion the now internationally experienced lawyer would spend time on legal work in England and elsewhere in Europe.

When Peck Senior returned to the United States, the firm of Sullivan & Cromwell was looking for a strong hand for the litigation department it intended to build. Its first thought was Thomas Dewey, but Dewey was in line to become New York District Attorney. So S&C invited thirty-year-old Peck Senior, already known to them through Buckner, to take on a department that at the time was 'one partner, two associates of advanced years, and one just out of law school'. The following year, 1934, two years before Scott was born, Peck Senior was named a partner. He was thirty-one. It was a considerable achievement for a young man from Indiana, and Wabash College. When John Foster Dulles brought his brother, Allen, into the firm, noted Dulles biographer Leonard Mosley, 'It was a time to count blessings, and to be grateful to Foster, and Sullivan & Cromwell from whom all blessings flowed.' A similar sentiment guided the head of the Peck family. 'My father's world was the WASP world of the 1940s, and he tried in every way and shape possible to keep the forties alive, the world when the East Coast Establishment truly ran the United States,' said Peck.

In 1944, when Scott was eight, Tom Dewey, with whom his father had 'a lifelong political association and close friendship', to quote Peck Senior, was New York governor. There was a vacancy on the New York State Supreme Court, to which, Peck Senior wrote, he was 'appointed and elected by the sheerest political luck. The previous occupant of the position was the only Republican on the court and the Democratic leaders were persuaded that the Republicans should continue to be allowed such representation and so gave me their nomination.' He was thirty-six. From that year on, when the court recessed, Scott Peck's father had long summers for family vacations, summers that Scott recounted sometimes with wonder and joy, and sometimes with misgivings. Whichever, few financially upper-crust children had as much summer with both parents as the Peck boys did – and with parents who loved to travel.

Judge Peck had no intention of spending his life on the bench, but two years into his term he was appointed to the Appellate Division, and, in 1947, designated Presiding Justice, the youngest in the state's history. 'I felt obliged to serve out my term, but not take another one,' he said. The first of January 1958 found him back at Sullivan & Cromwell after a twelve-year absence. As a 'glamour litigator', representing high-profile clients, he created a new avenue of business for the firm. In *A Law Unto Itself: the Untold Story of the Law Firm Sullivan & Cromwell*, by Nancy Lisagor and Frank Lipsius (William Morrow), Judge Peck merits two-and-a-half pages. The book tells of the judge's 'taste for limousines, the opera, expensive wines, and exclusive schools for his sons with connections at the top of New York society'. Those connections saw him involved with some of the major names of America's financial and political elite – the Astors, the Rockefellers and the Kennedys. Until his retirement in 1972, the much-written-about Judge Peck was a late-blooming celebrity in his own right.

The firm was one of the first major New York City law firms to have a Jewish partner. According to S&C records, Alfred Jaretski, S&C's sixth lawyer, in 1881, was Jewish. Scott Peck was newly married and in medical school when his mother, visiting him and his wife, Lily, in Cleveland, and 'well into her third martini', blurted out the family secret. They'd put Mrs Peck up 'in a very nice nearby hotel,' in Scott's words, 'and she immediately downed three martinis, one after another.' There had been difficulties over Scott and Lily's marrying so young, and Mrs Peck acknowledged that they were really ready to get married and said in these kinds of situations there were always upsetting moments. She even admitted that at one point she broke off her engagement to Peck Senior. When Scott asked why she did that, she replied '"Well, you know that your grandmother is a Jew." And I said, "Daddy's Jewish? No, I didn't know."' And Mrs Peck said, 'Well, he is. And I don't want you to talk to your father or ever mention this to him. Don't ever mention this again.' Scott's brother, David, was twenty-three before he learned it. He was on the dance floor of the Nantucket Country Club when his fiancée asked, 'David, why didn't you tell me your father was Jewish?' And in his protestations, David Junior learned the facts.

When the adult Scott Peck became aware of the Jewish heritage in the family, he said, other things began to make sense. 'At every family celebration, there was always smoked salmon. I didn't know until I was around twenty what lox was.' Early in their marriage, when Lily asked Scott what she could make for him, he asked for bread like his grandmother's. As they were living in a primarily Jewish area of Cleveland, he spotted the bread one day in a Jewish bakery and said, 'There, that's it. My grandmother's bread.' And

Lily replied, 'Well, it's challah.' Challah was as close as Peck came to connecting with his Jewish heritage.

Peck recalled, 'When Dad celebrated it was always with his mother's bread, kneaded over and twirled with poppy seeds, and the lox. Now, in my parents' defence,' he added, 'it was an anti-Semitic world in that day and age. Just up the road from here,' he said, referring to a village close to his Connecticut home, 'there's a wonderful inn that well into the 1950s used to advertise itself in the *New York Times* as a "gentile" inn.' Peck remembered another clue, unrecognised at the time, to the family's Jewish heritage. 'One boring, long summer day, we were in the living room of our country house in Sharon. David and I were singing the St Bernard's school song. A chorus which goes, "Come let us sing in a jubilant chorus. School days and college alike . . ." but there's great emphasis on the word or symbol "jubilant". Well, my mother came running out of the kitchen, through the dining room, into the living room and said, "Don't you boys talk about the Jews that way." And we said, "We weren't talking about the Jews." She said, "The Jews are ordinary people, just like us." Scott also surmised that when his paternal grandparents and his father as a boy, on their annual automobile pilgrimages to Vermont, made the side trip to Buffalo en route, it was to the German-Jewish community there. Of these side trips to Buffalo, Judge Peck, however, reminisced fondly to his sons only about the quality of the ice cream in his favourite shop there, but never about his relatives in Buffalo's middle-class German-Jewish community. Such was the chasm between father and sons that never once in the ensuing three decades did Scott or David raise the issue with their father.

Jews or not, when society came to 863 Park Avenue it was always WASP society in the swirl around Mr and Mrs John Foster Dulles, Sullivan & Cromwell folk, and high-ranking members of New York's Republican and economic elite. Not so incidentally, Park Avenue was *the* place to be, and the lower the number the more prestigious the address. During the course of their lives the senior Pecks gradually moved south, and therefore upward in the Park Avenue social register, finally settling at number 580, a prime location. For Scott, from the age of five until he left home permanently at twenty-three, his domestic world was the spacious apartment he shared with his mother and father at 863. 'I grew up with these high-powered people in our living room,' he said.

They were present because Judge Peck was good at what he did and was well accepted by New York's upper crust, from which he recruited future clients. His was an outgoing, and later somewhat flamboyant personality that brought business to Sullivan & Cromwell. Judge Peck, through Sullivan & Cromwell, represented *Look* magazine against Mrs Jackie Kennedy Onassis in her 1966 suit against the magisterial author William Manchester, whom she'd appointed to write the account of the JFK presidency, *The Death of a President*. *Look* was to serialise the book. She had been more frank with Manchester than she realised and wanted the final word, for she kept a censorious grip anyway on all books about the late president and herself. She was no less merciless in this respect than the Kennedy clan itself in its watchtower surveillance of anything affecting the Kennedy reputation and what would become the 'Camelot myth'. Judge Peck went line-for-line through the book with Mrs Onassis's lawyer until the matter was settled. And while they might have been on opposite sides, Judge Peck did everything he could to shield Mrs Onassis from the press on occasions when the suit brought them together.

Entertaining was part of the Peck household system. By a certain age, David Junior and Scott were marshalled in to be presented at the frequent dinners and gatherings in the Peck family apartment, then marshalled out again to eat in the kitchen or their bedrooms until they were old enough to join the adults at the table. Because they were impeccably trained, that came quite early indeed.

There was a difference between dinners and parties. At parties, 'My mother drank. I don't remember ever seeing my father drunk, but I heard tales of him being drunk in his younger days. At a couple of parties they threw I tasted my father's cucumber punch. It tasted very mild, but I can remember as a child stepping over the bodies of people who had passed out. And I can remember my father having a hangover one time saying, "I made a New Year's resolution, that is I'm not going to go to another goddamn New Year's Eve party in my life." But in terms of regularity he was a modest drinker.'

If Jewish high holy days were ignored, and religious observance limited to a perfunctory attendance at Christ Church, Christmas was nonetheless a major event in the Peck household. 'We were into huge Christmases, largely related, I think, to the denial of death. Huge family gatherings began during the World War II years – not only my brother and I and my parents, but my two grandparents, Uncle Herbie and Aunt Vicky and Uncle Al. They'd all be there. And then they began to die off. My father couldn't bear to see the pile of presents under the tree diminish. And so it became the custom that he'd give each person two presents, and then three presents, and then four presents, and then five presents, in order to see the big pile still under the tree.'

Scott celebrated Easter in his own fashion. There is a poem to his parents in a penmanship that suggests he was possibly ten years old:

> This weekend I have earned dollars four;
> Two of them give Dear Mummy for
> Some brand-new shiny clothes
> The rest to Daddy for some hose
> And as long as you are near me
> A song in my heart you'll all see.
>
> Happy Easter
> Scotty

In Peck's eyes, his father's standing worsened with each passing year. 'My rage at him always had to do with the ethics business. Ethics meaning he could not begin to see the holes in his own argument. And I suppose I can't separate that out because it was why my mother even thought of divorcing him.' Peck never would articulate a bill of specific charges against his father sufficient to explain his bursts of animosity towards him. One can only hesitantly conclude that perhaps Peck's troubles with him stemmed from the boy's need to protect and defend his mother. Whether there was more to what he saw or heard when he eavesdropped, whether he eavesdropped more than once, he would not say. Pressed on these matters, Peck would shift the conversation.

'It wasn't that life with Daddy was unpleasant, it was that life with Daddy was a puzzlement as to – well, was he a judge of great probity? Later there were times when I would confront him on issues and he would agree with me and say thank you. And the next morning wouldn't remember he'd agreed with me. It drove me nuts. It wasn't that he was generally unpleasant, generally he was very pleasant, but could he lose his temper! Ninety-five per cent of the time, being with Dad was a pleasant experience.' That there was a loving element to the parent–offspring relationship probably arose in many moments like the one Scott recounted from the period when he was about four and his brother David was hospitalised with appendicitis. Scotty and his father went up to 'the magical Hooper House' together for the weekend, just the two of them. It was in the late spring. They spent the mornings planting corn, his father drilling the rows of holes in the earth with a corn-hole driller, and Scott coming up behind him dropping four or five corn kernels in each hole. When the corn was sown, they returned to the house. 'My father made me butter and sugar sandwiches.' Later, the mature Scott Peck wrote a poem about that morning, which talks about the sandwiches his father made, sandwiches that *'gave me then my first blessed, delicious taste of sin.'* (*Fragments of a Future Work,* Okinawa, 1970).

Paradoxically, as only a young boy growing up can, despite his injured innocence Scotty fiercely admired his father. The lack he felt was one of reciprocity: 'My father never talked about his work,' he said decades later. 'And that was one of the grudges I had against him. He was at least as good a father as I,' said Peck, 'though there were times I felt I did not get enough from him, though he gave as much as I gave my children. He was a loving guy, though on his terms. So even when I was dealing with the bad part of him I could have a good time co-existing with him on every level. I used to deeply enjoy lunches with him at the Manhattan Club, on Madison at Twenty-sixth Street. My father never talked to me as much about his business as I would have liked. But if I did get talking to him, I had from this early age a penchant for being critical of him and his ethics.'

Peck still could not, or would not, cite precisely why he reacted so strongly against his father. Incidents he mentioned did not seem out of character for the reactions of many a hard-working, ambitious preoccupied high-priced lawyer facing family issues at the end of his day. When Peck said, 'I may not seem it, but under the surface I'm potentially a very angry man, as was my father,' the example he gave was almost trivial. Peck remembered as a boy meeting his father's train in Brewster, New York, his mother immediately complaining Scott had done something wrong. His father dragged him the length of the railroad station by his earlobe. Peck may on occasion have confused anger with exasperation.

'There were ways in which my father was almost extravagant, but there were ways in which he was distinctly cheap. Just before he was dying, one of our daughters visiting him made a call on her credit card, and was talking on the phone at some length. My father yelled at her for talking so long on the phone. And she said, "It's on my credit card . . . Grandad . . ." and he took his cane and whopped her, knocked the phone out of her hand.'

In an interview with psychologist Dr James Guy, Peck said, 'One of the moments of my own therapy (at thirty) which was dramatic was telling my therapist what a peaceful man my father was. My father wasn't as gentle and as peaceful as I thought. He, in truth, had a great deal of anger in him, which relates to several depressions he had at different times. Going through his effects I ran across correspondence between my mother and him about his depression, trying to get him to have faith and feel better and whatnot. I can remember being cuffed on the head, nothing serious like big-time beatings.'

National and world events, from the Korean War to Watergate, occasionally intruded into Judge Peck's life. On 25 June 1950, North Korea brought its tanks down to the 38th parallel, the stand-off line with South Korea. The move sent shock waves through the US Government which was already coping with a deepening Cold War in Europe and potential conflict with the Soviet Union. New York banker John J. McCloy, US High Commissioner based in Frankfurt was considering a review board for those Nazis imprisoned by the Nuremberg Trials. War-torn Europe still needed rebuilding, and the once industrially mighty West Germany, the 1950s' 'sick man of Europe', needed rapid revitalisation. The Cold War made it a necessity; the Korean War an imperative. The *New York Times* regarded North Atlantic Treaty Organisation (NATO) policy as contradictory, for the Western Allies wanted to revive Germany's heavy industry capabilities while 'holding down the industrialists'. One of those industrialists was Alfred Krupp, the Nuremberg Trials' imprisoned head of the centuries-old Krupp armaments maker. Krupp controlled vast resources of iron and coal and Sullivan & Cromwell knew that terrain well from its considerable involvement in German commerce up to almost the start of the Second World War. Furthermore, McCloy knew Dulles and other S&C principals. S&C understood, therefore, McCloy's anxieties and intent when, as high commissioner, he allowed Krupp to resume leadership of the decartelised Krupp empire though he was still a war criminal.

William Manchester, in his book *The Arms of Krupp*, reported that Eleanor Roosevelt wrote to McCloy to ask, 'Why are we freeing so many Nazis?'

The Korean War began. McCloy, three months before the outbreak, had formulated some ideas for what became The Advisory Board on Clemency for War Criminals. It short form, it was known as 'the Peck Panel', for Judge Peck chaired the three-member commission, which issued its report in forty days, in August, 1950. To put the commission in foreshortened perspective, it could be seen as a much-reduced follow-up to the Nuremburg Trials. It had a purpose – to establish whether certain war criminals should be released. It could reduce sentences, it could not inquire into findings of guilt.

National and geopolitical pressures swirled around the Peck Commission, in addition to the fact that the United States was becoming bogged down in Korea. The pro-German sympathisers in the US Congress, representing myriad financial interests and their own ideology, headed the movement urging the Allies to 'go easy' on German industrialists. It is an extremely murky period of United States history, with still-warm leftovers from the (pro-Hitler) American-German Bund intertwined with Cold War rhetoric and what would blossom as the McCarthy era. Indeed, Manchester quotes McCarthy's reaction to McCloy's decision to release Krupp: 'Extremely wise.'

In 1964, when Peck was twenty-eight and his father was sixty-two, Manchester's *The Arms of Krupp* was published. And while Manchester explicitly refers to Judge Peck's probity, the overall tone of Manchester's reporting is that at the highest levels of the US Government and Administration, the fix was in. It was a variation on an earlier theme when the United States had siphoned off Nazi Germany's rocket scientists for its own development programmes. Commented Peck, 'To give my father some room, at least, I have my own suspicion that [the decision] was ordered by John McCloy, and hence probably by [President Harry] Truman and [General George] Marshall. That's my suspicion. It doesn't let my father entirely off the hook.' Peck 'vaguely remembered' his father was angered by the Manchester book. Other than which, apart from Second World War rationing, neither that conflagration nor the Korean War interfered noticeably with the Peck family's daily world.

Nephew David, son of Scott's brother David, offers a nuanced

assessment of Judge Peck from two generations down. 'My grandfather was a titan: his brilliance, his drive, his charm and wit, his
capacity for work and play were remarkable. These passions leave
little time for family and I think that always rubs. He was very
ordered and I am sure controlling, with a real twist of anger. I think
he could be devastatingly cool and articulate, and can only imagine
that what I've countless times seen in my own father (and myself)
chimes in with descriptions of scenes I have heard Scotty relate
about his father.'

Nephew David, the Rev. Peck, is an Anglican priest who served at
Guildford Cathedral in Surrey, England, until transferring to
Lambeth Palace, as secretary to the Archbishop of Canterbury (Dr
Williams); he said, 'The vehemence with which Scotty speaks of [his
father] is something I have always felt strange. I do not think many
of us are as good or as bad as those who love or hate us think. But
Scotty feels, and I can imagine – but I really do have to imagine –
that Grandfather marginalised Scotty and his family in favour of my
father and our family. I am the youngest member of my family, with
Heather the eldest and Lisa my middle sister. Lisa adored my
grandfather and he her. I loved him immensely and it was a long
time before I knew there were anything but good things to say about
him. Within the firm [nephew David worked for a period at Sullivan
&Cromwell] and all around New York, indeed in Britain and France,
he was revered by those who knew him socially or worked with him
or faced him in court.' That Judge Peck's shinier side beamed
through at times was certain. He was a Brooklyn Dodgers fan, until
the Dodgers left Brooklyn in 1957 for Los Angeles. Judge Peck's
current and past law clerks of that time, known among themselves
as 'Peck's Paragons', held their annual gathering with him at the
Dodgers' venue, Ebbets Field.

Nephew David compared and contrasted the two brothers – his
father, David, and his uncle, Scott. He suggested that 'one thing
Scotty despised, I think, was charm and superficiality,' and 'as he
lived in a world that valued these things over the gifts he had, his life
resulted in his adolescent martyrdom. My father was "winning" in a
crowd, as an athlete, a joker, and one who rarely thought too much!
So [Scotty] must have felt badly underrated as a small, bright and
sensitive boy in a world of boisterous charm. No doubt he inter-
nalised the insecurity that I think my father and grandfather would
have felt in their own social aspirations – as relatively new and poor

comers to the world of serious old money they inhabited – and in my father's case, married into through my mother. Despite every cultural advantage, my father never reached his peak. He always said that Scotty walked to the sound of a different drum, long before Scotty wrote a book of that title, but my father never had a killer business instinct, great brains, or great drive. He liked a party; was fun and charming; relatively successful, but never seriously so. He lacked or recoiled from the risk-taking and strategic thinking one needs in the world. He was supremely clubbable. Scotty was the earnest, sincere, the driven and sensitive one – the suffering poet as opposed to the party boy. He was far more attractive to me than my own father. But that is what uncles are for!'

Scott Peck said there was an issue on which he and father were always in harmony: the importance of sleep. Peck said, 'I think I was born tired. I've always needed a minimum of nine hours of sleep. I can get by for four or five days on eight, maybe for one or two days on seven. One day on six. If I don't get enough sleep I feel terrible. I suspect I have a gene for schizophrenia. [Some researchers link sleep disorder patterns to schizophrenia.] On the sleep thing my father was very wise. During my early adolescent years my parents were liberal. Either that or they didn't want to deal with the issue where I'd come home on vacation from Exeter and it was nothing for me to stay out with the boys drinking and not stagger home until three-thirty or four a.m. Then I could sleep all day. But my father would always wake up, come out in the hallway – although I tried to be very quiet – and start lecturing the hell out of me. "What are you doing coming in at four o'clock in the morning? You need your sleep. Sleep is really important. You need your sleep." I don't think he did that with my brother. I just think he had some sense of how much I really needed my sleep.' Possibly, lying in bed wondering where Scotty was, the judge was also aware how much he needed his own sleep.

Another sentiment Scott shared with his father was that they both hated Washington, and its politics. Judge Peck knew it well for he'd argued cases before the US Supreme Court. During the Eisenhower Administration, in which his friend John Foster Dulles was such a star, Judge Peck was invited by the Attorney General, Herbert Brownell, to become the US Solicitor General, the government's deputy chief litigator. President Eisenhower, according to Scott Peck, told his father that if he'd accept the Solicitor General job he would be given the first opening on the US Supreme Court. Peck assumes his father turned down the offer for financial reasons – as a New York judge he was already earning far less money than he could in private practice, and the US Solicitor General earned less than a senior New York judge.

Even late in life, Judge Peck was not done with the prospect of further public service. In June 1972, there was a break-in at the Democratic National Headquarters in Washington, D.C., which in time was traced back to the White House of President Richard Nixon. A decision was made to create a special prosecutor within the Justice Department to investigate what became known as 'Watergate' and would lead to Nixon's resignation. 'We were on [one of Judge Peck's] family vacations in Bermuda at the time,' said Peck, 'and Father's name was on the selection list as a candidate.' In the words of the man appointed to the task, former US Solicitor General Archibald Cox, the prosecutor was needed to restore 'confidence, honour and integrity in government'.

Judge Peck, by that time seventy, declined on the grounds of 'urgent commitments to clients of long standing.' Scott, conscious of his father's fondness for Nixon, later remarked that it 'was just as well. To my father the whole issue was never criminal, never a matter of right or wrong. It was one of smart or stupid. I can remember him saying, "I can't say as I have ever liked John Mitchell. But he's not stupid and he simply would not have done anything like this (order the Watergate break-in). John just wouldn't have done this. I mean nobody in the club would have done this, and John, I never liked, but he's in the club."' Said Peck, 'The club, preserving the world of the forties, was all that mattered.

'I'm glad my father turned down that job. I don't think he liked the limelight of politics at all. He was, in some ways, very thin-skinned and didn't want to be criticised.' Then Peck went on to criticise his father again, because Judge Peck resented paying the employer's share of the Social Security to fund the retirement of the Pecks' housekeeper, Mrs Hooten, Scott's 'Aunt Sally'. 'I don't see why she needs Social Security,' Judge Peck would say.

As a boy, Scott carried his own varieties of deep grief about it all, and never fully shrugged them off. But the grief was also creative. To paraphrase writer Dennis Drabelle's comment about author Paul Bowles (who hated *his* father), young Scotty's strategy for dealing with his hurts was 'to cry, or to smile, and cultivate his interior garden'. The interior garden cultivated by the boy Scott Peck, seeded and watered by the finer side of his introspection and temperament, blossomed into the attractive elements of his personality as revealed through the sensitivity of his compassionate writing. The tears that seeped from the deep grieving created a rich loam in his fertile mind in which grew the words and concepts that, after his psychiatric training and experience, enabled Peck to assist millions of others over the same hurdles, millions who previously had found no interior garden to cultivate.

CHAPTER 3

SIBLINGS, SORROWS AND SEX

Scott Peck's relationship with his father was reflected to a lesser degree in his relationship with his brother, David, whom he found to be an equally 'very confusing character. We had a lot of fun playing together. I looked up to him and admired him, but then at other times he would treat me really shittily. He would jump on top of me, hold me down on the bed, put his finger up his ass and then take it out and put it under my nose. That's a little sadistic.' In most families with a couple of boys, the brothers have spells of major cooperation, as well as discord, but four years is a wide age gap in the pre-teenage years. Said Peck, 'Adlerians believe that siblings tend to define themselves off one another. Whether this happened or not, I don't know. My brother became a rabid Republican. I've been a lifelong Democrat.'

Peck's second wife, Kathy, said of her husband's acute self-centredness, 'He was so hurt because people in that family didn't know how to love. This is just my pop-psychology, but I think he developed a coping mechanism, and that was the narcissism. I really think that the damage was done in childhood. And that it was from a bullying father, a bullying brother and a mother that went along because she just succumbed to the situation she was in.' Christopher Peck said, 'My Aunt Greg [Nephew David's mother, David's first wife] said that Scotty's mother had pulled her aside, or had lunch with her, and told Greg she was just a terrible mother because she didn't keep Scotty and David from fighting.' Peck had no anecdotes about his mother to match those he told about his father. He'd mention a characteristic – that she smoked and his father berated her for it. But in failing to go through with the divorce, he said, she'd resigned herself to her fate and ever after existed in her husband's shade. As Peck himself described it, she more or less lost her personality.

If Scott Peck felt bullied and put upon, there must have been times David felt put upon in a different way, from having to keep an eye on a much younger brother. And when the younger brother got the better breaks, that could really hurt. The lawn at the Sharon summer home was the thin end of one such wedge between Scott and David.

'My father, the perfectionist, wanted the finest lawn in all of Connecticut,' explained Scott, 'so he consulted with the Department of Agriculture. He planted something, didn't like the result, rolled it over the next year, then replanted it with something better. Sure enough, by the time I was eight and David twelve, he had the finest lawn in the state. The lawn by then was so thick it was nearly impossible to mow – and that was David's job, with a hand mower. David was mollified only by the fact that when I became twelve it would be my job to do the mowing. That was the summer my parents bought the power mower.' Scott said David was furious and held it against him that he'd got a reprieve. 'I used to refer to David as having a lawn mower neurosis. But there was a reason for his neurosis.'

On reflection, Peck said, 'It often seemed to me that I got my parents' good parts and David got all my parents' bad parts.' In the early 1980s, Peck, already achieving fame with *The Road,* received a telephone call from Myron Madden, a pastoral counsellor and author of *The Power of Blessing.* Madden had recently read *The Road Less Travelled,* he told Peck, then he stated, 'You must have an older brother.' 'I said, "Yeah, that's right",' Peck recalled. 'Madden said, "So you're the second son. Any others?" I said, "No. I'm the only one. But how did you guess that?" Madden replied, "Because you got the blessing. The second son always gets the blessing."' Madden's statement, like his book, was based on the Jacob and Esau myth. Said Peck, 'Madden is cautious in his book to point out all the ways in which the formula may not work, but basically the first daughter gets the father's blessing; the second daughter gets the mother's blessing. The first son gets the mother's blessing and the second son, the father's. For boys, the father's blessing is always the most important.' If Scott Peck had it, he lost it. 'I had my father's blessing, I had my mother's too until I was an adolescent. My blessing was withdrawn when I quit Exeter. Until the day my father died I no longer got his blessing. But in my childhood there is a picture of me standing in the playpen at age one, just filled with light and my brother standing next to me, one and a half months short of four years older than me, looking depressed as hell.

'David was very bright but for much of my life, certainly during my twenties and thirties, I hated him. And yet, though we were totally opposite in personality, I admired him. He went from Princeton, where he majored in Arabic studies, to Arabia with Aramco, and was kicked out after two years for reasons never made clear. My brother had a way of doing atrocious sorts of things. He had lots of fights as a kid, fights as an adult. In New York City he was ganged up on by some people who wanted money. He was fifty or fifty-five and tried to fight them off. That was my brother. I would have run, or given my money and run. It was after Arabia he went to Harvard Law, flunked out, but went across the river to Harvard Business School and did wonderfully. He was a Republican, he was in business, he talked my father's language. So, from adolescence on, my brother seemed to be the favoured one, while I was doing flaky things like refusing to take Reserve Officer Training Corps, and dropping out of Exeter.' (ROTC is a university level pre-commission military officer recruitment programme, mandatory in some US colleges and universities as part of their federal land grant funding.)

In a sense, said Peck, David was 'totally unadventurous, never introspective. He was one of those guys where the peak of his life was at Exeter. He died at sixty-six – I outlived him. He was much older and bigger and he'd beat up on me, but on one occasion, I don't know what happened, I was suddenly tossing him to the other side of the room. Other than that, when I was in a fight I'd just curl up and protect my testicles, whereas he, after rotator-cup surgery on his shoulder, was white-water rafting two weeks later. I was a better tennis player, but sometimes he would beat me because when he went for the ball he didn't care whether he'd hit the fence, or how hard. Later, I thought my brother had been the sacrificial lamb – sacrificed to the WASP cause – the family scapegoat.'

The young adult in the making, the one with the air of injured innocence who appears quick to complain a lot about others, at thirteen began attending concerts with his parents, but also developed a summer social life separate from theirs. As a psychiatrist, Peck was quick to admit that children live psychologically and emotionally on several levels simultaneously, their existences an amalgam of private thoughts and dreams they entertain while adapting well or badly to changing situations on these various levels.

He applied the admission to himself. He could have a lot of fun playing with David, he said, and also hate him and admire him almost simultaneously. His multi-level relationship with David was not dissimilar to his relationship with his father, and not unique only to his life as a child. Most children live with variations on this theme. If in the adult Peck some of these variations appear magnified, they were.

He knew that what he said had consequences, and once or twice as a child learned that the hard way. During what he referred to as 'my musically abused childhood', at age six or seven, one passing comment backfired. One day he remarked to his mother, '"Gee, it would be nice if we had a piano." I wasn't really saying I wanted to learn the piano, just it would be nice if we had one. And my fantasy was there'd be some old upright maybe they'd put in my room. Well, a week after there arrived this baby grand in the corner of the living room, and along with the baby grand came Mr Johnson, a piano teacher. All I can remember Mr Johnson doing was telling me to practise, practise, practise these scales. And the only other thing he said was to cut my nails. My brother bit his nails atrociously; the only thing I had going for me was that I had nails. Mr Johnson was a poverty-stricken concert pianist. The only clients he had were a couple of kids like me he was dependent on. Every spring he would say to my mother I had great talent. In six years of piano lessons I never learned how to read music, which is a tribute to the human will.' Sixty years later, Peck said he discovered he had perfect pitch. Others more knowledgeable said he had 'good' pitch.

Scott loved his first summer as a teenager. It opened up experiences for him that would serve him well in later life. As that summer closed, it was with a transition into a situation that would haunt his later life, for his world turned grim. His summer was fun because in his class at St Bernard's was a boy called Carl Brandt, Junior, whose mother was the top literary agent of the day and, on a temporary basis, she was a vice president of MGM in charge of selecting books with potential as movies. 'Carl, her son, and I were both going to attend Exeter,' said Peck. 'Mrs Brandt thought it would be a good idea for the two of us to establish some friendship so that we would be able to support each other at Exeter. So she invited me for a week up to the mansion she and her husband were renting on Long Island. She and I became very fond of each other. It was not a romantic kind of love, me at thirteen and she in her mid-forties, but this very important powerful woman cared for me greatly. Every vacation we used to meet and she would take me to 21 [one of New York's top restaurants], and supply me with cigarettes, caviar and champagne, much to my parents' horror and chagrin. She'd invite me to quite a fair number of her parties in Manhattan. There were no artistic people in parties at my house, but there were indeed at her house, so I met a great number of the great authors of the day. She never really told me anything about writing but encouraged just by her interest in me. The only thing she did give me were little tips, terribly important, like save all your typewriter paper boxes because you'll want those to send the manuscript to publishers, and always have a duplicate copy of anything you're working on lest you lose the original. She encouraged me in bigger ways than just writing.'

Those pleasures ended as abruptly as the portcullis of boarding school crashed down to separate summer from the fall. His parents drove up to New Hampshire, to Exeter, to deliver him to the top-rated boys' prep school in the country, Phillips Academy. (In the United States, boys begin their boarding school years in their freshman high school year when they're fourteen years old. In Britain, Australia and elsewhere, they often start at an earlier age.) The emotional trauma of being sent away from home to boarding school, a stock feature of early twentieth-century English autobiographies and biographies, is not prominent in American literature. The starting age differential could account for Peck's trauma. He was a year younger than his peers because he'd skipped a class in elementary school. The disastrous Exeter years were so major a turning point that later, when Peck talked about his life, his key complaints would always emerge as Exeter and his father. If Exeter tended to disappear from the thread of conversation for a while, when it did emerge it was with the same old bitterness, even in an aside. In 2005, discussing his friend Omar Kahn, Peck said, 'Omar's much smarter than me, it took me two and two-thirds years to quit Exeter, it took him two and a quarter months.'

Scott was well aware David had enjoyed Phillips Exeter Academy for he'd been a brilliant success, at least in sports, the only Exeter student, Scott said proudly, to ever gain three 'letters' (similar to a 'blue' at Oxford or Cambridge) as a goalie in varsity soccer, varsity hockey and varsity lacrosse. Scott genuinely realised he was fortunate to have been accepted and set on the rails of success, hooked to a career locomotive that would pull him on to the best of the Ivy League universities, in the company of boys, soon men, whose careers in high finance and government and the professions were as guaranteed as his own.

Fifty-plus years on, Peck mused that while he felt embraced by the 'security which came from being a part of what was so obviously a proper pattern' and could revel in the fact that 'there are a whole number of prestigious WASP prep schools – though if one is more prestigious than any other it would be Exeter', and while he could conclude he was 'ready for the intellectual stuff', for he went in as a freshman taking 'sophomore-level courses', emotionally he was a little boy lost. 'I felt horrible there right from the start because I was so depressed and miserable,' he said. 'Right from the start, even before classes began, I can remember sitting around with a bunch of kids. A kid asked me, "Hey, you ever been laid?" I didn't know what being laid was. I was thirteen. I knew it was something good, so I said, "Sure, sure."'

Peck was in a situation over which he had no control. Exeter, he said, was a 'culture totally dictated by kids between the ages of thirteen and eighteen. It was like the book, *Lord of the Flies* [by William Golding]. That could have been written by an Exeter graduate. There was no interaction between the faculty and the students. You were appointed a faculty advisor. The entirety of my first year I never once met with my faculty advisor. The faculty had no real contact with the students.' Another 'big thing at Exeter,' he said, 'was tremendous homophobia where all the worst people in the out-group were called "fairies", or, "zoom! There goes a fairy". The living environment was deliberately harsh. You weren't really allowed any decorations in the room or anything to make your room comfortable.' The only respite, the only touch of home, was that every Sunday evening someone prominent would travel to Exeter to lecture. 'It was a voluntary kind of thing to go to,' Peck said, 'but after the lecture, those who wanted to could go to a large faculty home. In the living room they would gather around and talk with this famous lecturer and I would go faithfully, not because I was particularly interested in the subject or the person but for the opportunity to go to this house that had sofas decently upholstered, curtains, warm and soft and gentle. I would go just for the opportunity of going into a real living room. Exeter took, and as far as I understand still takes, great pride in being harsh. The race is won by the swift and hardship will teach you to be swift. If you can't deal with this kind of hardship then you better get out. It was the most un-nurturing place that I have ever seen.'

Exeter's 'in-group' had immediately pegged Peck firmly with the 'out-group'. He hated his general predicament and despaired further in being among the 'outs'. When his parents came to visit during the first Thanksgiving they saw he was depressed. They asked why. Peck denied it was so and said he was getting along fine. He said the same in his letters home.

Fifty-plus years later he said that he felt so much pressure to succeed at Exeter he couldn't acknowledge his depression to his parents. He endured the first year and 'went back for the second year because I was expected to. It was what I was supposed to do. Here was this great school with a great reputation and I was supposed to tough it out.' In fact, he was doing poorly academically and lived for the vacations. Away from Exeter, at ages thirteen, fourteen and fifteen, he was becoming critically aware of the world around him. He was already well along the road to holding strong opinions based solely on personal reactions.

His parents occasionally attended Christ Church on Park Avenue, 'a weird church that was built around one guy [the Rev. Ralph Sockman], *the* minister for the upper-crust Park Avenue types. He was smooth, he was oily.' At fourteen, Peck struck out on his own and several times attended the Madison Avenue Presbyterian Church, presided over by the Rev. George Buttrick, a famed preacher, and later 'Preacher to the University' at Harvard. 'Buttrick would weep during his sermons, I remember one was "come with me and I'll make you fishers of men". I decided that sounded like a good idea, to become "fishers of men". Spiritually marooned somewhere between Sockman and Buttrick, Peck found only confusion in religion. 'The reason Christianity made no sense to me,' he said, was here were 'two famous ministers. One, I knew, I was spiritually ahead of, while the other, slightly less famous, was light years ahead of me spiritually. It just didn't compute.' On the religious front at Exeter he paid 'no attention to God'. His best friend at the school, he said, was Rene Tillich, son of the noted US theologian Paul Tillich, and he and Rene had 'great intellectual discussions late into the night'.

Peck said he found himself reacting to ethical issues that ranged from his adverse reaction to hearing Senator Joseph McCarthy on the radio, to suspicions about his father's home away from home, Sullivan & Cromwell. During Peck's first summer break from Exeter, he said, he was at home, sick and bored. He rarely listened to the radio but turned it on and 'heard someone by the name of Joseph McCarthy speaking. I didn't know who he was, or anything about the issues of communism or whatnot. I just caught about thirty to forty seconds of a speech he was giving. The voice was so ugly I turned it off and I remember going down the hall from the bedroom thinking "that was the voice of evil".'

The summer he was fifteen Peck briefly entered the competitive tennis arena and, more lastingly, also discovered girls. 'One of the reasons I was never a better tennis player, never a great tennis player, was I went on a tournament that summer, but I hated the tournament circuit and I hated the kids. Stuck-up. I'm very competitive, but I had none of the killer instincts the great tennis players have. There were no ball boys or lines people, you had to make your own call. Whenever I called a ball and was questioned did I really see it, I'd wonder could it have been my imagination that it went out. And I would invariably lose the next point.'

That same summer, staying on Long Island, he French-kissed a girl and decided he had met the love of his life. She ditched him and dated all the other boys. 'And I spent much of the summer watching the waves come in from the ocean and pondering the mystery of it all.' When, towards the end of the summer, she'd run through all the boys in town and asked if they might date again, he took her out. They necked and kissed. 'She said, "You're distant, don't you love me any more?" And I said, "No I don't. Frankly, my dear, I don't give a damn."' But he was not unmoved. In 1965, in San Francisco, he memorialised that summer by writing two poems, one on death called, 'Life Wish', and one on sex called, 'Death Wish'. At that point, he was also watching the fledgling hippie 'Free Love' experience open up around him. He was not part of it.

Back at school in the fall of 1951, the lonely confines of Exeter gave Peck time and reasons to brood about his father's shortcomings, and on his father's reaction to what schoolboy Peck felt was an inevitability – his need to leave Exeter as an act of personal survival. 'My lungs were hurting. I'd no idea how my father would respond. I was depressed. I felt I was a failure. It wasn't any of the masochism of rebellion,' a fact that 'almost confirmed that my father should respond that way because I was such a *failure*,' he said.

But as a thirteen- to fifteen-year-old at Exeter he felt 'daily my life appeared more meaningless and I felt more wretched. The last year I did little but sleep, for only in sleep could I find any comfort. In retrospect I think perhaps I was resting and unconsciously preparing myself for the leap I was about to take.' He was more than despairing, though, he was angry.

Decades after Exeter, he'd decided his malaise at the school was a 'heritage from his father's deepest motive in life, to look like a WASP and to raise his children to be the ultimate WASPs. Father succeeded in David. In retrospect I would be walking out of the WASP culture into the absolutely unknown.'

Teenager Peck's later character is shaped by Exeter in several ways. Despite his relentless disparagement of the place, he had his achievements. His writing ability was praised. 'I have got a swelled head. My English teacher thinks I am a genius as a writer. We had to write a description a couple of weeks ago and I wrote about the reflections of the headlights of cars on the walls of my room at night. The other day in class he handed them back, he read it to the class saying that the paper showed genius and compared me rather favourably with John Steinbeck. Now he is keeping it to read to the English department. On the first theme we did I got a C and on the last one, which we just did I got a B, which was the highest mark in the class.'

He broke into the school's theatrical world. He was fifteen when, in the winter semester, he entered the 'in-group' through being cast for a small part in *Billy Budd,* the school play. It was a minor role but he enjoyed it. He wrote home, 'Last Sunday I went out for the Fall play which is "Billy Budd". I was called back for a second tryout on Wednesday and made it. I have the fifth largest part, that of Lietenant [sic] Ratcliffe [sic]. I am pretty pleased about it of course, although it takes all of my Wednesday and Sunday afternoons. Tim [Childs] is going to be Billy and a boy by the name of John Poole is going to be Captain Veer which is the part I cherish. You have seen the play, haven't you?'

One of the co-authors of the play was John Chapman, the drama critic for the *New York Times.* He was a friend of one of Exeter's teachers and came up to see the production during one of its two nights, he then reviewed it for the *Exonian,* Exeter's newspaper. 'The review was full of kind praise,' said Peck, though as his eyes raced down Chapman's column searching for his own name, Chapman 'mentioned everybody in the play in his review, everybody but me. As I kept reading I wasn't there, I wasn't there, I wasn't there. Then I came to the last paragraph which I thought he would use for summation. Instead he wrote, "I would like to end by making special mention of Scott Peck, who although in a minor role as Lt Radcliffe, as far as I'm concerned, played that role better than it was played on Broadway." That helped me get into the in-crowd.' Peck's triumphant acceptance into the ruling elite did not play out the way one might expect. Rather than his new status making his continuance at Exeter likely, he felt that being accepted into the in-group gave him the emotional freedom to pursue his plan to quit the place. 'When I got into the in-group I felt I could leave, as a success. I couldn't have left as an out-group failure.'

To his parents he wrote, 'How did you like my reviews. They were pretty great. Did you save the *Exonian*?' He was delighted that 'in the in-crowd was Tim Childs, a very eccentric and wonderful man, quite potent in the intellectual circle of the in-crowd. Timmy was in class with me and took me under his wing and let it be known I was a friend. We remained good friends for half a century' until Childs' death. In fact it was more than 'good friends': Peck was in awe of Tim. Down the years Peck would find and periodically befriend or be befriended by the strong, father-figure types he could admire and look up to, and indeed depend on. And Scott, in turn, was known as a good friend once he became one.

At Exeter he had developed hypochondria into a minor art form. His illnesses, both feigned and real, revolved mainly around the infirmary, a stay in which gave him more time to read. He wrote, 'All Sunday night I had a beautiful headache so I came in Monday morning to make my weekend a long one. I have just finished having the first of fourteen nice penicillin shots. I have a little sinus trouble but it is nothing to be worried about and I will soon be out.' Peck was developing a coping mechanism as he oscillated between his detestation at his situation and the need to survive in it. 'Well, life is just about the same as usual, not depressing but frustrating because I cannot read English all the time. Probably I will zip off to the infirmary and read a couple of books sometime soon.'

So, determined to leave Exeter, he first went to see his advisor, Mr Lynch, 'a kindly person who had barely spoken to me in the previous two and a half years.' At that meeting, Peck had barely begun speaking when Lynch broke in and told him it would be preferable to graduate from a superior school like Exeter with lesser grades than from a lesser school with better grades. 'And your parents would be quite upset, just go along and do the best you can.' Peck next went to 'the crusty old dean of the school who cut me off straightaway, told me Exeter was the best school in the world and I was a damn fool for thinking of quitting.' Finally Peck went to see his maths teacher, a somewhat younger man. 'I chose him not because we had any relationship or because he seemed to be a particularly warm sort of person – indeed I found him a rather cold mathematical kind of fish – but because he had a reputation for being the faculty genius.' The maths teacher let Peck talk for five minutes then asked him questions for three-quarters of an hour. Then the teacher leaned back in his chair, and, with a pained expression on his face, told Peck, 'I'm sorry. I can't help you. I don't have any advice to give you. You know,' he continued, 'it's impossible for one person to ever completely put himself in another person's shoes. But insofar as I can put myself in your shoes – and I'm glad I'm not there – I don't know what I would do if I were you. So, you see, I don't know how to advise you. I'm sorry that I've been unable to help.'

Five decades later, Peck said, 'It is just possible that the man saved my life. I was close to suicidal, but when I left his office I felt as if a thousand pounds had been taken off my back. Because if a genius didn't know what to do, then it was all right for me not to know what to do.' It was a fine rationalisation. Peck had been desperately trying to survive at Exeter on his own terms. Now, headed home for the Christmas vacation, he was prepared to leave on his own terms. Back in Park Avenue he told his parents he hated Exeter and wanted to quit. His parents asked him why he hated it so; he could give them no rational answer. When they asked which school he wanted to attend, he said he didn't know. 'They worked on me and convinced me to stick it out for at least one more semester and if, at the end of another semester, I still wanted to quit, well, then I could.' Much later in adult life, Peck would insist he had identified the cause of his Exeter unhappiness, his reaction against the dominant WASP culture so cherished by his father, 'for Exeter was one of White Anglo-Saxon Protestantism's formation centres,' he said. Equally, the WASP bogeyman may have been a handy scapegoat for a Peck genuinely unhappy also because he was a young boy away from familiar and comfortable hearth and home, and had a strong tendency to want things his own way. Contrary to impressions, his parents were far more attentive to him at Exeter than later conversations suggested. His letters show a high level of interest in him, with quite frequent parental trips to Exeter, New Hampshire and the facilitating of his weekends at home in New York City.

'First of all, Dad,' he wrote, 'I want to thank you for a really great weekend. I will never forget the food, glass flowers, and viva sabata [sic – the movie *Viva Zapata*]. We had better start arranging about Thanksgiving [the fourth Thursday in November]. Of course I would like to come to old New York as I have numerous invitations for dates on Wednesday night.' On another occasion his letter opened, 'Dear Mom and Dad, first of all I want to thank you for a most wonderful weekend. It was so nice of you to bring me all the way in just for such a short time but it was certainly worth it. I didn't get much sleep coming back on the train as you can imagine. For the last four days I have been pretty much of a wreck and today is the first day I have felt fine. I have been sleeping about fifteen hours a day so I am all caught up now but I have a hell of a lot of work to do. I am almost already out of money. I have spent $7 for my bill at spa, $2 for a carton of cigarettes which will last me until you come up anyway, $2 for a pen, 50 cents for a tube of toothpaste (I should have stolen one from home) and 75 for food. The food in the dining hall is putrid. Something ought to be done about it. So counting George's money I have about three dollars which will last until you come up for the play. As for that I think it is a foolish thing. I really think I am getting to be pretty good in my little part.' The schoolboy plaint. In another letter: 'You said Daddy will send me some money. At the moment I am broke.'

He made it through Exeter's winter semester, had a small role in another play [*L'Ecole de Maris* – the School for Husbands], and the lead role in the spring play [*Yellow Jack*]. 'On Monday and Tuesday Timmy, John Mueller, Dave Beer and I worked like dogs on the winter play,' he wrote. 'The faculty wanted to do the most god awful fantasie [sic] called "Noah". It is supposedly a French comedy-tragedy about Noah and his ark and a lot of animals. It was the most absurd thing I ever read. So we protested it and spent the two days doing nothing but reading plays and calling New York about them. Things are not really decided yet but it is definite that we are not going to do "Noah", thank God. Whatever it is I am going to try out for a good part. We were debating seriously about "Twentieth Century" [a play about showbusiness] and Dave Beer wanted me to do the part of Gloria Swanson, heh, heh. I don't think we are going to do it though.' [Swanson starred in the play's 1952 revival.] Of the spring play, *Yellow Jack*, the ever-competitive Peck was able to write home, 'Guess who got the lead, your own little son. I'm the enthusiastic young scientist and it is the best part in the play besides being the longest. I have 350 lines, 75 in Billy and 20 in *L'Ecole de Maris.*' But Peck had determined on another course. In later conversation he said that although he hated letting the school and the spring play down, when he came home for the spring break – before the last semester of the academic year – he said to his parents, 'You said I could leave Exeter and quit if I wanted to, and I still want to.' When, again, they asked where he wanted to go and he could give them no answer, they said, 'Well, you must be crazy not wanting to go to Exeter, you ought to see a psychiatrist.'

Judge Peck had a classmate from Wabash who was a psychiatrist with a posh residential treatment clinic, Silver Hill, in southern Connecticut. So, at his father's behest, Scott went to see the man. He took an instant liking to him, despite being told, 'You're depressed and I think you ought to come into hospital here.' The doctor told young Peck that he was not so depressed he could be committed, Scott had to admit himself. 'It's your choice, but my advice would be that you come into the hospital.' 'And that night,' said Peck, 'he made an appointment to see me again the next morning for my decision.' No matter how many times he has told the Exeter tale, Peck contended that leaving Exeter was the bravest thing he ever did. (And, given he was a teenager opposing a mighty father, there's no reason to doubt him.) He would also add that making a decision that night to enter Silver Hill was the hardest thing he ever did. He again had thoughts of suicide, he said. 'I couldn't sleep until, finally, as I recounted in *The Road Less Travelled,* these words came to me, that "the only true security in life lies in relishing life's insecurity."' And so he told himself he would go into the unknown. He went into Silver Hill and stayed for five weeks. Apart from his daily meetings with the psychiatrist, he mainly read, slept, and mused. It could be that in these five weeks, as he mused on life's insecurity, and about life being difficult, that the seed of his first book was planted. Was it as happenstance as he'd later suggest, that he became a psychiatrist?

'The biggest thing that happened in my therapy was the

psychiatrist – who was very good,' said Peck, 'asked what in relation to Exeter was I most angry about. I said, well, I was angry at Exeter. He said, "Well, I'd like you to think about this question when we see each other tomorrow so you can come up with another answer."' And the next day Scott told him, 'Well, I guess what I was angriest about was not Exeter but angriest about myself for being a failure at Exeter.' The psychiatrist said, 'Well, I think that's correct.' At Silver Hill, Peck had been given psychological testing. The only thing the psychiatrist said about it is that it indicated Peck had a certain fear of sex. 'He asked did I masturbate and I said no. And he said, "Well, you know it's perfectly normal to masturbate."' So, having gotten permission, I went off and immediately started masturbating.' He was not quite sixteen. He'd also got permission to leave Exeter. But was Exeter leaving him? In one sense, according to his nephew, David (the Rev. David Peck), it was Judge Peck, Sullivan & Cromwell, Park Avenue and Exeter that prevailed. 'Scotty has a real snobbishness that is straight from the same flask as my father and his father!' The WASP culture had enfolded him. He could poke holes through it, but he never escaped it. Like it or not, however, Exeter had told him he could write, at least descriptively. In one of his final letters home he noted, 'This weekend I have a free expository theme in which I will try to work as much description as possible. I hate expository writing as there is little room for the imagination.'

Scott Peck left Silver Hill shortly before his sixteenth birthday and went to work early that summer on a farm attached to a school out near Sharon, work for which he was paid. There were others his age he made friends with in the evenings and on weekends. He worked, he said, a gruelling forty to fifty hours a week on the farm. 'That's how I became familiar with what it's like to get the stones out of the field.' He was living at the school. The only thing that upset him was that two or three weeks before the end of summer, he learned his father was paying the school 'to have this position where I was working my balls off. I got furious at my father, furious at the school', but not at the farmer he worked for. 'He was close to a mentor to me, a beautiful sort of gnarled, weather-beaten huge man, strong as an ox. He had a son about seven or eight. I used to be impressed by how he always called his son "dear", or "sweetie". He obviously just loved his son. He was also very good to me and I praised him for the way he would lift a full can of milk, three or four feet tall, probably weighing when full about 150 pounds, with what looked like a couple of fingertips. He was always clapping me on the back and saying, "You've got to know your business. You've got to know your business."'

When Scott left Exeter, David was already in college. 'My brother and Timmy loved Exeter and would go back for reunions and whatnot. I never would,' he said. 'One of two great ambitions of my life was that when my twenty-fifth college reunion rolled around I'd be too busy doing more important things than attend. That was fulfilled. The other ambition, which looks like it is going to be fulfilled, is that until the day I die I'll have someone like Gail [Puterbaugh, his office executive] filling out the [government required health] insurance forms [that follow each doctor's visit] and be unlike my father who was beginning to get confused and old and shaky. He spent hours over Medicare forms and I'm damned if I'm going to spend the last few months of my life fussing over Medicare.' In the 1950s, both Peck sons were still very much dependent on their father, and their father's standards were high. He expected, indeed demanded a rigorous adherence to them. Said the Rev. David Peck, 'My father was certainly stunted by his need to perform according to certain [parental] norms and by his inability to do so because his heart so often lay elsewhere. I see so much of my father in Scotty it is amazing, the man who Scotty must, in so many ways, feel unlike. I find it utterly uncanny when we are together.' Both David and Scott had tales of their father's mischievous – Scott called it sadistic – streak. Scott had the 'crybaby' newspaper headline to haunt him. David had the sweetheart ring. His father usually played a joke on one of his sons at Christmas in a Christmas stocking gift. Scott said that when David had a crush on a local girl called Josie, there was a little present from her in his stocking. 'It had a card, signed Josie, that read, "David, here's a ring, love Josie." David opened up the present and it was a tiny bathtub with a ring around it.'

Scott was admitted to Friends Seminary, a day school on the border of Greenwich Village, in New York City. It is the oldest Quaker school in the city. He repeated his junior year, eleventh grade. In conversation both his eyes and his voice lit up when he talked about the school. 'Friends Seminary was an extraordinary place. I'm sure it had something to do with the Quaker Meeting House and Quaker background. It was the opposite of Exeter,' he said. 'A day school, small, co-educational [Exeter was not during Peck's years], liberal [Exeter was conservative], and loving. And I just blossomed. Part of my guilt at leaving Exeter the last semester was that I had to write a ten-page paper for American history, fully annotated with bibliography, end notes and footnotes. I was aghast at the prospect. I just didn't feel I could do it and I wondered if I quit Exeter just because I didn't want to write that paper. Then I repeated the American history course in eleventh grade at Friends and sailed effortlessly through full forty-page papers, fully annotated, all of them about religion. They particularly specialised in Jonathan Edwards [an eighteenth-century American theologian] and the Great Awakening [a surge in religious feeling at that time]. Now I was not a Christian and I was approaching this as a historian or sociologist, but it's still interesting that I chose to write about religious history.'

Peck's mention of Edwards is an essential element of what, a quarter-century into the future, would develop as his particular brand of Christian inquiry. Born in 1703, this American Presbyterian divine provides a marker for Peck's own intellectual journey. Edwards, in *Personal Narrative,* his account of his conversion, reveals he was seeing God's visible glory – placing God in the human context afresh. He saw God reflected in nature that, in the words of one scholar of American religious experience, combined in a complex way 'philosophical idealism and Lockean psychology'. Peck would similarly plunge into the interface between belief and psychiatry.

There was also something in the Quaker approach to religion that triggered a response in Peck. 'Once or twice a week we had meetings in the Meeting House. Once or twice a month those meetings were traditional Quaker silent meetings. It wasn't that you couldn't speak, but you could only speak if you felt moved. And it was there I had my first experiences of being moved by something that the Quaker would call the "inner light", which today I would call the Holy Spirit,' he said. 'To stand up and speak and say things that were wiser than I even knew I had to say. That was a very powerful spiritual experience and indeed became a foundation of FCE [Scott and Lily Peck's Foundation for Community Encouragement].' In his senior year Peck would have described himself as an agnostic. He found the religious studies textbook a problem, so much so that 'the stuff about Christianity, Judaism and Confuscianism made absolutely no sense to me.' What did make sense were some of the Hindu and Buddhist and Taoist mystical writings. 'I felt that I had intellectually come home,' he said, 'and of course, they're filled with paradox. It wasn't that I discovered paradox through them, but I discovered I wasn't the only person that ever thought about paradox and I was really turned on. If you'd have asked me at nineteen or twenty what I was, I would have told you then I was a Zen Buddhist. That's very fashionable now. But back then, in the 1950s if you told people you were a Zen Buddhist they'd think you were either queer or pinko. But I just found it very, very exciting stuff.'

At sixteen he'd also discovered something equally exciting – sex. There had been no sex play of any kind among Exeter boys, he said – homosexuality was the great taboo. He may have made a pass at a boy, on one occasion, he thought, but he wasn't sure what he had in mind, and nothing came of it. The incident was not repeated. Peck was sixteen-and-a-half when he fell deeply in love with a girl he referred to only as 'Q'. He felt then, and still felt a half century later when he spoke of it, that he treated her shabbily. When talking about Q, he spoke with an obvious sense of remorse not evident to the same extent when, on other occasions, he talked about his marital infidelities. Q was spoken for – she had a boyfriend in some distant state and wore his ring on a chain around her neck. Peck initially kept his distance. In late 1952 they were together in a library. 'I was looking at her and I said, "God, I'd really like to date her."' He passed her a note asking her for a date that weekend. Her note back said yes, and they had their first date, with follow-ups the two following weekends. A couple of nights after the third date, 'I came to the sudden realisation I had fallen hopelessly in love. I called her and said, "I've got to talk to you," and went down to see her.' She reminded him she was still in love with the other man. Even so, she and Peck continued to date and she gave up the other fellow. 'She taught me about half of what I needed to learn about sex. I was a slow learner. I don't know, maybe it was Oedipal stuff with my mother, that I somehow thought women were off-limits, or untouchable, or that they didn't like sex. I don't know. Part of it, too, was about the holiness of sex. The first time she touched my penis it was like my experience of French-kissing – I mean I just never dreamed that a woman would have any interest in touching it. So that became a ritual and, eventually, it went all the way to intercourse. I perpetrated this terrible lie on my parents that, because New York subways were dangerous, it was dangerous for me to take Q back home at night and return alone. I might get hurt. It would be nicer if Q could stay the night at our apartment.' His parents agreed. Q slept in what had been David's room. 'Until one day my mother had a friend who was staying in my bedroom and I was relegated to one of the tiny maids' rooms off the kitchen. Early the next morning, my mother and her friend were in the kitchen, about seven a.m., banging pots and pans around. I stumbled out all rumpled in my pyjamas and my mother's friend said, "Oh, Scotty, I'm sorry we're making so much noise. Go sleep in my room if you want." I said, "Oh, that's all right," and stumbled into David's room where Q was and crawled into bed with her. And that's how my mother found out. My mother was furious that I'd done that in front of her close friend. "How could you do that?" she kept saying, "how could you do that to my friend, my close friend?"'

Peck's regrets regarding Q, whom 'I loved as deeply as I've ever loved anyone,' were several. They dated for two years, but there was 'nowhere for our relationship to go except to get married, and it was not necessarily a neat idea to get married at eighteen.' Even so, he would have considered it, he said, had there not been some major differences between him and the girl that convinced him it was a marriage that would never work. They broke up. Six months later the relationship resumed when he met her again at a dance. 'I was still desperately in love with her.' But nothing had changed, and after a year the relationship faltered on the same grounds as earlier. 'I feel badly,' Peck said, 'I'd stolen her from this guy – although I don't know who the hell he was. But the big point was she was deeply in love with me and deeply caring. I had the experience of twice ending a relationship with a woman who I know loved me to the hilt and who I loved as deeply as I've loved anyone. The only time I ever cried between the age of eight and the age of thirty-six was those two times when I broke off with her. Lily, to this day, thinks I carry a torch for Q.' Even in the 1990s, Peck could say that besides his wife, Lily, 'She's the only woman that I love until this day.' Once he'd become famous, he said, 'All my old girlfriends, including the one I French-kissed, made contact. Except Q. I'm glad I didn't marry Q, but it wasn't for lack of love.'

There was another side to his sex life. From the age of sixteen onwards until his marriage, Peck had casual homosexual encounters. He got the idea, he said, after witnessing a young man masturbating in the men's toilets at Grand Central Station. 'It was a real turn-on,' said Peck. After that Peck would pick up men in the streets in New York City and 'go back to their place. It's the easiest way to get it off in the world. They don't want any responsibility. You don't want any responsibility and you can just arrange it with your eyes. When I was feeling horny, I'd go out and do that. But there was never any romance associated with it. It was a turn-on.' He never paid for sex: 'I was too cheap. For a few years I wondered whether I was a homosexual or heterosexual.' That issue was resolved with Q, he said: he was heterosexual. But whenever he was horny and girls were unavailable, he'd cruise, and pick up a man and go back to his place. 'There was nothing either emotional or romantic about my hour-long homosexual contacts,' he said. Later, 'stopping cruising was easy because sex was available with marriage, and Lily was never one to say, "Oh, I've got a headache tonight, dear."'

In conversation, Peck was ill-at-ease discussing homosexuality. There was no inkling he'd ever sought a homosexual relationship once marital sex and, later, a series of one-night stands and affairs kept him sexually satisfied. He did seem to believe that because he'd had homosexual contacts simply as a sexual release, that for some homosexuals that's all it was. That they were really heterosexuals. Later, a New Yorker who read *The Road Less Travelled* objected to a Peck comment about homosexuality, much as other readers would challenge his view that romantic love didn't exist, except as a by-play to the sexual chase. The New Yorker, who said he'd enjoyed the book, nonetheless continued, 'I do want to air one bad feeling I had and that was to a remark about "passive homosexuals" who might benefit from the risk of asking a woman out. I am a homo-sexual and I don't feel that this is a disease or a lack of development psychologically – that "old" Freudian stuff is something I, and most healthy people in your field, don't believe in any more. I am in a lifestyle that was chosen for me by a High Power, and one that takes as many risks and disciplines etc. to grow in as in a heterosexual lifestyle.' It was a topic Peck omitted from future books and talks.

He and Q had avoided pregnancy, he said, by using coitus inter-ruptus. He hadn't begun using condoms. That started the following summer when his father said he was taking him to Europe. 'I knew I was going to get laid in Europe,' Peck said, 'and that I'd better have some condoms.' When he went to his father to enquire about the best brand, his father gave him a lecture about not doing anything that would require condoms. 'By that time,' said Peck, 'I'd learned how to stand up to him. I said, "Listen, I came to you for advice, not for some kind of moral lecture. Answer my question about what's the best condom or it's the end of the conversation."' His father replied, 'Well, probably Ramses.' Peck could not explain the process by which he could at one remove be intimidated by his father, and at another deal with him man-to-man on the question of reliable condoms. But the WASP culture in which they both operated could explain it. Father–son issues dealt with emotions, and the culture frowned on anything emotional. Condoms were a manly practical matter and, therefore, could be straightforwardly discussed.

The Ramses brand name may have solved Scott Peck's immediate plight, but it didn't prevent some subsequent embarrassment. Buying condoms in the sex-doesn't-exist 1950s was a blush-producing venture, and not all pharmacies stocked them. Peck decided to seek a pharmacy far from the ones near home. There was one about a mile away that looked sufficiently disreputable to stock condoms. He stood on the opposite side of the street waiting for the light to change. Then he went charging across the road, eyes downcast, straight into the store and up to the counter. He raised his embarrassed eyes to ask for Ramses and was face-to-face with one of the few female pharmacists in New York City.

When it came to choosing a college, Peck decided to stick with what he knew. Friends Seminary was small and co-ed, he would go to a small co-ed college, to Middlebury College in Vermont. 'It was dull, dull, dull. The faculty were terrific but the students were mostly there just to get their degrees so they could buy what was then the ideal house, $60,000 [probably $600,000 today]. Drinking and fraternity life was the big thing. I was involved in that but took no joy in it. I also felt that the women were dull. Every weekend I went down to date Smithies [at prestigious Smith College, North Hampton, Massachusetts], a considerable drive.' He would also be dating women of his own social class.

When Peck went home to New York City during a break in his sophomore year, he called Carol Brandt and asked her if he could take her out for lunch. 'In her typical commandeering way,' said Peck, 'she said, "Oh, I'll take care of it all."' The result of that lunch for Peck was an apprenticeship under one of the most prominent and successful writers of the day, John P. Marquand. Brandt told Peck the name of the restaurant, he got there a little early and there were three chairs. He later surmised that Brandt was having an affair with Marquand and Peck provided good 'cover' for their public meeting. 'When she showed up, it was with Marquand. They were

in the process of trying to make a movie out of Marquand's *Sincerely,*
Willis Waide, and they seemed to be stymied when talking about it
during lunch. I had about three martinis and Marquand had about
five and I don't know what I said but suddenly they were both
clapping me on the back, saying, "You've got it, you've got it."
Apparently a plot idea. And the next thing Marquand says was,
"Well, young man, if you want to write, why don't you come live
with me this summer?"' Peck thanked him and returned to college,
presuming it was something of a five-martini invitation. 'Two days
later in the mail comes a letter saying, "I'm quite serious about
wishing that you would come live with me this summer."' It was a
two-and-a-half month apprenticeship under a master. 'The only
thing I wrote,' said Peck, 'was a romantic sort of thing set in Mexico,
which I didn't know anything about. He thought it was pretty
terrible.' If Peck regarded Carol Brandt as his first mentor, the first
adult who had taken him seriously, Marquand was a close second.
Among other things, he taught Peck about the discipline of writing,
for Marquand left his house at 9 a.m. each morning, walked a
hundred yards to his study in a little barn where his secretary
waited. He'd dictate until 1 p.m. on the dot and then left to go to
play golf or bridge. Said Peck, 'I realised that if you're going to be a
professional writer, you don't write just when the spirit moves you.'

Marquand had started as a Boston newspaper man, was a First
World War artillery commander, and served as a civilian top secret
intelligence consultant during the Second World War. He was a
national figure who had a popular national following through his
'Mr Moto' stories in the *Saturday Evening Post,* an audience less
rarefied than those who read his novels. (Mr Moto was a Japanese
martial arts expert who tackled international crime. The stories were
made into movies starring Peter Lorre.)

This was a novelist whose best writings were his books that deftly
skewered the Boston upper class and the New England elite's
manners and mores. Peck who, like Marquand, was putatively born
into their class, was severely wounded by the same WASPs. Peck
likely picked up some fuel for his own fires from Marquand, and not
just by osmosis. Marquand's 1938 Pulitzer Prize had been for his
novel *The Late George Apley,* in which, remarked one reviewer, the
satire is slow to emerge but no less stinging when it does. Peck was
stinging, satire was not his suit.

As an international traveller, Marquand also wrote articles from around the world for major American magazines. The Marquands and Curzons, his forebears, were early on to the American scene, with property and wealth – at one point – in Newberry Port, Massachusetts. The money, but not some of the holdings, was gone by the time Marquand came of age. As an author, his fame and writings did not survive his death, for he wrote for 'an entire generation of Americans from the 1920s to the 1950s,' wrote Jonathan Yardley in 1988 in the *Washington Post*. And, said Yardley, 'Nobody seems to read him now except Yardleys and other superannuated White Anglo-Saxon Protestants. That is a pity. He deserves better.'

In 1952, Marquand's son, Johnny Marquand, under the name John Phillips (a *nom de plume* quickly penetrated by reviewers), had written a novel, *The Second Happiest Day*, to some acclaim. Since when, Johnny had been working on his second novel. In 1956, when Peck met Marquand, Marquand senior had invited his son and his wife to come home for the summer from Europe, where they were living, to spend it with him. They remained in Europe until the fall; Scott Peck spent the summer instead.

Marquand may have been lonely, equally, he had heard in Peck's table talk his erudition, intelligent assessments, strong opinions and nuanced summations that are the prerequisites of a first-class writer. Peck in conversation on a topic he held close to his heart was a masterly reasoner with a great grasp of supportive evidence and a skilled use of language. It was precisely that which Elizabeth and John Allen heard on the snowy days in front of the fire in the Peck home in New Preston.

To Peck, Marquand 'was always a form of social critic, and I think that may have been why we got along so famously. A biography years ago described him as very angry, hostile and difficult to deal with, always having affairs and whatnot. That summer he was only absent from the house twice, that I remember, and was one of the kindest, loveliest people I have ever known.' It was Marquand's insistence on productivity in a writer that was not lost on Peck who, at Harvard, within a year was researching his thesis.

Peck stayed only two years at Middlebury College before transferring to Harvard. What put the finishing touches on the Vermont college was that it couldn't produce enough volunteer students to make a Reserve Office Training Corps unit viable. So Middlebury mandated attendance at ROTC for all freshmen and sophomores. 'They left that out of the college catalogue,' Peck said. The requirement infuriated Peck and never more so than when, in his second year, there was to be a parade that conflicted with his favourite course, an advanced seminar on modern British poetry. He went to the dean to explain the conflict. The dean listened and said come back in a day or so. When Peck returned he was told he'd have to relinquish the seminar and go on parade. Peck disputed the decision, the dean wouldn't budge. Peck said he was quitting ROTC, and refused to attend. Middlebury docked him one-third of an academic credit for each missed parade or class. By the end of the year he'd lost most of his academic credits, though he'd also become much beloved by the faculty, who hated as much as he did the ROTC and the cancellation of scheduled academic meetings.

Later, Peck would make it appear that his ROTC protests were in some way an anti-militarist stance. It was nothing of the sort at the time. He objected to ROTC interfering with a course he wanted to take.

Peck's application to Harvard was accepted, most probably because his father was active on Harvard alumni committees. 'Anyway, Harvard restored all my academic credits [dropped by Middlebury]. I mostly loved Harvard. It's just a magnificent college and university, the exception being the teaching. The teaching is terrible. I was in the department of social relations. It included psychology. There was a mandatory statistics course one semester taught by a German statistician who Harvard had gotten for a year because he had some new statistical technique they wanted to use. He barely spoke English and during the entire semester never changed his shirt. Today, students wouldn't put up with that. We were part of the silent generation. Going to class was ridiculous. I just read the book as best I could and got a passing grade. Not all the teaching was that bad, but the teaching at Middlebury was far finer than Harvard's. What makes Harvard so distinctive is not its teaching but its location, ambiance and the student body. In Middlebury hardly anybody was interested in intellectual stuff, whereas at Harvard everybody was. That was a great plus. It didn't matter whether you were in class or sitting out on the campus. Everybody wanted to talk.'

Peck also did volunteer work in prisons and, for his first Harvard summer, and admittedly using his father's name as entrée with the head of the department, he worked himself into a summer job with the New York State Department of Corrections. 'I proudly came home to announce to my father I had gotten a job working in New York jails for the summer. He threw a quiet kind of fit. I knew something would happen. Three days later he came to me and said, "I know you got this job, and I'm very proud of you, my boy, that you got it. But I just happened to have found a job that might interest you more.'" It was in Geneva, Switzerland with the International Labor Organisation, run by David Morse. ILO Director General Morse was an old political pal of Judge Peck's from their US Attorney General's office days. During Morse's tenure, the ILO, the United Nations agency that promotes human rights and justice for workers, was awarded a Nobel Peace Prize. Peck was encouraged, envisioning he'd be shifted around from department to department as training in organisation and management.

Not at all. He travelled to Switzerland to find himself in an office in the bowels of the ILO building with twenty-five women to the right of him, twenty-five to the left, collating papers for reports. He was in the 'one thousands' division – pages 1001, 1002, 1003, 1004, 1005, which he fastened with a rubber tie and passed on to the next collator. There was little conversation, Peck could not speak French beyond a few halting phrases. When there were no pages to collate, he operated the Roneo, a messy duplicating machine, to spin off thousands more copies of the pages. After six weeks he asked Morse for something more challenging. Morse said he didn't have anything. Peck's parents were arriving in London on vacation. He handed his resignation to Morse and left for Britain. 'I figured my father owed me a substantial living for having given up the Department of Corrections job, and could fork up for me to live a good life for the rest of the summer in England.' Then it was back to Cambridge, Massachusetts, and Harvard.

What made Harvard for Peck was an honours programme that required a thesis. He spent a lot of time on it but, as he hated academic writing and was too lazy and uncaring to be bothered with bibliographies and footnotes, he said, it was a total armchair thesis. It was entitled 'Anxiety, Modern Science and the Epistemological Problem'. Jake Severance was Peck's roommate at Harvard during his senior year. Judge Peck and Severance Senior, who was in the New York District Attorney's office, were acquainted, which was how the two young men ended up rooming together.

Hope Childs, wife of Tim Childs, Peck's friend from Exeter, recalled she and her husband visited Scotty in that room. Everything was painted red, she said, and it looked dreadful. Severance described the honours thesis pressure Peck brought down on himself and provided a cameo of Peck at that moment. 'At six foot he'd attained his full height and even then wore the round lens glasses that are his trademark, the ones he seems to have worn all his life. He didn't party. He dated at least two different women, but he was very, very serious about the work he was doing. He would stay up until three or four in the morning writing on his yellow legal pad. In wintertime there was usually a six-pack of beer sitting on the windowsill outside, keeping cool. That was the extent of his party-ness. Every now and then you'd hear a little "pop!" that meant he was having another beer to help him think.'

Peck had a habit that irritated Severance. Severance had a bridge [floor] lamp next to Peck's chair and Scott would keep sliding its adjustable arm up and down the pole. Severance told him, '"Scotty, I spent a lot of time trying to get that thing painted so it would look nice, and what you're doing is chipping the paint off." He said, "Oh, sorry," and promised not to do it again. Whereupon he started doing it again right away. I said, "Please don't do that or there's going to be a catastrophic reaction." "Catastrophic reaction" was a term Scotty had taught me only the week before. It's a sociologist's term, I believe. It basically means a temper tantrum.' Peck was so amused by Severance's use of the term he stopped fiddling with the lamp. It was scarcely surprising that in the thesis dedication, Peck thanked Severance 'who suffered admirably through this busy year when I have undoubtedly not been the easiest person to live with'. Severance recalled Peck as someone given to telling jokes, 'usually rather erudite, usually to do with psychology or sociology. Occasionally quite bawdy. He had a wonderful sense of humour.'

His humour was not limited to telling jokes. That same year, Peck was a member of the Timothy and Hope Childs wedding party. Tim, later a foreign service officer, was always intensely keen on military history. Prior to the Childs' wedding, Peck had acquired 'a bunch of swords somewhere on Third Avenue', with which the wedding party formed an honour arch as the newlywed Mr and Mrs Childs emerged from the church. Hope Childs, who told the story, recalled shielding herself behind her husband when she saw the display.

Peck's thesis, said Severance, 'was a story in itself because when it was submitted to a review board of three people in the department,

two of them rated it summa cum laude. The third rated it unacceptable, which created all kinds of problems in the department, and not
just for Scotty. He had to spend a week or two weeks, I think, going
to daily sessions to defend his thesis which the one person found
unacceptable because, I think, it was not particular enough. It was
too general.' But Peck was already what he became known as – an
able generalist who liked to range across themes that interested him.
He had little interest in relying on the informed opinion or asides of
others, beyond seeing what reactions they provoked in his own lines
of thought. Further, the opinions of others, quoted in a thesis, would
require them being footnoted as references. With only two or three
exceptions in each, neither in his Harvard thesis nor his books did
he go the footnote route. And that was a sticking point with the
academic who would not accept the thesis. (Consistency was one of
his attributes: Peck's style hadn't changed much since Exeter when
as a fifteen-year-old he'd written, 'I hate expository writing as there
is little room for the imagination.')

A Harvard undergraduate thesis usually had only two readers,
one of the student's choosing, and one chosen by the department. If
there was a discrepancy of more than three grades, they called in a
third reader. Peck, decades later, said of his own choice of reader
that 'I knew it was kind of a weird thesis but there was this teacher,
Charlie Slack, who seemed to be a fun-loving guy and off the wall,
so I selected him. Well, Charlie Slack, for some reason, designated
my thesis to be "unacceptable", the worst you can get. The guy who
I hadn't selected, don't even know who he was to this day, graded it
summa cum laude, which is the highest grade you can get. So
obviously there had to be arbitration. Gordon Allport gave it a
summa and sent a letter congratulating me on it. They averaged it
out and I graduated magna.' Allport was no small name, he was an
important social psychologist with his doctorate from Harvard.

The thesis was in major measure a precursor to *The Road Less
Travelled*. What the thesis tackled in the society, *The Road Less
Travelled* targeted in the individual. Peck was taken by the poet W. H.
Auden noting that the West was mired in the Age of Anxiety. (Peck
would return to 'Age of Anxiety' as part of a subtitle to a later book,
*The Road Less Travelled and Beyond: Spiritual Growth in an Age of
Anxiety*, 1997.) At Harvard he decided to explore Auden's assertion.
In his thesis he developed three neologisms on the grounds that
everybody who tried to explain society and the way it worked fell

into one of three camps. One camp believed in the *intra-organismic* theory, that the impulses that govern the behaviour of the organism rise from within the organism. The second group believed in *extra-organismic* theory, that the organism's behaviour is governed by external forces, like God or perhaps one's upbringing. The third camp, which Peck liked the most but still had problems with, was the *inter-organismic* theory, which said that the nature of things is dictated by the relationships between organisms. Peck then pointed out that in the age of modern science none of these theories work, and when human beings realise they don't know something, that produces anxiety. Twenty years later, *The Road Less Travelled* focused on those humans individually, not in the group, but the topic was still the Anxiety that had fascinated Auden.

The newly graduated magna cum laude from Harvard wanted to be the great American writer. He admitted to himself, however, as his senior undergraduate year drew to a close, that 'I still wanted to be the great American writer – but I had absolutely nothing to write about.' His career choice was made when his father later suggested medicine. 'This was one of father's better suggestions,' Peck said. 'I gave up the dream of writing and thought I would do something responsible like my father advised.' A half century later he said he had never regretted becoming a medical doctor and a psychiatrist, though he admitted that he'd 'copped out' by not pursuing the writer's life. Medicine or not, the writer's bug had bitten deeply and burrowed in. It had simply gone dormant.

CHAPTER 4

MED SCHOOL, MARRIAGE AND MOTHER COURAGE

L ooking back over Peck's high school and college years, he moved around a certain amount. He was at Exeter until he was fifteen, and Friends Seminary until he graduated at eighteen. Next he had two years at Middlebury (1954–1956), then two years at Harvard (1956–1958). On graduating he attended the required pre-med courses at Columbia University in New York City (1958–1959). He applied to both Harvard and Cleveland's Western Reserve (now Case Western Reserve) medical schools for the fall of 1959.

He'd graduated from Harvard with no pre-med requirements fulfilled beyond basic chemistry and basic biology, 'which I'd forgotten.' He went out to Cleveland for an interview. Western Reserve Associate Dean John Caughey heard Peck out, glanced at his academic record and told him he'd be admitted the following fall. 'But I have one problem,' he said, 'and that is that your scores on your medical scholastic aptitude test were rather low.' Peck told him, 'Well, that may be because I haven't yet taken any physics or organic chemistry or biology or embryology.'

Caughey said, 'My God, you haven't? Well, anyway, you're in.'

There was no word by then from Harvard Medical School, so Peck decided 'the hell with Harvard', and accepted Caughey's offer. Then, for the next academic year, he lived at home while he took pre-med courses at the School of General Studies in Columbia and worked twenty hours a week at Bellevue Psychiatric Hospital.

At Columbia, said Peck, 'We had one of the greatest teachers I ever experienced. Fascinating man on loan from the University of Buffalo. He began his first class by saying, "My name is Dr Payton. It rhymes with Satan. I have certain principles by which I teach.

And one of them is that all students cheat. And so, henceforth, to remove you from this temptation, you're going to have assigned seats, three seats apart from each other in this much too large auditorium. In addition on these hot summer mornings, it will help to circulate the gases amongst you." And then he was off on the circulation of gases.'

It was an amphitheatre. A young Chinese woman, Lily Ho, almost twenty-four, was assigned to a spot three seats down and ahead of the twenty-two-year-old Scott. So he looked down on her nape. 'I think I became a nape man,' he said. 'She was also working in the lab so she was always five minutes late. We palled around a bit that summer with a couple of other people and then in the fall began to date.' When Peck started at Bellevue he thought he might want to be a psychiatrist. At Harvard he'd majored in social relations, which has a large psychology component. But Bellevue was 'such a hopeless place' that when he left and finally got into medical school, he said a psychiatrist was the last thing he wanted to be.

During the summer he'd discovered something else, too, that he'd fallen in love with Lily. 'She was lithe, beautiful in a Chinese way, intelligent and fun to be with,' he said. After he'd taken Lily to his home several times for dinner, his father one day suggested he and Scott walk down to the 68th Street Bloomingdales department store. 'I liked to walk with him,' said Peck, 'it was the only time we really got along well.' On that walk Judge Peck talked 'about how wonderful it was to get to know people of different cultures. That it was broadening. But one should definitely not get too serious about it. That was the beginning,' said Peck. 'From the time we announced our engagement, from then on there were the violent fights, both with Lily's parents and mine. Finally, I knew I was going to be disinherited. I was not looking forward to that fact in medical school.'

To resolve the growing impasse, father and son met with the psychiatrist who had originally talked to Scott after he quit Exeter. 'I was feeling vulnerable,' said Peck, 'and agreed at that time to try to make it through medical school before marrying. Then, a month after I got to medical school, I felt I had sold out, and told my father that I felt it was a dishonourable agreement I had signed on to.' Peck contended his father had earlier vacillated over his oft-repeated dictum to his sons that they shouldn't marry before the age of thirty, and at a point when they were able to support their wives. Despite that parental dictum, twice, even when Scott was 'twenty at most', there were two girls among the several he brought home of whom his father said he'd be willing 'to make an exception and support me if I chose to marry one of them'. But not Lily. She was not a WASP.

It was December, 1959. Scott Peck had just completed his first semester as a medical school student and was home for the vacation. Christmas was barely two weeks away, yet the scene at the senior Pecks' household on Park Avenue, where Scott was still living when not in college, brought no promise of yuletide joy. Scott and Lily Ho were at the apartment together to meet the Peck parents in yet another attempt to gain parental blessings for their forthcoming marriage. Instead, on hearing their voices, a visibly annoyed Judge Peck emerged from the bathroom wearing only a bath towel. He wanted none of these wedding plans. When he saw Lily, he wagged his finger at her and roared, 'You! You! You adventuress!' The pair left, defeated.

A day or two later, they girded themselves for a visit to Lily's equally hostile parents. In contrast to the high emotional drama on Park Avenue, the scene at the Ho family apartment in the modest high-rise on the edge of Chinatown played out more like slapstick, said Peck. The Reverend and Mrs Ho, on seeing Scott and Lily at their front door, let them in but wouldn't let Lily leave. 'They were clutching Lily. There was no way for me to get Lily out of the apartment without physically fighting with them,' said Peck, who went to another apartment where he used the telephone to call the police. The Peck and Ho parents were responding to the same impetus – the emotional upheaval that can result when adult children who are not quite independent want to live their own lives. The Peck parents had made it quite clear they did not want Scott to marry a Chinese. Whether Judge Peck also knew that Lily was almost two years older than twenty-three-year-old Scott is uncertain. The judge thought he had a binding promise from Scott not to wed until he finished medical school. On the Ho side, Lily's parents were opposed to her marriage to a non-Chinese. Indeed they expected her to become a doctor – she, too, had been taking pre-med classes.

The senior Hos were born in Canton, China, as was Lily's brother. The family moved to Singapore, and Lily was born there. The family survived the Japanese Second World War occupation. Ten years before Lily left Singapore, the Hos had sent their son to the United States to become a pharmacist, and he'd switched to engineering without telling them, said Peck. After about ten years in the United States, while working as an electrical engineer, the son wrote to inform his parents he was marrying an American woman. Peck said Lily was fifteen when she went alone to the US Embassy to apply for a visa to the United States. 'She wanted to get the hell out of the traditional Chinese culture.' She arrived in the United States at age seventeen.

With her brother thoroughly Americanised and going his own way, the Hos were not about to let Lily choose her future, said Peck. According to him, they'd supported Lily's application to leave Singapore for the United States, dreaming that she'd become a doctor – 'She'd been programmed for medical school. When we met she kept forgetting to take the medical aptitude test,' Peck said. The senior Hos had arrived in the United States several years after Lily, when Pastor Ho took over a conservative Baptist church in Chinatown that needed a Chinese-speaking minister. The Ho parents' ambitions were further assaulted by Peck's spiritual interests. Lily knew of Scott's interest in Zen Buddhism, and had bought two books on the topic for him for Christmas. Her parents had seen the books. Peck said Pastor Ho was outraged and railed at his daughter, 'We have not been Christians for four generations for you to marry a Zen Buddhist!'

This was the backdrop, said Peck, as two New York policemen arrived, knocked on the Hos' apartment door and demanded they open it. The Hos complied. The police asked to see Lily. She came to the door. The police asked if she was being held against her will and wanted to leave. She said she was, and she did want to leave. The burly cop in the doorway stood with his arm against the doorjamb in such a way that Lily was able to quickly duck under it into the corridor, and race towards the elevator. Scott said he followed immediately behind her but then the Hos broke past the police. Lily and Scott ran into the stairwell, and headed down, with seventeen floors ahead of them. The police, to keep her safe, came down behind Lily. Mrs Ho, not to be deterred, joined in the descent while the Reverend rang for the elevator. If he intended to get there first, to catch Lily at street level to prevent her from leaving, it didn't quite work out that way. What happened instead, said Peck, was that Mrs Ho caught up with a policeman and bit him. The Hos apparently then had to rely on a persuasive Peck – for the Hos did not have Peck's English fluency – to plead and reason with the cops to prevent Mrs Ho being hauled off to the precinct house and charged with assault. The police agreed, and Scott and Lily were out of the door. The Hos gave no further pursuit. Nor, said Peck, did they speak to their daughter for the next six years, by which time Lily was a mother with daughters ages four and five.

All this time, Scott was still living at home, and Lily would stop by to visit. During the uproar over the marriage plans, Aunt Sally in the kitchen would say to each of them, 'Give me a hug,' and console them. 'Don't you worry, Miss Lily,' she'd say. 'It will all work out. Don't you worry, Miss Lily, I'll see to it. You're a dear girl. They'll realise it eventually.'

Scott and Lily became Mr and Mrs M. Scott Peck on 27 December 1959 in a high Episcopal ceremony at Grace Episcopal Church. Lily was nominally a Methodist at the time. They chose Grace Episcopal because the minister had a brother who was married to a Filipina, so the minister was familiar with racially mixed marriages, still a rarity in the United States of the 1950s. Among the few friends in attendance were Timothy and Hope Childs. The only parent to attend was Mrs Peck. 'It was an act of real courage. The only time my mother directly defied my father,' said Scott. None of Lily's family was present at the wedding. Among Lily's friends were the Grangers. Lester Granger was president of the National Urban League, the 1910-founded organisation for African–Americans. 'The Grangers were lovely people and had formed a friendship with Lily,' said Scott Peck, 'which gives an idea of her talents right from the early days. Lester said he would be happy to give her in marriage if her family did not attend.' Judge Peck may have bridled further when he learned that his now daughter-in-law had been given in marriage by a black man.

With the wedding date set, Peck called a college friend who lived with his family in an apartment near the church. He asked, could the wedding group bring a couple of bottles of whiskey and have a celebratory gathering at the apartment? The friend checked with his parents, who said yes and donated a case of champagne. 'They were Orthodox Jews. That wedding was about as ecumenical as you could get,' said Peck. That was a high point for Scott and Lily; otherwise, Scott's relationship with his father had descended from an all-time peak – Scott graduating from Harvard magna cum laude, and accepting his father's suggestion to go to medical school – to an all-time low. He was cut off financially and his father refused to speak to him.

Following the wedding, with the breach between Scott and his father complete, the not-so-happy pair headed off to Cleveland. They were given to singing, 'There's a place for us, somewhere a place for us' – the plaintive song from the musical *West Side Story*. They headed West not quite broke. Scott had $800 in the bank, Lily had nothing. They bought a bed and a bureau. They had no food, no dishes, and no car. Lily worked full-time as a lab technician at the university hospital. And three evenings a week they both worked as lab techs in the main laboratory. About a month and a half after his marriage Peck received a letter from his father which read, 'Scotty, if you send me the bill I will pay your tuition. And please find enclosed a check for $100 which I will remit same monthly till your graduation.' It was signed, 'your father'.

Scott wanted to tear it up, write back and say, 'Take it and stuff it up your ass,' he said. But the very day they received Judge Peck's letter, he and Lily had dinner 'with an older and wiser couple'. The couple pointed out the obvious, that not only did Scott desperately need the money, but at that point the money was the only real way his father could express his affection. By refusing it, Scott would be cutting off communication completely. Peck wrote back and said, 'Dear Dad, I thank you very much for your generosity, and I accept it.' Less than eighteen months later, when their first child was born, Judge Peck increased the allowance to $200 a month. His father may have eased up on Scott, but, said Peck, he didn't speak to Lily, 'or even look at her directly,' for the first five years of the couple's marriage. 'Then he started treating her like an ordinary human being – though he favoured my brother's wife, Greg. Later, my father came around and would send Lily roses.'

Scott and Lily were living in the attic of the Two Sisters Nursery School for forty-five dollars a month. It had a back yard with swings and slide, 'which made for great parties,' said Peck. As part of the rent Scott had to mow the lawn and shovel the walk. The walk was twenty yards long and the lawn was all of twenty yards square – 'It wasn't much of a task.' One hot summer evening under the eaves of the Two Sisters, sweating away in those pre-air-conditioned days, Scott said to Lily, 'I don't believe there should be any secrets in a marriage.' Lily replied, 'Well, I do.' On Peck's side, there wouldn't be any serious secrets to keep for another fifteen years, until he began his philandering. But one Peck family secret was about to come out.

Sometime around Scott's twenty-fourth birthday, in May, 1960, when he and Lily had been married six months, Elizabeth Peck travelled out to visit her son and his wife. It was on this occasion she told Scott his father was Jewish.

The Pecks' first child, Belinda, was born in 1961, her name prompted by the movie *Johnnie Belinda*, said Peck. Fifty-one weeks later, in 1962, Julia Alison was born. Her name, he said, was adapted from his maternal grandmother, Juliet, while Alison 'was conjured up out of the stars'. At the time, June Allison was popular among earthbound stars. Their third child, Christopher Scott, was born on Okinawa in 1969. It was when Lily was pregnant with the second child, and after a particularly rowdy party for adults on and around the nursery school's swings, that the landlords kicked the Pecks out of their apartment under the eaves. By that time, having scrimped and saved, the couple had $5,000, mainly from Lily's wages. She was no longer working, and there was just $200 a month coming in from Judge Peck. One of the Western Reserve faculty, a medical doctor and his wife, had a thirty-room home in a prime part of Cleveland. They rented the Pecks seven rooms to themselves. The bonus, with two babies in diapers, was the use of a washing machine. And probably on the off-chance there'd be future parties, there was a refrigerator, too.

Peck said he'd chosen Western Reserve not only for its highly regarded medical school, probably one of the top ten in the country, but also because it was liberal and non-competitive. At most medical schools, he said, grades were posted each week along with class standings. At Western Reserve there were only thirteen exams during four years of medical school. The grades were E for excellent, S for satisfactory or U for unsatisfactory. Peck said that generally, on any given exam in the class of eighty students, six or seven would get an E, five or six would get a U, and the middle sixty-five or so would get an S. During those three years Peck had thirteen Satisfactory, not one Excellent, not one Unsatisfactory. 'I was obviously no medical genius,' he remarked. Until two or three months before the completion of medical school, Peck had proceeded along 'with the delusion that I was going to be a general practitioner, a missionary type, working in the Deep South or Burma.' However, at the point in his clinical year when he was 'doing a lot of emergency room work, I realised I didn't really like most of medicine, that it was cookbook kind of stuff: you followed the recipe. I realised that what I really liked to do was talk with people. So I revived my desire to become a psychiatrist.' As he would later acknowledge, he preferred talking to hands-on patient-care medicine.

Peck's own financial survival was an issue at this point: how to afford to live during an internship and psychiatric residency. 'At that time,' said Peck, 'all medical school graduates had to take what was called a rotating internship, to rotate amongst different specialties. Then they could become a general practitioner or go on to residency to become a specialist. At good hospitals they were paid nothing. At Brigham Hospital in Boston, as an intern, they got thirteen dollars a month. And it ranged from about thirteen dollars a month to a hundred dollars a month at other universities. The only place you could get high-class post-graduate medical training, and survive financially, was in the Army, Navy, Air Force medical corps or public health services. And so with some misgivings, not knowing anything about Vietnam, except it was some place in the other hemisphere, I joined the Army where there was a livable wage. I could get by without being financially dependent upon my father – there were all kinds of strings attached to being so dependent.'

When it came to his US Army medical military career, Peck never fared badly as far as location was concerned: Hawaii as an intern, San Francisco as a resident, Okinawa as a psychiatrist, and Washington, D.C. to conclude his service career. First, from July 1963 to July 1964 he went to Tripler Army Medical Center, at Oahu, on the island of Hawaii. The huge medical building was known as the 'pink palace'. Medical corps officers did not participate in basic training. The closest Peck got to 'boot camp' was two weeks of learning how to salute and listening to some general rules concerning army life.

Peck entered the military for financial security while he became a psychiatrist. The near-decade came with other experiences, and some benefits, including marching in anti-Vietnam protests, living overseas, developing as an administrator, deeper immersion by default into the Vietnam War as soldiers were sent to Okinawa for R&R (rest and recuperation), or to Okinawa's stockades as prisoners, and surviving high-wire confrontations with top military brass as a psychiatrist. Peck said he did not wear his uniform when he marched in Berkeley and San Francisco anti-war protests. In conversation he seemed to have enjoyed this aspect of his life, recounting his days as an anti-war provocateur within the military establishment. But in sum it didn't seem to amount to much. What he wouldn't say was whether he'd detached himself from the military and his family on his peace marches to take advantage of the rapidly relaxing sexual mores that the intersection between the anti-war movement and the hippie revolution represented.

In San Francisco, not yet fully engaged on a new spiritual search, he nonetheless was still sufficiently connected to mainstream Christianity to write a poem dedicated to an ordinand to the priesthood at All Souls Episcopal Church in Berkeley, California, on 12 February 1966. Under the poem Peck wrote, 'This poem was written at a time when I had already developed religious passion but long before I understood anything about the church, and fourteen years before I myself was non-denominationally baptised. The poem reflects some of the anger associated with my confusion about religion at the time, and may be compared to the different tone of my poems after 1977.'

Peck's time in the Army meant learning practical politics in Washington, D.C. on the staff of the Office of the Army Surgeon General, and insider fighting with the Nixon Administration. When he left the military, it was to plunge himself back into financial insecurity.

After Hawaii, Peck was posted to the Army's Letterman Psychiatric Hospital in San Francisco for his three years of psychiatric residency, rotating shifts at the hospital, on hand for psychiatric emergencies. Whenever Letterman came up in conversation, Peck had unstinting praise for the quality of the faculty during his years there. In his not unusual flights of hyperbole they were 'geniuses' or 'giants'. There was no shortage of practical experience in the military psychiatric hospital and soon the fledgling psychiatrist was stretching his professional wings. At home in the Officers' Married Quarters, the situation was somewhat different. He refused to have his wings clipped, and was less successful in applying the new psychological insights he was gradually acquiring to himself and his family situation. He was unusually absent from wife and family. During a medical residency, it is not abnormal for a doctor, military officer or otherwise, to work long shifts. Peck, however, was gone from home even more than most other residents, a clear indication he wasn't handling his workload well. He had something else to learn besides psychiatry – time management. Other residents were out of the office by 4 and 5 p.m.; Peck wasn't getting home, he said, sometimes until nearly 10 p.m. When he asked for fewer patients, on the grounds he spent more time with his patients than other residents did with theirs, Dr 'Mac' Badgely, director of the outpatient psychiatric clinic, simply implied Peck had a problem that Peck had to resolve himself. Peck said he left Badgely's office in a huff and it took him months to realise Badgely was right. Peck may have learned to manage his time better to his own or the Army's satisfaction, but never to Lily's, he said. Peck knew what he should do to placate Lily. She was home alone with two very young children. But he couldn't or wouldn't or didn't change his work habits. It became a source of fairly constant friction in the household. Captain Peck was busy, he was also a male chauvinist, a man of his time, and he never achieved a work and family–life balance that met his wife's needs.

Of greater lasting benefit to Peck was the fact that the Letterman experience propelled him into therapy during his final year of residency. To an onlooker, the series of incidents that led him to therapy in a single day evoke a sympathetic amusement, especially the climax that had Peck on his knees in front of the residency programme commanding officer, General Jingles. He and Jingles did not get along.

This particular working day, as Peck recalled it, opened badly. It began at the reaction he experienced when, during an early morning seminar, he'd played for his peers and supervisor a tape of an interview he'd conducted with a patient. They 'raked me over the coals for the clumsy way I'd handled it.' He took his lumps, he said, and rationalised the incident out of the way, though it still rankled. He told himself, 'Well, they always rake you over the coals, that's standard operating procedure.' After the seminar he had some free time. 'I thought I'd use it to get a haircut – I didn't feel I needed one, but I knew General Jingles would think I needed one. Off I went, and as I had to pass the post office I thought I'd check my box. And there, to my dismay, I found a traffic ticket.' The ticket dated back many weeks earlier to an afternoon when Peck ran a stop sign on post on the way to play tennis with the post commander, Colonel Connor.

Normally one's commanding officer (Jingles in Peck's case), fixed the tickets. Peck had been loath to approach Jingles, and Connor said he'd fix the ticket with the Military Police's Provost Marshal. Some six weeks later, however, the Provost Marshal was fired without time to clean out his desk. In one drawer there was a stack of fixed tickets. The authorities had 'unfixed' the tickets and the miscreants were now being held liable. Feeling 'worse and worse' – raked over the coals and with an unfixed ticket surfacing – Peck went for his haircut. He was in the barber's chair, halfway through the cut, 'when in walked General Jingles to have his hair trimmed. In that situation,' said Peck, 'even a general has to wait his turn. To show you what bad shape I was in, the last minute or two of my haircut, all I could think about was, "Should I say hello to the bastard, or shouldn't I?"' When my haircut was finished, with great aplomb I passed by General Jingles and said, "Good morning, General Jingles," and went straight out of the barber shop.'

Peck hadn't paid for his haircut. 'The barber came running out after me, "Doctor, doctor, you no pay for your haircut. You no pay for your haircut."' Peck returned to the shop, but he was so unnerved by Jingles' presence, 'I dropped all my change on the floor, right at General Jingles' feet. So there I was, kneeling at his feet while he was laughing uproariously at my predicament. When I finally got out of the barbershop my hands were shaking like crazy. I said to myself, "Peck," I said, "you're not okay. You need help." It was one reason I always disliked the title of that book, *I'm Okay, You're Okay*, because one of my finest hours was when I could say – painful as it was as a breaking moment for me – "Peck, you're not okay. You need help."'

Peck, reflecting four decades later on his therapy, said what he was suffering from at the time was an authority problem. 'In every job I'd had, for years, college, or General Jingles, there was always some son-of-a-bitch in charge of me whose guts I absolutely hated. Always a male, always an older male. So that's how I went into therapy.' It was a one-year, three-times-a-week therapy programme with a Dr Aikers. It proceeded well. The therapist accepted 'all of my stuff that my parents didn't accept, my weirdness and uniqueness and whatnot, and I just felt less and less anxious,' Peck said. At about the ten-and-a-half-month mark, Peck was feeling so good he said he talked to Aikers about stopping.

'You know, I feel so much better. You've been such a great help to me that I've been thinking maybe we really don't have any more work to do.'

Aikers said, 'I wonder if you're not angry at me.'

And Peck said, 'No, I'm not angry at you. I told you that. Actually it's because you've been so kind to me and the excellent work has made me feel so much better. I'm not angry at all.' The therapist continued, 'Maybe you're angry at something that happened last session?' Peck denied it. 'As a matter of fact, it was such a dull session that I was writing a paper for this course I was taking – an evening course on Buddhism – and asked you if you knew anything about Buddhism and you said you didn't. So I spent the whole hour talking to you about Buddhism, and actually it was kind of a wasted hour. As a matter of fact, come to think of it, for somebody who has been to the Jungian Institute in Zurich, it's a little hard for me to believe the fact when you said you didn't know anything about Buddhism. I'm not sure you weren't withholding from me. Matter of fact, I'm pretty sure you're probably holding yourself from me just like my father, just the way my father used to.'

Looking back on his outburst, Peck said, 'I, who used to think I was much too smart ever to fall into the trap of "transference", realised I'd done it.' (Transference Peck described as ways of dealing with the world in childhood inappropriately carried into one's adult life.) 'Dr Aikers and I worked it out. The basis of my neurosis – and I needed help from him to see it – was that my father was such an attractive man, in looks, in his brilliance, in his sense of humour when he was in a good mood, so loving, that I deeply wanted to be dependent on him as a young child. But I also knew that to be dependent on him would be to be emotionally steamrollered by him. He would have just obliterated my psyche and made me who he wanted me to be. And the only way I could deal with that was to say, on a very deep level, "Who needs him?" And to say that I had to say, "Who needs anybody?" So I'd become this hyper-independent individual. But at the same time I was going around unconsciously, totally unaware of this, looking for a good father figure. And whenever somebody who was a potential father figure for me turned out not to be the good father I wanted I'd get furious at him. As soon as I became aware that I was, in some ways, a dependent person, and where some of this rage was coming from, and that I did want a father figure, then I was able to do things in the military and in executive life that I just never would have been able to before.' Peck liked to insist that this therapeutic year 'cured' him of his father and childhood neuroses. His behaviour and attitudes in the years ahead belie the claim.

The Army was freeing Peck from some major constraints. In the closing months of his military career, it would enable him to cry again. What couldn't have been anticipated was that the Army, inadvertently, also helped Peck further along a road he had not yet embarked on: towards Christianity. Truly, Peck's nine-and-a-half years in uniform created the Scott Peck of future fame, through its accidental role in his faith formation, and its deliberate moulding of him as a psychotherapist. In 1966, as he prepared to depart San Francisco for service in Okinawa to honour the required 'payback' period for his medical training, he had been a student constantly for twenty-five years. Peck, emotionally less constricted than at any period in his early adult life, was about to step into a freedom he had neither experienced nor anticipated. He had psychological and physical distance from his father, and, in a modest way, was financially independent of him.

The freedom and independence, his increasing experience and sureness as a psychotherapist and a commander of men, and his travels towards Christianity, was the combustible admixture which, a decade ahead, exploded into the creativity that produced *The Road Less Travelled.*

CHAPTER 5

OKINAWA AND THE NEW PSYCHIATRIST

The Japanese province of Okinawa is a sub-tropical cluster of 161 islands, halfway between the Japanese mainland and Taiwan. The United States, since the end of the Second World War, has maintained a large military presence on the main island, which meant, when Scott Peck arrived in 1967, that Kadina Air Force Base, Okinawa was home to 115,000 troops and their dependents, plus US military psychiatric patient evacuees from Vietnam. It was before post-war governance of Okinawa had been returned to Japan.

If his island home and this posting represented some potentially formidable problems to the newly promoted Major Peck, the climate wasn't one of them. Work aside, he and Lily and the two girls had an idyllic family life in a place where the summer temperature rarely exceeds 73° Fahrenheit (22.4° Celsius) or drops below 60°F (16°C) in winter. They were an American family, not a quasi-Asian or Asian-American family. It was still an era in the United States when rapid assimilation into the mainstream culture was the sine qua non. A full-time local nanny was available for sixty-five dollars a month. The nanny also loved to baby-sit, at the rate of one dollar a night, and for the entire night, if required. An evening at the movies was twenty-five cents each.

At work, Peck's first challenge was he had to immediately become a top flight administrator. He led a department with some forty personnel who handled thousands of cases. Peck's senior staff was a veteran non-commissioned officer, a sergeant considerably older than he was, three psychiatrists about his own age, and two junior officers in their late twenties. The remaining thirty-five personnel were enlisted men and women in their late teens or early twenties.

89

For the number of military personnel at the base, the department was understaffed with psychiatrists. In a novel departure, Peck started training enlisted personnel as 'psychiatric technicians', quasi-psychotherapists, to shoulder some of the load.

First, however, he had to get a handle on his new responsibilities. Until he arrived in Okinawa, Peck 'had never managed anybody. Through college, medical school, internship and residency I had always been at the very bottom of the hierarchy. Nor, typical of such schooling, had I ever received anything faintly resembling management training.' The one thing he was determined to be was 'Mr Nice Guy, as different as possible from every authoritarian boss who had ever been in charge of me.' Because it was a medical professional department, he felt rank could be ignored. He discouraged all ranks from addressing him as 'Major Peck'. He was soon 'Scotty' to one and all. His daily operating model was that no decisions would be made until everyone involved had been consulted. Wherever possible, his subordinates were encouraged – within the constraints of professional competence – to make the decisions that affected their own work lives. The mood was euphoric, everyone congratulated him on his leadership, morale was superb, and the mood held for about six months. Then things began to sour.

The euphoria dissipated, bickering started. By nine months Peck could see that the situation had markedly worsened, but couldn't account for it. Admittedly working conditions were cramped, but those would shortly be addressed when the new outpatient complex opened. He anticipated morale would improve as the moving date approached. It didn't. 'The staff grew worse,' he said, 'files fell behind schedule. Finally, it was my responsibility to do something about it.' He told the entire staff there'd be meetings each morning in the new building's conference room 'until we got to the bottom of the problem.' What he got, in two four-hour morning sessions, 'were the stormiest meetings I ever attended. Everyone took potshots at me and everyone else. Yet all the complaints were picky, superficial and seemingly unreasonable.' An innocuous remark from an enlisted man on the second morning set Major Peck off on a fresh tack. The soldier said, 'I feel I don't know where I stand.' Asked to elaborate he couldn't and became inarticulate. 'It's like we're all at sea,' was all he could offer.

That lunchtime, Peck sat in his office in the old building and stared at the ceiling, lunch uneaten. Was it possible the department needed more structure than he'd provided, he wondered. Were they really asking: what's going to happen to us in this new building, and where will we be in it? Who got the better offices would determine who was who in the pecking order. He called in the senior sergeant and asked for the plans for the new building. Then he set to work and assigned everyone on his staff to an office in the new psychiatric department. Job done, he handed it to the sergeant and said, 'Now go inform.' The result was 'you could practically hear the howls of dismay across the island,' he said, but everyone knew where he or she stood, or sat, and 'by evening morale had began to improve. Then escalate. By the end of the week it was back to where it had been.' They still called him Scotty, his overall leadership was still relatively non-authoritarian, but everyone knew who was in charge. And morale stayed high for the remainder of his tour of duty.

Typical of Scott Peck's preference for a paradoxical 'yes and no' view of life, he said the story could be seen as a success story. But he preferred to regard it as a failure because the organisation and individuals in it suffered for six months before he diagnosed the problem and took corrective action.

Having dealt with the staff, it was now time for Peck to deal with the Pentagon – the US military's removed and remote US Department of Defense in Washington, D.C. on the other side of the world – regarding the shortage of psychiatrists on Okinawa. He had already pleaded long distance by military mail to no avail. When a crisis erupted in Vietnam that affected Okinawa, he was quick to read its signs and make his move. Long Binh Jail, Vietnam – known as the 'LBJ' as a pointed reference also to the Vietnam War's main proponent, President Lyndon Baines Johnson – was a major brig (military prison) that held US servicemen found guilty of extremely serious crimes. The prison population was predominantly black troops, and by that time the brig was holding at least twice the numbers of prisoners it was built to accommodate. When there was a race riot in the 'LBJ', the Army tried to hush up the affair, but the news got out. The Pentagon had to make a move to show it had the situation in hand. The president ordered a large contingent of black militants shipped to Okinawa, sixty of them as prisoners. The Secretary of the Army ordered a psychiatric evaluation of a dozen or so of the key militants.

Peck made his move or, rather, his slowdown. 'My only other psychiatrist had just gone on leave. I was the sole psychiatrist on the

island. A colonel, aide to my commanding general, Major General
Michael J. "Mickey" Finn – he and I were friends – called me and
said he wanted the twelve particular psychiatric evaluations of the
militant prisoners requested by the Secretary of the Army straight
away. I said, "Well, fine, let's see. It's the fourth of September now.
I'll see the first one or two on the seventh of October. And then I
can see one on the eighth and then maybe two on the ninth." He
said, "No. These are urgent evaluations.'" Said Peck, "'I hear that
they're urgent. I'm giving you the first times I can possibly give
you." He said, "Look, this is the Secretary of the Army who wants
these things." And I said, "I hear that very well, great priority." The
guy hung up on me in a fury. I called my colonel at the hospital and
I said, "Colonel, I just wanted to warn you that shit is going to hit
the fan." He knew we were way understaffed at about one-fifth the
number of psychiatrists required. The next day there was a
psychiatrist en route from Hawaii TDY, temporary duty. Within six
months there were nine new psychiatrists.'

That was only the first wave of trouble emanating from the
Okinawa stockade, however. The military police staff there proved
no more adept at understanding the problem on their hands than
had the 'LBJ' staff. Then one day, in a six-man cell occupied by five
blacks and one white, one of the African–Americans, who'd
embedded a razor in a toothbrush, held it to the white prisoner's
throat and kept it there ready to slit it if the black troops' grievances
weren't addressed. The Okinawa stockade had a rebellion on its
hands.

The Okinawa stockade staff didn't know how to handle these
black prisoners. Peck was called in, by which time the stockade was
surrounded by a SWAT team, a fire crew, and armed soldiers. Major
General Finn told Peck no one knew what the riot was about, and
the issue was how to end it. Then Finn asked Peck if he'd be willing
to go into the jail to discover why the prisoners were rioting.
'Mickey Finn was a two-star general when he should have been
four-star. He was a man of considerable courage but somewhere
along the line alienated somebody or other. The first time I'd been
his adviser he was talking angrily about hippies in a stereotype kind
of way and I said, "Mickey, you know I'm not much of a soldier but
it seems to me there's an old saying, know your enemy. You talk
about hippies in a terribly derogatory tone. I'm not saying they
don't deserve it, but I honestly don't think you know anything about

hippies, and I think you ought to learn before being so definitive."
He looked at me with a scowl and I thought he was going to kill me,
then he said, "By God, you're right." And that was the beginning of
our friendship.'

Now, when Finn asked Peck to go into the riotous jail, 'I did,
scared as hell. The reason for the riot was eminently clear, and
eminently cruel. The stockade had run out of segregated disciplinary
cells, those used for solitary confinement to isolate particularly
unruly prisoners. Short of cell space, the military police had taken to
using conex shipping containers.' These commercial conex containers were multi-purpose metal boxes used for anything from
shipping furniture to storing ammunition. The police had punched
holes in the containers for air, thrown a mattress in the bottom and
started putting prisoners in them out in the broiling sun. 'Not only
was this illegal,' said Peck, 'for there are specifications for disciplinary segregation cells, but furthermore the blacks believed that
this was the last step before their extermination. Which was not true,
but it was what they believed.'

The military commanders gathered to discuss the situation. There
were sixty people present, 'almost all of whom outranked me and
the African–American sergeant,' said Peck. 'We told them, "We
think you ought to get rid of the conex containers." The other fifty-
eight people said, "We can't get rid of the conex containers. That's
giving in to their demands. You just can't do that. You'll lose the
authority of the guards. You simply can't do that."' Peck went to
Finn and assured him the prisoners were 'going to cut this white
guy's throat unless they got rid of the disciplinary conex containers.'
Finn asked Peck, 'What do you think we ought to do?' and Peck told
him, 'Well, they're illegal. If you do get rid of them you are going to
have a riot on your hands on the part of the guards. But nonetheless
I think you ought to get rid of them.'

Finn made the decision to go with the two against the fifty-eight,
and ordered an end to the containers. The guard population was in
an uproar, said Peck. Finn addressed the uproar. Said Peck, 'I
witnessed Finn give one of the most eloquent speeches I have ever
heard about rightness and law and about America. Everything. It
was an extraordinary moment.' That there was a degree of racism in
the uproar would go without saying, which brings the topic round to
Peck and American blacks. His attitudes were apparently a mix of
wholesome equality with an element of romanticism to it, peppered

by the oddest sort of occasional racist observation. He certainly seemed to have an easy-going personal relationship with black people, a fact he credited not only to Aunt Sally, the Pecks' housekeeper of his childhood, but to an affair he had with a black woman who enabled him to cross cultural lines.

This apparently occurred early in the 1980s when he was beginning to gain some initial prominence as the writer of a bestseller. He also said that until that experience, he'd had a deplorable habit of not seeing black women except to undress them with his eyes. Entering into what he described as a two-year relationship with a black woman, he said, introduced him to his own unconscious racism and stereotyping, lessons he learned and did not forget. It was not clear where this liaison occurred geographically, or whether he was comfortable being seen as one half of a bi-racial couple in public. From the gist of the conversations, and given the fact he liked to confront the prevailing culture, he was likely not particularly uncomfortable. If that was the case, his open attitude would have shocked most people of his generation and class, even in the 1980s.

Aunt Sally had been loving and open, but she was a paid employee in a household run on class system lines. Later, when Peck was prominent and invited to speak in churches, he found African–American church groups open and capable of offering 'instant community', which he enjoyed. But there was a place in that community which a white man could not reach or enter, he said. As a student of social relations and a psychotherapist interested in groups and community, he was as critical of black groups as he was of whites, when he felt criticism was justified.

Peck himself was still learning. About himself, about being family, about life, about psychiatry and psychotherapy. He was candid about his learning experiences, including his residual racism. 'My big education in prejudice came when a black soldier was transferred from Vietnam for exposing himself. I learned he'd also exposed himself in the United States, and that was why he'd gone to Vietnam – either Vietnam or the brig.' Peck decided the soldier was not simply a man who exposed himself, but a chronic, low-grade schizophrenic who did not belong in the Army and would expose himself again. 'I told him I was going to put him in the hospital and prepare him for evacuation to the United States where he would get a medical discharge and it would be fine.' The soldier was bitterly upset but Peck told him neither of them had any options. Peck said he didn't put the soldier under observation or restrictions, but confined him as a regular, unlocked-door patient.

'That was at two p.m. on the Tuesday. At ten a.m. on the Wednesday,' said Peck, 'the hospital's adjutant general, who usually called me Scott, called and asked, "Peck, what the hell are you doing? What the hell have you done?" I said, "What? What?" And he said, "I've got forty Okinawan women in my office all shouting at me at the same time. Apparently one of your patients was hiding himself in the mop closet, and whenever one of the cleaning ladies would come and open the closet door, there he was, all exposed. You get your ass over here and do something about it."'

Peck went, and through an interpreter gave a lengthy apology for his stupidity, carelessness and the trouble he had caused. And he assured the women there would be no more trouble, the man would be kept under very strict surveillance. He concluded, 'I am sorry this happened and I thank you for being so gracious about it.' Thirty years later, he added, 'But I realised it was the first time I had ever looked at these Okinawan cleaning ladies. I really had not seen them. They had been invisible for two years.' Scott the non-racist who saw every black as a person 'had never noticed an Okinawan. They had just faded into the wall. For my last year, I'd always say, "Good morning," or "Hi!" as I passed the women in the corridors.'

With the conex crisis resolved, and plenty of psychiatrists to shoulder the work, 'I took up golf and had a lovely time. Okinawa, I still dream of it. It was such a heaven. Beautiful facilities, a comfortable life, all at next to nothing in cost. We figured, heck, if we're ever going to have another child, this was the place to have it. So Christopher was our Okinawa child, born seven years after the girls.' It was probably the happiest period of their family life. Soon Scotty, a Lily pregnant with Christopher, and the two girls travelled to Singapore and Thailand, and then spent eleven days in India. Life was pleasant now, not difficult for the ambitious military psychiatrist who had shown he did not lack personal or moral courage, and who possessed sufficient wit to baffle and battle a bureaucracy into meeting his needs. But it was still only 1970, and Peck had remained mired – despite the changing times – in many of the mores he had grown up with. Not least among his still unchanging ways was his attitude towards women.

Terry Paiste was a military dependent in Okinawa, her husband,

Gary, was one of Peck's 'psychiatric techs'. She worked for the military base education office and hosted a Friday afternoon television show, *The Teahouse,* on the Armed Forces Radio and Television Service. 'People could watch my programme on the only station that broadcast in English, or they could watch Japanese television,' said Paiste. 'I scoured the islands for guests who would expand the minds of the military personnel and their families. Women's Lib was a hot topic. I'd had a woman teacher speak, but I wanted to find a male guest who would promote the same cause.'

Paiste, who made these comments in a talk she gave decades later at a Toastmasters Club gathering, said she had a problem – that apart from her husband she didn't know one man on Okinawa who was a feminist. She was about to give up when her husband suggested Dr Peck. 'He'd make a great guest,' said Gary Paiste. 'He's intelligent and articulate, and he'd make a terrific spokesman for Women's Lib.'

'Are you sure he's in favour of Women's Lib?' she asked her husband.

'Well, we've never actually discussed it,' Gary admitted. 'But he's very open-minded. I'll ask him if he wants to be on the show.'

The arrangements were made. On the air, when asked about the Women's Liberation Movement, Peck said he didn't think much of it because it was the invention of a few malcontented females. Most women, he said, had no interest in equal rights. Said Paiste, 'I couldn't have found a less sympathetic guest if I had placed an ad in the *Okinawan Times* for a Male Chauvinistic Pig.'

She never saw Peck again, but in the 1980s noticed his name on the best seller list for *The Road Less Travelled.* She ignored the book. A decade later, his name came up in conversation with a co-worker who liked his books, Paiste said. 'I should read them, the friend said, because he talks about what a sexist he had been, and how he'd changed.' Paiste said that, more than a little sceptical, she thumbed through a couple of chapters 'wearing gloves so I wouldn't be contaminated.' She read *The Road,* and his other books. 'There wasn't a sexist line or thought in them,' she said, 'and I learned a lot. The most important thing I learned was that people *can* change.'

In Okinawa, Peck proudly declared, he developed psychiatric technicians as 'mini-psychotherapists' to handle the case load. Later, he would train his wife, Lily, and remark that she was, in fact, a better therapist than he was. As Peck's three-year 'payback' time for

his medical training would coincide with the end of his Okinawa
tour, the thirty-four-year-old psychiatrist now had some decisions to
make. He knew what he wanted if he remained in uniform –
Washington, D.C. And he'd learned about working the system to his
own advantage, to the extent anyone could move such a ponderous
bureaucracy. So, typical of Peck, he added a bargaining chip to his
demands for a Washington posting: he successfully applied for a
fellowship at Harvard. (This was a paid academic position that
would allow Peck study time while requiring a minimum teaching
load from him.) 'It was a magnificent fellowship,' he said. 'They
would pay me eight thousand dollars a year. I could take whatever
four courses I chose, and provided I got a B or better I'd have a
Master's in Public Administration.' Peck wasn't shy about letting it
be known in military circles he'd already received an offer from
Harvard. He was asked what it would take to have him stay in
uniform, and he told them.

'One of my dreams in wanting Washington was to try to stop the
Nixon push for an all-volunteer Army,' he said. 'I regarded it as a
very dangerous idea. We felt that the draft kept the US Army sane.
When we were marching in protest in San Francisco, we'd go, "Boy,
look, there's seventy thousand of us here, the war will be ended in
five months." And of course nothing happened. There was a draft
even in the 1960s, but only those who volunteered for Vietnam
were sent there. Things began to happen only when the government
started sending to Vietnam those who did not want to go there.
Those who had not volunteered. Those whose mothers and fathers
and sisters and brothers didn't want them to go. Only then did
opposition to the war become powerful enough to do something.
And that's one reason I was very much against the very popular
idea of an all-volunteer Army.'

In December, 1970, his military masters gave Peck the nod and he
flew to the United States to be interviewed for available openings.
The thirty-four-year-old en route the nation's capital was a markedly
different young man in several respects from the one who'd flown to
Okinawa. Key among them was that Okinawa had given him
geographic and emotional distance from his father. He'd had time to
see his parents in a clearer focus than before. He was returning to
the United States as an adult, as a professional, who'd grown on his
own. That was soon to be tested. While he intended to visit his
parents in New York, Peck had decided to stay with his old friend

from Exeter, Tim Childs, and his wife, Hope. Peck went to see his parents on New Year's Eve, and combined the journey with a shopping expedition in New York to buy gifts for Lily and the children. Holiday festivities still in the air, he went into a New York department store, 'and as I did so an incredible wave of depression came over me, so powerful I just had to run from the store. Walking back to my parents' apartment, I said to myself, "God, what happened there?"' He decided that 'searching for presents for the kids just reminded me how much I missed them, and that I was almost exactly on the other end of the world from them.' When he went into the Pecks' Park Avenue apartment his mother was present. He told her about the feeling he'd had while looking for presents for his children and said he was a bit depressed by it all.

'No, you're not,' she said.

'Not what?' he asked.

'You're not depressed,' she said.

'And I said, "What do you mean, I'm not depressed?"'

She said, "Well, you've got no reason to be depressed."'

Peck summarised the incident this way. 'Fortunately by that time I realised some of the stuff I'd grown up with, and that there was some of this stuff – this capacity for denial – that I'd just been unaware of. I'd been away. I'd had therapy. [Mother's attitude], that I could not experience depression, was just a mind-blower to me.' It was as if, he said, he was not allowed the simple emotional expression of admitting he missed his wife and children, that it was a somehow unacceptable weakness to feel depressed about being absent from them after being with them constantly for three years.

He hadn't realised, he said, quite how tightly governed were the emotional constraints within which he'd been raised.

CHAPTER 6

WASHINGTON, D.C.

His military masters in Washington, D.C. granted Peck his preferred assignment – Assistant Psychiatry and Neurology Consultant to the Surgeon General of the Army. The Army Surgeon General is commander of the Army Medical Department, which provides healthcare for the entire military and their families. The nation's capital was a fast-track career move, if Peck was interested in climbing up the military ladder. Though he'd have a long way to go, for generals were as commonplace in Washington as archbishops in the Vatican. That he only gave himself odds of one in a hundred of achieving anything significant in deflecting the all-volunteer Army programme didn't deter Peck: 'I was very ambitious,' he admitted. Under his poem, 'Leaving Washington' (1972), he wrote, 'It was exciting to walk along those marble corridors of power. I felt privileged to be in a position to participate at the very centre of our government. Twenty-seven months later I left with my spirit crushed.'

Peck once assigned, had to find somewhere for him and his family to live. He bought a small house in southeast Washington in the District of Columbia, not far from the US Capitol, and reported for duty. The house's location suited him: 'I could walk to work, and I wanted to be close to the black population rather than be totally isolated from it.' Whether his remark about the black population was a gratuitous aside, or well meant, is hard to determine. Unless one lived in northwest Washington or Georgetown, the near-all-white enclaves well beyond the purse strings of a major, it was difficult to be isolated from the African–American population in a city then 65 per cent black. On Peck's second night in town, tense from the trauma of moving and facing a new job, 'I got really nice and mellow drunk. I went into the office the next morning with a hell of a hangover and asked the secretary, "Well, what's up today?"

She said, "Well, you're supposed to be over in the Pentagon at ten o'clock for a meeting with the morale and discipline committee of the Army." This was a regular task that our office had, apparently. So I said, "Okay. How do I get to the Pentagon?"'

The Pentagon, the largest concrete structure in the world, headquarters to the entire Department of Defense leadership, is south of the Potomac River, in Virginia. Peck arrived early enough to learn how to find meeting places, and to get to the assigned room before the others arrived. In the cavernous meeting room there was an enormous table with place plaques, including one for the Army Surgeon General. High-ranking military types arrived and took their seats, Peck suddenly aware that practically everyone else was two to four ranks above him. In Washington it was a condition he'd have to learn to live with. A three-star general bustled in, took his seat, called the meeting to order, went around the heads at the table asking if anyone had any business, no one did, and he came to Peck. Given the committee was 'morale and discipline', Peck, 'through the cobwebs of my hangover', introduced himself as representing the Surgeon General, as newly arrived in Washington to work exactly on these kinds of problems. The general continued on around the table. No one had anything to report. The meeting ended with the general closing it and adding, "'Major Peck, I'd like to see you in my office right after this meeting." And I thought, oh, my God, he knows I'm hungover.

'I went into his office, a huge waiting room with a secretary in it. He kept me waiting for about ten minutes, wondering what the hell was happening. And finally I was ushered in and he was sitting behind his desk and he said, "Close the door, close the door." So I closed the door. He said, "Sit down." Then he looked piercingly at me and he said, "What do you know about transcendental meditation?" Out of the cobwebs of my mind I recalled some article I recently read, and said, "It may help people get off drugs." His eyes lit up and he said, "Oh, God, finally somebody I can talk to about this. There's nobody in the whole Pentagon I can talk to about this and I think this Maharishi Yoga programme is going to be the salvation of the Army."'

At which point, said Peck, he decided he'd better quickly become an authority on transcendental meditation. He did, he said, 'and that way became a favourite of his.' In such ways, Peck said, 'I was very successful politically.' But transcendental meditation had no spiritual appeal for Peck, he was setting aside that element of his religious life for something 'more earthly, something more carnal and flesh-and-blood real than Buddhism.'

Peck also regarded as 'good and graceful' the advent in his life of his newly arrived boss, Colonel Stewart Baker, the chief psychiatry and neurology consultant. 'He turned out to be just the right kind of person – we were co-conspirators.' As 'sort of consultants' to the military, he and Baker were 'in a hot spot because we were the centre of any kind of dissent against the Vietnam War, the centre for examining drug abuse problems and the centre for racial problems.' There wasn't much attention being paid to racial antagonisms in the military, though whatever surfaced spilled over into Peck's domain. The Pentagon's anxiety about drug abuse among the military in Vietnam was reaching fever pitch.

In Washington, D.C., Peck, a student of social relations, found himself alternately amazed or entertained by the institutions around him, the military with its doggedness for detail and congressional politics with their momentary passions. 'I was interested in the psychology of politics, and the psychology of power,' he said. He was in the thick of things in the Surgeon General's office because the Army was petrified by what he called the Vietnam War 'drug thing. I guess they got scared because of *The Man With the Golden Arm* syndrome [a 1955 movie starring Frank Sinatra that dealt with heroin addiction and the difficulties of overcoming it].' The current Army General Staff reasoning, he said, was that because some 50 per cent of all US military serving in Vietnam had tried heroin, ergo, 50 per cent of the military would return home addicted. 'My boss and I kind of knew the actual figure would be around 1.5 per cent, but we couldn't get that through anybody's head,' Peck said. It became an issue of enormous consequence, and even though Baker and Peck disagreed with the Army General Staff premise, 'the paperwork started to fly. So, the thing I became most involved in was one that interested me least – the drug abuse problem,' he said.

Most majors shared a secretarial pool, two or three majors per secretary. Because of the drug paperwork blizzard, reports and testimony for meetings and hearings, Peck had three secretaries, he said. By rank he nonetheless remained the low man on the structural totem pole. He testified before the United States Senate, and when information he deemed important wasn't circulating fast enough, or indeed surfacing at all, Peck wasn't above leaking useful tidbits to the press – through Jack Anderson, a leading and respected Washington, D.C. syndicated columnist. Colonel Baker and Major Peck developed an anti-drug proposal to deal with the problem as they envisioned it, and forwarded it up the chain of command with a request for $8 million, to run at a cost of $1 million a year. It was not funded.

The issue itself was far from dead, however, because the Congress, alerted to and alarmed by the heroin topic, began investigating. Peck contends that the military is just about the only population Congress can study with impunity. 'If you're [a Congressman] investigating drug abuse in somebody else's state you're going to step on your colleague's toes. If you're going to investigate it in your own state, you're going to step on some important toes in your own state. But you're home free if you investigate it in the military, the federal population.' Part of the heroin scare's being blown out of all proportion, he said, 'was because everybody under the sun wanted to investigate it, there were like six [Congressional] committees all investigating it at the same time.

'It just escalated and escalated until [President Richard] Nixon had to take action and bring in a guy by the name of Jerry Jaffe, and form a new office that reported directly to him: SAODAP, or Special Action Office of Drug Abuse Prevention. He took this initiative with great drama and flair.' Jerome H. Jaffe, MD, had pioneered a mix of methadone, detoxification and therapeutic programmes in Chicago. In Peck's assessment, 'Jaffe was a sort of hardliner – "By God, we'll get these guys to pull out their peckers and pee in the bottle no matter how humiliating it might be."' An evening meeting was called in one of the Pentagon situation rooms. 'Down in the bowels,' said Peck, 'a huge room with one of the longest tables I'd ever seen, fifty feet long. The room was just jammed. Anybody who was anybody of importance sat at the table, the less important on seats away from the table; me in particular in the darkest, furthest corner, and my boss was also about three seats from me. These guys told how the urine testing would work and the guys would be tested just before they got on the boat or the plane to leave Vietnam. And then if they tested positive they would be held over and put in a drug rehab programme of some kind or another, either in Vietnam or someplace else. And questions came up about managing these guys. Well supposing they didn't want to be in a drug rehab programme. Supposing they ran off, what do you do, and so forth, to detain them. It got more and more ridiculous. I had a friend who was sitting at the table who was an assistant secretary of the Army and I passed him a note that said, "John, this is getting crazier and crazier and it's really got to be stopped." So, John spoke up and said, "Well, on some of these issues maybe Colonel [Stewart] Baker would have something to say." Stu [Colonel Baker], much as I loved him totally, was kind of overawed by the high rank of the assemblage and just had nothing to say, and it just kept going on and getting worse and worse. Finally, I stood up in my little dark corner, the lowest ranker by two ranks of the hundred people or so in the room, lots of two stars and three stars and whatnot, and I think I just said, "Stop. This is getting out of hand, getting totally insane," and they said, "Who are you?"'

Peck explained he was from the Army Surgeon General's office, that he and his boss knew 'a fair amount about drug abuse, and I'm glad Dr Jaffe is here. But one of the things not mentioned thus far,' said Peck, 'is that most of these people that you're going to be urine testing are leaving Vietnam, many of them draftees because their tour of duty is up in the Army. And it is highly unclear – at least it's not clear to me yet, perhaps you would tell me – what legal authority you would have to hold these people past their tour of duty?' Peck continued, 'Well, that sort of put them back a little bit but made them pugnacious. So they got in after me and I got more eloquent. I said, "Look, I've been in the Army nine years now and I am really very, very proud of the Army and what it can do. It can do extraordinary things, but that does not mean that it can do everything." And I sounded off and said, "Incidentally, there is no way that the media is not going to get a hold of this and won't have a field day with the violation of civil liberties going on."' Peck said the meeting turned into a shouting match, not least between Jaffe and himself. Three-plus decades later, Jaffe said he remembered the meeting, recalled that it was an extremely high-level gathering, but had no recollection of Peck or the scene he described.

The doings in Vietnam were not Peck's only Washington contretemps over drugs: he was using them himself. 'I was turned on to pot by a colonel in San Francisco in the 1960s. Tried it a couple of times, and I didn't smoke any again until my last year in Okinawa.' In Okinawa Peck worked on drug abuse in conjunction with the Army Criminal Investigation Division officer who gave drug lectures. 'One day, in a joking sort of way, I said to the CID officer, "Do I really know what I'm talking about? I ought to smoke some of this stuff. Can you sneak me a bit to smoke?" He snuck me quite a bit, and I smoked with some regularity, I'd say two to three evenings a week, for the next, oh, dozen years.'

Pot-smoking wasn't something Washington condoned for people with a high secret security clearance, and Peck – serving in the Office of the Army Surgeon General – knew if he told them he smoked pot he'd never get one, unless he made himself essential. He'd been granted a temporary security clearance on his initial arrival but had never filled in the forms for a permanent clearance, until the day a man came to his office and said he was from 'the Company', meaning the CIA. He talked to Peck about his clearance and asked if there was anything he needed to reveal. Peck said he'd marched in peace marches, and that he'd smoked pot. When the CIA man asked, 'When was the last time?' Peck replied, 'Not recently.' They each had different notions of how recent 'not recently' was. Peck received his clearance. He'd smoked pot three nights earlier, and continued to do so until he was in his mid-forties. He saw no conflict with his pot use and the fact he was creating military drug counsellors to preach against just that. Later one of his stock answers in interviews regarding drugs was, 'I think marijuana should remain illegal for everyone under thirty and made mandatory for everyone over thirty. Fortunately I didn't start smoking until I was thirty-three. If I'd smoked during adolescence I think I would have blown my brain out.' Most of the soldiers were under thirty.

To get the question of an all-volunteer Army on the agenda so that arguments against it could surface, Peck usurped a military psychiatrists' annual conference by promoting his programme there with a panel that included as speakers 'the Israeli ambassador, the chief military sociologist from academia, a senator and a couple of other big people'. Once the invitees had accepted, it was difficult for the Surgeon General, 'who looked at it very dubiously', to cancel it. As a meeting, said Peck, it worked well, 'but it had absolutely no influence on the president. The psychiatrists, justifiably I think, resented me for what I had done because what was normally their sort of private conference had half of the General Staff over.' In these ways Peck played his own games in a Washington era known for Nixon's 'dirty tricks'.

Washington tricks never ceased to amaze Peck. 'About the time the first potential graduates of the military drug abuse counsellors school I'd helped organise and develop down in Texas were in place, I heard that they were being yanked out of their programmes. Well, the drug programme was always in jeopardy because the Department of Defense didn't want the military to get involved in any kind of serious way. But everybody we just trained and assigned was being reassigned to Germany. Indeed, suddenly a very large number of enlisted men was being sent to Germany. And I kept trying to find out what was going on in Germany. They'd brought in a Brigadier General, Gard, to run the drug programme, a lovely guy. Then right after him a three-star skinhead who was a real right-wing son-of-a-bitch. If Defense wanted to kill a programme they'd bring in a horrible person on top of it, which is what they did. Finally I was at a cocktail party, someplace in Washington, and Bob Gard was there and I talked about how our programmes were being decimated. Why on earth were these people being sent to Germany. And he said, "Oh, you don't know that? It's because they are quite sure that [US Senator William] Fulbright is going to get like a two-thirds reduction in troop strength in Germany. And so they are just sending three or four hundred thousand extra men over to Germany so they can just send them back again when Fulbright gets his cuts." God, a horrible story. Think of the costs, plus screwing up four hundred thousand people's lives just to play a paper game with Congress.'

Whatever his personal grandstanding in recalling some of his battles, Peck, in an instance he's quite modest about, almost changed how the US military polices itself and monitors its internal conduct. Had Peck been successful in getting the Army to deal with the psychology of brutality in one war, Vietnam, he might have been able to help prevent the brutalities that, at Abu Ghraib, Guantanamo and elsewhere, were a sideshow of brutalities in another war, Iraq. The atrocity in Vietnam was the massacre at My Lai.

On 26 November 1969, while Peck was still serving in Okinawa, General William C. Westmoreland, chief of staff of the US Army, directed Lieutenant General William R. Peers to investigate 'the nature and scope of the original US Army investigations of the alleged My Lai incident, which occurred 16 March 1968 in Quang Noi Province, Republic of Vietnam.' The massacre and cover-up had been made public by an American reporter called Seymour

Hirsch. The Peers Inquiry concluded that US troops had massacred a 'large number of Vietnamese . . . that efforts were made at every level of command from company to division, to withhold and suppress information.' Despite numerous officers and enlisted men being charged with a wide range of offences, the Army authorities dealt with My Lai by dismissing the charges as they surfaced. Out of an initial three dozen charges, only one made it as far as a court martial. And he was found not guilty.

In 1972, Westmoreland decided to retire. Peck had decided that he, too, was nearing the end of his military career. Not only was he tired of the game, there were reports circulating that the Office of the Surgeon General of the Army was to be relocated from Washington, D.C. to Texas. And Peck had even less interest in being in Texas than he did being in Washington. Westmoreland had remained deeply disturbed by My Lai and, prior to leaving military service, picked up on a sentence in the Peers Report that stated, 'We have made no effort to investigate the psychological and sociological implications of My Lai, which is something that ought to be done.' The general said something ought to be done, which left the Department of the Army trying to figure out what to do with Westmoreland's request. 'So,' said Peck, 'we, or rather I, went over to the Pentagon and essentially grabbed this floating paper and said, "We'll take care of it."' The result was 'Recommendations for research and training changes in response to General Westmoreland's request relating to My Lai and the report of the Peers Inquiry', with eight recommendations listed. Three men produced the response – Peck, Baker and another colonel, head of research at Walter Reed US Army Hospital, who filed a minority report disputing the Baker-Peck recommendations.

Peck was insisting that the first step was to authorise a study of atrocities of brutal behaviour by US troops both elsewhere in Vietnam at that time, and in other wars; that actually such a study was quite feasible, and that the Army General War College was quite willing to undertake it. Recommendation by recommendation, with the relentlessness of a man who understood the significance of what had occurred, Peck said he outlined how to research the atrocities issue and how to arrive at some conclusions that could lead to change. The Department of the Army immediately shelved the Baker-Peck recommendations and they were never heard of again.

If Peck was foiled in his attempt to give the Army a lasting gift, the Army in its turn munificently dropped two gifts in Peck's lap that were distinct personal direction finders.

By the early 1970s, increasingly dissatisfied with Zen Buddhism, he was exploring – reading a little and cogitating a lot. In November-December of 1971 Peck was assigned to a high-level inspection tour, with a US Senator's aide, of the military anti-drug programmes he'd helped establish. Because of the Senatorial and Surgeon General rankings, the expedition meant a high degree of eager-to-please attention from his hosts at whichever military base they visited. One was Fort Jackson, near Columbia, South Carolina.

Part of the attention was that the military would arrange some evening programme to keep the guests entertained when the inspecting was done. At Fort Jackson, said Peck, 'the people who were supposed to take care of us were terribly embarrassed, all they'd been able to get was tickets for something called *Jesus Christ, Superstar*. If we wanted to go, the tickets were available. I knew nothing about it except it had been talked about a lot. I didn't know whether it was heretical or not.' They decided to attend. 'It was fascinating going to the show in Columbia because I noted that in the huge audience there was not one black person. So we were there, and for the first, oh, twenty minutes all I could think of was, I can't stand all this noise. But then, after about twenty minutes, I began to hear it. And for the first time Jesus really became real to me.' He said he was able to get the message because of the music, the music opened him to the words.

He carried the feeling, or realisation, away from Columbia with him, and began to explore Christianity more thoroughly, 'for that was the beginning of the journey,' he said. Religion and psychology had melded in Peck in the Army in a new way. The Army was not particularly interested in religion's role in the military, but it was certainly keen to keep abreast of the relevance of psychiatry-psychology to its everyday needs. Military psychologists studied everything from psychological warfare to indoctrination, from improving race relations to maintaining morale. Consequently, in 1972, the heyday of 'encounter sessions', which could be a some-what demeaning and sometimes brutal psychological immersion programme, the military was weighing the possibility of a contract with the National Training Laboratories in Bethel, Maine. NTL had developed a twelve-day 'sensitivity group' programme which, in

June that year, newly promoted Lieutenant Colonel Peck went to
Maine to experience. It did more than bring tears to his eyes.

In *The Different Drum: Community Making and Peace,* Peck glosses
over the worst aspects of encounter sessions, some of which have
been criticised for having a strong element of psychological coercion
to them, sufficient to drive many people to tears. Shouting and
hectoring, verbally pillorying people for their weaknesses and failings
were not unknown in the early encounter session days. Sessions could
produce some semblance of community evolving out of the mutual
exploration, revelations – and evident emotional pain. To a psychologist like Peck, this experience was something to file away for later.
But he did not come through unscathed. At the end of ten days he,
too, was in tears. He was so wracked by the emotional release and the
flow of tears that one woman became concerned. He assured her, he
said, it was because he hadn't cried in thirty years, since the 'crybaby'
headline in the newspaper his parents gave him.

'Within a month' of the encounter session, said Peck, 'Lily and I
were house-hunting in an area where I could establish a private
practice. By Labor Day we had found our house, and I submitted
my resignation. We left Washington on November fourth, four-and-
a-half months after that night I had first sobbed.' Few people have
been so happy to leave Washington that they wrote a poem about it.
Peck did. In part, *Leaving Washington* (1972) reads:

> The rugs were taken up,
> The cleansers like wooden soldiers in formation stand waiting
>   for action on a cardboard battlefield
> Plymouth Van Lines will rescue us tomorrow
>   from this soul-sucking sterile marble town.
> The sapless trees bear National Trust Blossoms
> And the mean, ugly real blacks mock us all.
> Do I escape to the wild hills to lick wounds and return?
> Or retire to sit early old in the sun
> Recounting brief honors and showing shallow scars.
> Or are we being maneuvred there by some distant general
> To fight a war more elemental yet than little skirmishes for
>   position?
> I do not know.
> I know that if the fight must again be here
> I will need a better army or greater love.

With his decision to leave the Army, Peck had to be willing to fail, for, as he and Lily talked over the decision, they agreed he should go into private practice. The question was: where? For location, he said, it came down to Santa Fe, New Mexico, Maine, or Western Connecticut. They decided on Connecticut, somewhere in the region of his boyhood summer home at Sharon. They'd saved $10,000; 'We couldn't even handle the down payment on the houses we liked, they were well over a hundred thousand dollars.' They kept looking.

Before resigning his commission, Peck had had options beyond going to Texas with the Surgeon General's office. Peck had been ambitious when he first arrived in Washington. He was genuinely opposed to an all-volunteer Army. Now he was more bored than tired, disappointed at how resistant was an enormous bureaucracy to acknowledge its problems and seek change. Further, Peck had absolutely no intention of living in Texas. One option was to head the Veterans Administration's drug treatment programme. The VA, as it is known, is the medical care provider for all former members of the US military. It operates hospitals, rehabilitation centres and nursing homes. For Peck the offer was a last 'piece of glory. At my glory night in the bowels of the Pentagon, they tried to enlist me for this, to be Chief of the Outlawed Drug Abuse Programmes for the Veterans Administration. And I turned them down. It would have put me up in a sort of Brigadier General rank, which would have been nice, with a hundred and eighty-seven million dollar budget.' The Army also dangled before him another alternative, Medical Military Attaché at the US Embassy in London.

Peck was not inclined to accept either offer, he was done with military life. He said, 'I'd learned everything the Army and Washington had had to teach me. It was time to move on.' He was thirty-six.

CHAPTER 7

THE COUNTRY DOCTOR

Though his plan was to become 'an ordinary country psychiatrist', Peck said, 'I was terrified – terrified I wasn't going to find enough work to support myself. Practically everybody I know who has left the practice of medicine under the aegis of an organisation to break free and go into private practice has been terrified. There's something about having to deal with the paperwork, the insurance, your own health insurance that's terrifying.'

The couple had decided on Western Connecticut. An expensive decision. Prices of homes in those rolling hills and dales are kept high because New York City-oriented East Coast wealth wants a place in the country as well as in town. And prizes rural Connecticut. The Pecks kept looking. Finally, in the village of New Preston, the Pecks 'stumbled across a house' at a price they could consider. It was a few steps across Bliss Road from Lake Waramaug. 'Unoccupied, it was on the market at a low price because it hadn't been painted in twenty years,' said Peck. 'The grounds were overgrown, the inside neglected. It was one of the many acts of grace in our lives. We bought it for 79,500 dollars. It was a wreck, but it was gorgeous.' The house is a typical structure for the area in that its core is eighteenth century with nineteenth-century additions. The Pecks would add more, until it became today's five-bedroom house with a guesthouse to the rear. At the time, in the downstairs configuration, they wedged in a sizeable home office for Peck. Later Peck would say setting up his office in his home was a huge error. 'The children would see Daddy at home but not available. It would have been much easier for them had I had an office and then, when I came home, be available.

'I'd chosen New Preston because of my terror I wouldn't make a living – there was a dearth of psychiatrists here. The town of Torrington is about twenty miles north and Danbury's about thirty miles south, and there was no psychiatrist in practice within perhaps forty-five to fifty miles of Danbury. It looked like a place where I'd be in demand. Before I even got here I had employment arranged at a clinic in the Torrington hospital, and two days at a clinic in Milford, and a two-hour set-up to be psychiatrist at the jail in Litchfield.'

New Preston village is about a ninety-minute drive from the nearest major airport, Hartford-Springfield, Connecticut (Hartford is the life insurance capital of the United States) and an almost two-hour drive from New York City. New Preston village's popularity comes from its lake, the second largest natural lake in the state. The house, rimmed by hills, sits in the sheltered Bliss Hollow up from the lake edge. Peck insists the previous owners had named the house, 'Hollow Bliss, would you believe it?' 'Hollow Bliss' may have been prescient. For the first the time in his adult life, Peck had to answer to no one other than himself: he was paterfamilias, the head of the household. And as head of the household, he wanted things his way. Further, he was a psychotherapist, he understood the art of manipulation. Later his wife and children would regard him as particularly controlling.

Peck decided to call the house Imladris, the place in Tolkien's Middle Earth magically protected against the forces of evil. Imladris was not protection for the occupants against some of Peck's developing whims and demands. Against his will, against his wishes, against his deepest intents, he was not just transplanting his family close to his father's summer home, he was admitting some of his father's behaviour into his own household. In later conversations about these early years in New Preston, Peck was frank about many of the issues, and careful to turn the account his way. For example, an early Peck childhood phobia about being lost mutated into always wanting to know where Lily was. He said he realised that when Lily went shopping and he asked her where she was going and when she'd be back, it would look to his wife as if he was always trying to control her. 'I'd say, "What's the latest time that you'll be back?" And if she wasn't, I'd begin to worry like crazy that something had happened to her. I'd remember that when I was young and my parents were late I was worried something had happened to them; this was fear of losing them, not of being deliberately abandoned by them.' On its own, the exchange about 'where and when' was innocent enough, and not uncommon in a marriage. As a constant, however meant, it could be galling, and controlling – and often seemed so to Lily.

Terrified though Peck might be about losing Lily, or not making enough money, he was fortunate in other ways. This era, as his friend psychologist James Guy later remarked, was indeed 'the Golden Age of psychotherapy'. Within six months of arriving in New Preston, Peck could report more patients than he could handle with more money coming in than he'd ever made. 'I came with no ambition higher than that of simply being a country psychiatrist who played golf, hopefully, on Wednesday afternoons. It was one of the times in my life that I've been truly without ambition.' Indeed, with more patients than his schedule permitted, he asked Lily if she would like to take on a patient. She agreed to try, and the small summer house to the rear of Imladris became the practice waiting room and Lily's office. 'From the word go I knew that Lily was a born therapist. She had a practice, fifteen to twenty hours a week, for the next ten years, maybe fifteen. The first patient I sent her turned out to be the sickest patient she ever treated. She didn't do very well by her but she was a born therapist,' said Peck. Lily was also the linchpin in ensuring the practice operated efficiently and that the patients were welcomed and comfortable. 'Lily made everything work,' said Hope Childs. The Childses and Pecks were close during these years, their children being of similar age.

In the Peck family, the girls were early teenagers, Christopher was in school locally. Said Peck, 'Back when the kids were very young, I mean up to two, two-and-a-half or so, parenthood was a lot of work, but I enjoyed that work. Lily wasn't so keen on faeces, I didn't mind changing diapers, washing them, taking the girls for walks. As soon as they began to talk, and started telling those endless sorts of stories that children can talk about that never go anywhere, I found taking care of them very difficult. I would do some of it, but I thought it very boring. I really had to work at it until they became old enough to have dialogues. Christopher, we've always been close. We used to dance incessantly and had great fun. I spanked less than I was spanked. The oldest, maybe five times when she was a kid. The next one, three times. Christopher not at all. I would be hesitant to say never spank a child.'

Later he'd say he regretted that he competed with his children too much, that in horseplay he wrestled with them too hard, that he'd given them the same type of joke Christmas presents his father had visited on him and David. But he couldn't take his time away from his own drives, he *had* to write. 'I didn't pay them enough attention. If you asked them they would say, "Well, Dad was really good in a crisis, but you had to have a crisis to get his attention." I regret not having paid them, particularly the girls, more attention than I did. By the time they were adolescents they were exciting. I gave them lots of attention. Of course, they had lots of crises then, too.'

Not-so-gradually Peck had become 'extremely focused on his work,' he said, 'whereas Lily had the great capacity just to flow with the kids – and she loves to shop, which I hate. She'd play dumb games with them. She loves to flow. It's rather hard to flow with children when there's a paper you want to write on religious ecstasy.' By the time they'd moved to New Preston, 'I left ninety-five per cent of the burden of raising the children to Lily. I put in my five to ten per cent.' At weekends, there were the children, and he and Lily were keen to develop the land around the house into a fine garden. Just as Judge Peck had been able to boast of the finest lawn in Connecticut, so, in the decades ahead, Scott, with a wave of his arm, would be able to introduce visitors to 'one of the finest gardens in New England', due in major measure to gardeners who created and maintained what Peck and Lily envisioned. Peck had his own patch, for growing pot, which he would offer to friends and guests. 'He was the only man who ever offered me pot,' said Hope Childs. She declined his invitation.

Connecticut neighbour and fellow Friends Seminary scholar Elizabeth Peale, now Elizabeth Allen, recalled of this period: 'snowy afternoons in our home when Scotty would expound on his latest train of thought and my husband, John, and I would marvel at the range of his dynamic thinking. We would always come away aware we had been in the presence of a great mind.'

At the point Peck opened his practice he was, at thirty-six, still a young man. He had learned how to command, or at least how to manage men and women, and how to press his case, sometimes quite successfully, against an impressively unyielding institution, the military. Nonetheless, while these skills and challenges may have added a fillip to his uniformed days, in the Army he was still under orders and his days were mainly filled for him. In Okinawa he had been able to have a comfortable family life; in much busier Washington it was more work and less play.

To New Preston he had carried some things with him from the

Army. His heavy smoking and drinking had not lessened, and he'd continued his three-nights-a-week pot habit. In New Preston, he said, his relationship with the children improved with pot. 'It made me more playful and more able to flow. Simon and Garfunkel music would have left me cold, but suddenly, under pot, I began to hear it.' But he tuned out what he didn't want to contemplate, such as the effect on his children of rolling his joints for him. He had a few stock phrases as quick defences when tackled with questions about his drinking, his pot-smoking and his ability to see everything in terms of his own needs first. He would say he was nicer to have around when he was drinking, 'I get mellow,' he said. And then he'd deflect the question by adding, 'whereas [brother] David was a nasty drunk,' and go off on a riff about David. Or, he would take the issue to its natural conclusion: 'I wished I could drink and smoke more,' leaving the conversation nowhere to go.

Decades later, psychologist Guy asked Peck 'if, looking back, you find yourself being kind of sadistic towards your kids the way your folks had been?' Peck replied, 'Yeah. Not to the same degree. But that's some of the stuff I would take back.' He provided an instance. 'I never learned to roll a [marijuana] joint properly. On the other hand they loved to roll my joints for me because Daddy was so much more fun when he was on pot. And again, that's something I wish I could do over again, it gave them the added burden of the secret they had to keep.' Many around Peck have chosen to keep their secrets secret.

Regarding pot, he said he felt marijuana allowed him to become more passive, and 'get more in touch with my feminine side. I also think it had a great deal to do with my spirituality. Talking in terms of a masculine God, C.S. Lewis said, "In relation to God we are all feminine." I became more able to more or less "hear" God, and for the first time, while stoned, I began to carry on serious conversations with Him – or Her. No great revelations, just an ever increasing closeness. I was still smoking marijuana when [about 1983] I first listened to the music of Marilyn Von Waldner, and was turned on to the Christian core of her music and lyrics in a way I don't think I would have been otherwise.' (Sister Marilyn von Waldner was a discalced Carmelite nun known for her sacred compositions and joyful songs of praise. In 1987 Peck and Von Waldner produced *What Return Can I Make?* a multi-media liturgical celebration kit subtitled *Dimensions of the Christian Experience*.

What he would add was, 'Once again, I don't want to recommend marijuana to everyone. I am damn glad I did not start smoking it until I was in my thirties and with a very well developed lifestyle and clearly focused. Under those circumstances it did have the effect of loosening me up so that I could become like a little child, and emotionally a child of God.'

On the seasonal calendar, as Lily and Scott moved into Imladris that first year, the ice on Lake Waramaug had begun to freeze. They settled in. The lake thawed, the work for both of them continued. There was the steadying routine of normal middle-class professional life: school for the children, work for the parents, and much effort put into family vacations. For Christopher, particularly, the contrast between vacations funded by his grandfather's easy munificence and those paid for by his father rankled.

'The odd thing with Scotty,' Christopher said, 'was there was generally enough money for luxuries but not enough for comforts. He had this strange way with money. He was a Depression-era baby, his father was doing well financially, but the Depression had an effect on everyone's psychology. So, when we went to Europe, we often stayed in very grand hotels, but the three of us would pile into one room. I guess our last family trip was we went to Paris one Christmas. Julia and Belinda both brought their fiancés, or they became fiancés during that trip. And they were given separate accommodations. I was the fifteen-year-old having to share my parents' bedroom and it was kind of odd in a very nice hotel. Obviously, I'd rather we'd stay in a cheap hotel and I'd have my own room. This was typical.'

'He was very tight with Mom,' he continued, 'but on the other hand she'd buy a lot of cheap things, that was her rebellion. They were always fighting over all this stuff she was buying. I think they only installed air-conditioning in the mid-nineties. It's an old house so air-conditioning was kind of spotty in places so Mom bought a couple of window units which actually worked really great. Dad on principle didn't like the idea, even though he was sweaty and miserable. He could be very Spartan now and then.' That account contrasted with Christopher's 'warm memories of my grandfather. He was a grand old gentleman by that time. Both Scotty and David were still burdened with memories of the way he'd done things, the way he'd been before. We had Thanksgiving at Grandfather's apartment and watched the Thanksgiving parade from one of his office windows.'

Peck, with a minimum fifty-hour work week, kept himself fully occupied. Those vacationing breaks from the routine included extended annual family gatherings in Bermuda, organised and paid for by his father. 'We were often together as two families,' said Scott's nephew, David (David W. Peck III), 'but almost always with my grandparents as hosts, whether Easter holidays in Bermuda or in the country.' It would be Judge Peck and grandmother Elizabeth, David Junior and his wife, Greg, and their three children, Heather, Lisa and nephew David III, plus Scott and Lily, and their three children, Belinda, Julia and Christopher. Said nephew David, 'Some of my happiest memories are of us playing, singing or dining as cousins in Greece or Bermuda. They were also shadowed on all sides by family dynamics of which one is only vaguely or subconsciously aware. But there were shadows only because the light was so bright.' Said Christopher, 'The Greece trip – we cousins had a great time. It may not be relevant but it's amusing, the sailors on the yacht were always perpetually fondling each other. It had a profound effect on my cousins and perhaps this side of the family. Some were entertained, the others intrigued.' Peck said he enjoyed turning a vacation into a learning experience. When the Pecks *tous ensemble* were in Greece, Scott said he 'laughed at the notion' that the Greek Isles, the Cyclades, might be the site of the lost city of Atlantis. But after hearing the tales, he said he sought out the Akrotiri (sunken city) exhibit in the Athens museum. And after viewing it decided he was a believer.

Peck said he regarded vacations and travel as a time for family bonding, whether taking Belinda, his eldest daughter with him to a Salt Lake City conference ('a time together to enrich our relationship'), or he and Lily taking Christopher a few years later to Puerto Rico for deep sea fishing. On a more modest scale, for parental relaxation and refreshment, Scott and Lily would go into New York, to catch up on art and music, or to hear speakers such as the Afghan writer Idries Shah, a Sufi mystic, teacher and storyteller (1924–1996). 'He was a brilliant man,' said Peck, 'he turned me on to the wonderful explosion of thirteenth-century Persian mystics. He talked about false Sufis and true Sufis – very important because there were a lot of New Age people floating around calling themselves Sufis who weren't.'

Shah awakened Peck's interest in Sufism and Peck, the anti-WASP, discovered in Sufism more ammunition for his blasts against the Establishment's idea of the proper social ordering of things.

'Muslims tend to believe there's seven levels to everything,' he said, 'and one [Sufi teacher] said that aesthetics is the lowest appreciation of the Real, with a capital R. And I suddenly said, "Aha!" The number one ultimate value of WASP culture is good taste, and in worshipping good taste WASPs have caught on to a little piece of the Real. The only problem is that WASPs don't realise – and generally don't care – that there are six further levels higher than that.'

The drift of young Westerners to India and elsewhere was symptomatic of a spiritual search Peck had already discovered as a late teenager, and Idries Shah an example of those who brought the Eastern experience to the armchair traveller. Religious studies departments being introduced to university curricula spoke to the depth of inquiry that gripped many young adults, while at Harvard, physician Dr Herbert Benson was about to found the Mind/Body Institute at Harvard Medical School, which grew into a focal point decades later of the examination of alternative therapies for medical treatment. 'By the time I was fifteen I looked like a WASP because certain things get tattooed into your skin, but under that skin I'm half black and half Mediterranean,' said Peck. Asked to explain, Peck would say he was a reverse Oreo. (The Oreo is an American cookie, black biscuit on the outside and white cream on the inside. Like the use of 'coconut' in some circles in Britain, 'Oreo' is a criticism some people of colour have of others who behave like whites or consider themselves in the white mainstream.) Peck was saying he wanted the release of the passionate senses, the release Latins and African–Americans ostensibly experience, a Peck comment laced with stereotyping.

Peck liked the challenge of new ideas, whether generated by others or himself. Idries Shah, for example, was hailed for his skill in introducing the West to classical spiritual thought. He was regarded by *Psychology Today* as 'a major cultural event of our time'. It was almost natural that because of Shah, Peck, the former Zen Buddhist, took his brief detour into Islamic Sufism, on his journeying towards Christianity. He was a seeker, but he was seeking enlightenment, not dogmatism. He read Shah closely, and studied the writings of Jelaluddin Rumi, the thirteenth-century scholar and teacher known to history as a fine poet. It was probably not lost on Peck that Shah blended Eastern teachings Peck himself had followed with Western needs Peck understood, to produce a viable vehicle that was simultaneously motivational and spiritual.

One of Shah's aphorisms may have lodged in Peck's conscious or subconscious to later be used to great effect by Peck himself. Shah's response to a person complaining about life's problems was, 'It is my view that your real problem is that you are a member of the human race. Face that one first.' Peck opened *The Road Less Travelled* with 'Life is difficult' – same thought, tighter construction. *The Road Less Travelled* was an instruction to 'face that one first'.

Peck was always a little skimpy in his early days in his books, in acknowledging the contributions of others. This was certainly the case with *The Road Less Travelled,* dedicated to his parents. The book had no acknowledgements, and in its Introduction mentioned only Lily by name, with a nod to helpful colleagues and teachers. Idries Shah may have deserved better. On 2 May 1976, in New York City, Shah addressed a conference on Traditional Esoteric Psychology. Peck in a 24 June letter to Shah in London reminded him that 'I thrust upon you in the hallway my professional card and asked for your address, explaining that I thought I might have need of your help some day, and offering myself to be of service to you if the need should arise.' [Peck offered his home as a retreat if Shah needed one during his American visits]. 'I began in January this year to write a book, the title of which is *Spiritual Growth,* and which is subtitled *Psychiatric Analysis of Discipline, Love and Grace.*' Peck said he 'intended to take the liberty' of sending Shah his ninety-four pages on discipline. 'Please forgive me if this represents an impingement upon your privacy, and please understand that I am fully aware you have no obligation to me to read it or pay it your attention.'

Shah did read it, and did more. He wrote to Peck and offered to talk to him about it. He was to be in New York in the November and would meet with Peck, or, if time constraints prevented it, at least they could talk by telephone, which they did. In December 1978, Peck sent Shah an inscribed copy of *The Road.* There was no further correspondence.

From America's earliest days, its population was accustomed to a seemingly unending stream of men and women, prophets and pundits, charlatans and charmers, who emerged to guide, cajole, or command them into a better way of life. Almost invariably there was a spiritual or religious overtone or origin to it all. And within this succession of social influencers there was always, fortunately, a leavening of the serious, the sincere and worthy. By the mid-1970s, Americans had become *serious* about their spiritual and religious quest. While Americans were individually exploring Eastern religion and making pilgrimages to sit at the feet of mystics, in the United States there was a slightly more prosaic approach to the spiritual. World religions scholar Melissa Jones, PhD, explained the two-step developments that further created tilled ground for what Peck would plant. Academically, religion was no longer simply confined to divinity schools, theological colleges and seminaries. For more than a decade, major US universities had been creating Departments of Religious Studies. They were filled, filled in part because the United States is one of those countries where religion is a matter of everyday life for the majority. In America, religion and the spiritual had become acceptably hot academic topics. Further, this was all in keeping with a nation that prides itself on, almost insists on, education, higher education, self-education and self-improvement.

That suited Peck, he was a serious fellow. Said Melissa Jones, 'Religion education used to be in seminaries. Suddenly it was everywhere. The Religious Studies departments were populated by disenchanted Protestants and Catholic seminarians and by people who had a religious urge but no prospect of taking vows or being ordained and yet wanted to pursue studies. To be authentic in the academic community you have to be scientific. Academics were trying to turn religious studies and theology and that whole area of inquiry into a social science. Dr Peck [with *The Road Less Travelled*] would make that connection. He did have the scientific credentials, he was an MD and a psychiatrist.' Peck had his own addendum to this. When he was on the lecture circuit he'd frequently be asked why he didn't go to divinity school himself. His view was that while he'd have loved to take time off to attend, 'it would be the bloody stupidest thing I could possibly do for my career because it would almost de-credential me.' In other words, people paid attention to the spiritual side of psychotherapist Peck's writing and lectures precisely because he was not shackled by theological academic trappings, only scientific ones.

The man who gave up thoughts of a writing career for medicine in these years in New Preston couldn't keep thoughts of a book out of his mind. 'We'd been here about two years, say 1974, a year before I got the idea for the book. I was sitting in bed, one summer afternoon it seems to me, I don't know why I had nothing to do. I was sitting in bed sort of meditating and suddenly the thought comes to me that "I am God." Well, that's the first thought. The second thought I had was, "Scotty, you better not go walking down the streets of New Milford telling anybody about this." The third thought was, "Why did you have that thought?" The fourth thought was, "Well, in a sense it's up to me to decide the kind of God I want to believe in," and in that kind of sense it put me in the role of being God's creator. And in a sense – by choosing what kind of God I wanted to believe in and stand for – I was creating what God would be for me. But the next thought was I basically got the inkling at that time of co-creation. That I was responsible for creation with God.'

In the period before *The Road* took firm shape, Peck's Connecticut world offered an active and rewarding professional life and lifestyle, with golf for play and, even better, the opportunity to explore psychotherapy on his own terms at work. 'There is a good reason for the Freudian training [in psychiatry] and the tradition of being aloof [from one's patients],' he said. 'But it has to be broken at some time or another, and the first time I broke it my patient suddenly started getting better. She was dating a man who himself was in therapy. Over dinner one night her date said that his psychiatrist thought he was "a bit of a shit". She told her date that her psychiatrist agreed with his psychiatrist, that he was, indeed, "a bit of a shit". By a bit of pure luck,' continued Peck, 'I said to her, "perhaps you want to know whether I think *you* are a bit of a shit?" And she said that, yes, she did. Well, I'd put myself in a terrible corner because a psychiatrist is never supposed to say such things to a patient, to make any kind of judgement really. So I said, "You've been coming to me for a year and a half now. You've come regularly and on time. You've paid what is a price to you financially. You've made hardly any progress yet, but you have been very faithful and you're clearly devoted to making improvements. And no," I said, "I do not think you are a bit of a shit." And zoom, she just made a total turnaround at that point. She started getting better by leaps and bounds.' Continued Peck, 'Myron Madden [an authority on pastoral care, and author of *Blessing*] says that the way good psychotherapy works, when it works, and this is very true, is that the patient gets the therapist's blessing. It is very powerful when it happens.' Asked if that meant the therapist was playing God, Peck replied, 'The therapist either as God or substitute father, or substitute parent, I would say. You don't have to go to God for it.'

Peck's patient clientele was predominantly female, with more divorced than married people coming to him in therapy, 'though some came in conjunction with their pain in going through divorce. My general feeling was that the divorced patients I saw were healthier than the people they'd divorced or who had divorced them. But then, people who come into therapy tend to be healthier – unlike the stereotype that sick people go into therapy.' Peck said he is comforted by the fact that 'most human beings function amazingly well in spite of themselves.' He countered that by adding that perhaps 20 per cent of people 'are walking Greek tragedies. You say of them if they continue to function this way they are doomed. There's no way but that things are going to get worse. Though only a minority.' He felt he had been 'unbelievably fortunate' in his career in that 'I've had only one patient directly under my care who committed suicide, somebody who was refusing to be helped.'

Peck said a great tragedy for him as a psychotherapist was when he found himself unable to help a certain type of adolescent: the ambitious, talented lower-class children who were held back by social class considerations. 'They were, seemingly, genetically upper-middle-class children, but they were born into lower-class homes where their abilities and ambitions and aspirations were squashed.' Over the years there were about eight adolescents, he said. 'Most of them I hospitalised briefly. I lost every single one of them – they would give up, become dulled. Their surroundings pulled them back.'

Meanwhile his own late adolescents were about to see less of an already busy single-minded father. Regarding his practice, Peck later told a newspaper reporter that he would not allow his patients to say they weren't selfish. He said, 'I am a totally selfish human being. When I water my flowers I don't say, "Flowers, look what I'm doing for you." I water them because I like to see pretty flowers. When I extend myself to my kids every so often it's because I like to have an image in my mind of being a reasonably honest person, a reasonably caring father, and in order to keep those two images together in my mind with any integrity, every so often I have to extend myself to the little . . . brats.' The article, written by Gary Dorsey, was one Peck singled out as among his favourite pieces on him.

By 1974, Peck, at thirty-eight, was living on several levels. There were the two obvious ones of family and professional life, which touched each other constantly but did not intertwine. There was the spiritual search, inconclusive as yet. There was the creative life, relatively quiescent since he'd abandoned ambition on leaving the military. Like water behind a dam, however, the creative urges were building back up. Peck's mind was busy, busy, busy, and though he didn't quite know it yet, a book was in the making. That year he also started an affair. It was a twice-a-week liaison that lasted some two years, he said.

It is not a diversion to mention Peck's sexual liaisons at this point, because from now on, until he is in his mid-fifties and, he said, his libido disappeared, his clandestine sexual life is a muted, unseen, unspoken backdrop to his marriage with Lily, a more corrosive backdrop in the long term than Peck actually wanted to admit. How one assesses the fact that Peck could conduct this sexual relationship, and subsequent affairs and flings, while working on, believing in what went into *The Road Less Travelled* on love and marital love, is a personal call. And there is a quite personal answer. Years later, Peck's friend the Rev. Stephen Bauman said a good preacher preaches out of his own needs. Seen in that light, *The Road Less Travelled* and his other writings are a multi-volume emotional, spiritual and psychological autobiography.

When Peck later revealed in his books the adulterous aspect of his personal behaviour, the immediate reaction of some readers and admirers was to condemn him. He was a sinner. To others, the fact of the affairs illustrated the disconnect between what Peck saw was needed in life, and what he was able to adhere to himself. In describing his own situation, Peck later told psychologist Guy, 'I had wet dreams starting at about thirteen, and so I instinctively knew what sex was about. I would not masturbate, but I had wet dreams. And I said I would never have sex or enter a woman. I can remember my first couple of dreams clearly. I was with my father and we had picked up a couple of Hawaiian girls, beautiful Hawaiian girls, and we were in my parents' bedroom, which had twin beds. And he was in the bed with one of these girls, and I was in bed with the other, and penetrated her, and had the sense that I was going to urinate in her. I can't do that. I can't do that. I tried to withhold myself and I exploded. I woke up and there was all this semen around. So that was my first. I don't know exactly what to make of the fact that my father was there and the girls were Hawaiian.'

Psychologist Guy, referring back to fifteen-year-old Peck's five weeks in Silver Hill psychiatric clinic, and the psychiatrist detecting a certain fear of sex, said to Peck: 'The issue of the fear of sex came up again in your thirties, when a mentor mentioned it to you after seeing one of your poems [*Death Wish*].' Peck said, 'I just don't think the poem shows it. The poem on death I called "Life Wish", and the poem on sex, "Death Wish", and the last couple of lines have to do with sinking into that dark furry hole where I will expire. Of course, orgasm is referred to by the French as "le petit mort", the little death. But there's no question that in my earlier years I was plagued unconsciously with a fear of sex, which I don't know to this day where it came from. It never surfaced in the course of my analysis.

'Marriage was not an intimacy issue,' Peck told Guy, 'it was a boundary issue. Lily proposed we have separate bedrooms; three years later I was ready for it and proposed we stop having sex [in the mid-1980s]. I think our marriage began to get better as a result. My infidelities were never about searching for a new wife or a better wife. They were some relief time from marriage, but not a substitute for marriage in my mind. They were primarily about sex, not intimacy. The majority of them were very brief, if not one-night stands, two- or three-night stands. One woman I had a two-year relationship with, really quite constant, say twice a week anyway. The other was much more occasional, limited to when I was on speaking engagements – eight or ten times a year, but lasted close to ten years between the time I was forty-five and fifty-five. If I could have lived without being unfaithful to Lily, I wish I could have, I would rather it had been that way.' By the very early 1990s when his libido dropped, he said, 'I stopped my infidelities.' Since when, he said, 'my relationship with Lily has been great. One of the reasons our marriage has survived and feels so glorious is that we are both growing people, very different from the young couple that married forty years ago.' At the same time, Peck said that the two longer-term liaisons in particular – 'we're still in some communication, not much' – were 'rich relationships. They gave me a great deal and I think that if they were talking to you they would say I gave them a great deal.'

Whatever the private practice in the United States, Peck's public rationalising of his infidelities did not reflect a view widely held by the American public. He could say that his affairs were 'never about searching for a new wife or a better wife but relief time from marriage' and served as personal enrichment but, as will be seen, he was not allowed much leeway by the class of women who wrote in response to *The Road Less Travelled.* Many were not afraid to tackle him for his views on sex in marriage even then, even though they'd enjoyed his book. A group of seven women in Oregon who formed a study group around *The Road* wrote, 'We have really built up a trust level and felt your guidance in our lives. But we are stumbling on our interpretation of your ideas on open marriage. In our varied experience we find that fidelity is a necessary part of all marriages. Even though an open, trusting relationship may survive an outside sexual experience, it does not contribute to the spiritual growth of your partner. It does reduce the amount of trust and openness with your relationship.'

Decades after these events, on St Valentine's Day Eve in 2003, the American essayist Michael Dirda (not with reference to Peck), addressed the topic of marital love in France in the *Washington Post*'s Book World. Dirda spoke of 'settled men and women who realise that a well conducted liaison can enrich and refine the spirit like a work of art. At the very least, wit, attentiveness and delicate flattery – all the social graces – enhance every encounter, whether over dinner or in bed . . . At its best (or its most cynical), the relationship could be less a betrayal of marriage than its safeguard. Such measured delicacy is probably not for Americans, burdened by a Puritan past . . .' To most Americans, this is a concept that speaks more to French sexual orderliness or Italian marital practicality than to their own US lives, 50 per cent of which, in the event, nonetheless end in divorce.

Peck had shrugged off his Puritan and WASP past. He had grown into a man of great strengths and some compelling matching weaknesses. His weaknesses he had phrases to excuse himself with. He was manipulating his listeners when he said such things as, 'if I could have lived without being unfaithful to Lily, I wish I could have, I would rather it had been that way.' The fact was, had it truly mattered, as the most important thing in his life, he could have lived without being unfaithful to Lily. Certainly he was trapped in narcissism, but he was satisfied enough with its gratifications, and had an addictive enough personality, not to cut his way loose. His marriage wasn't the most important thing in his life. He was the most important thing in his life. That's what narcissism means.

Yet Peck could be very supportive of others. In 1979, when the Moonies were making a concerted effort to prove themselves a serious religious movement, in the face of much Western scepticism, the Reverend Moon organised an international conference in

Portugal. Peck, already delving into 'evil', decided to go to see if he thought the Moonies were evil. At the conference, he met W. 'Bill' McNabb, a writer for one of the more unusual and highly appreciated religious magazines in the country, *The Wittenburg Door* (later known as *The Door*), a simultaneously hilarious and serious publication from the liberal wing of the evangelical church. It was noted for its extensive and penetrating interviews, and it three times featured lengthy pieces on Peck, including his views on the topic of evil. Peck became fast friends with McNabb and other *Door* editors. Peck was a good friend to have, kindly and concerned, and liable to do surprising things. Two examples cover many. When McNabb and his wife, Maureen, were wed in the 1980s, the by-then famous Peck nonetheless took the time to fly out to the West Coast for it. In the mid-1990s, when Peck's friend Tim Childs was seriously ill in a Washington, D.C. hospital, Scotty and Lily went to Washington, moved in with Hope Childs while Scott advised on Tim's medical care and Lily provided support and companionship to Hope. 'They saved both our lives,' said Hope Childs in a 2005 interview.

In his descriptions of his life at this time, it seems Peck was experiencing constant friction, raw edges were rubbed more raw by ambition and restraint, searches and lapses. It could be that out of that friction came the spark that ignited the mature writer. He would try to write honestly, meaning from what he knew about life being difficult, about love being difficult, about what he understood of sexuality and sex, and its demands; about what he was experiencing in family life as husband, father and son. Peck – the bruised healer – diligently and energetically sought to stick earnestly to the truth in his writing, no matter what the pain, though away from writing he'd expend far less energy trying to correct his ways. The outside observer might see Peck taking the easier road, accepting himself as he was too readily.

Peck in New Preston, still in his thirties, was a maturing profes-sional fascinated by social relationships, skilled as a psychotherapist in dealing with them. He was a self-centred man with an extremely lively intellectual curiosity about God, belief and the spiritual life, all wrapped in a yearning of almost compulsive proportions, to write; and a growing need to control everything around him. He'd tried writing a book before. In the 1960s, during a three-week break from his residency, Peck had penned his version of an environmentally aware type of book, he said. He sent it to a publisher, there wasn't a nibble, and he went back to being a medical resident. He would continue to occasionally take the time to write. He had his pen and pad busy during the period when he'd travelled from Asia to Washington, D.C. for his interview with the Army Surgeon General's office. In his introspective way, he'd create scenarios for possible themes he'd like to tackle. Nothing ever came of these efforts, they were little more than the equivalent of a pianist's five finger exercises. Something to stay limber with.

Another year. Lake Waramaug froze again, thawed again. And another, until it was spring, 1975. The undercurrents of needing more than being a rural psychiatrist continued to ripple the surface of Peck's calm. In an ambitious person who has exhausted his or her drive, it rarely means the end. By drop and by dribble, like gentle rains falling on a lake behind a dam after a drought, the ambition begins to return to its previous level. So with Peck, until the ambition that had evaporated in Washington, D.C. was back. If he felt he had a sense of destiny without a decided destination, it was because, he said, he knew there was something coming. And knew it had to do with writing. Months into 1975, when he was supervising a pastoral counsellor, Peck remarked to him, 'Gee, it would be good if somebody wrote a good book for patients to tell them what psychotherapy is about. What to look out for, and what to go with.' The conversation led nowhere, the thought died (except that in 1984 Peck did write an introduction for the *Clinical Handbook of Pastoral Counselling, Volume One*). A book for those entering therapy did not emerge.

In his Harvard thesis Introduction, Peck described his writer's *modus operandi*. It was a method of operating he would carry into *The Road* and all his other non-fiction. In either case, his explanation would certainly not defuse his critics. 'My efforts have been severely criticised on two counts,' he wrote in the 1958 Introduction, 'first, that existentialism is a philosophical topic and it is not the function of a social relations thesis to deal with philosophy; second, the subject is much too general and theoretical ever to be dealt with adequately by an undergraduate.' This was the future psychologist who, without any deep background in religion, and no under-pinnings as a theologian, in *The Road Less Travelled* wove life's strands into a cord around human woes that he believed only faith was strong enough to tug forward.

In his 1958 thesis, he hammers home a version of his non-fiction writer's creed: 'I am of the belief it is unrealistic to divorce one area of study from all other areas, to divorce psychology from philosophy or the "natural" sciences.' He believed for his thesis, as he believed for *The Road*, 'that the eclecticism practised in this paper is necessary to my approach. The question in regard to the second criticism now becomes one of whether an undergraduate is justified in attempting a molar [large mass] approach.' Suddenly one hears the voice of the boyhood neighbour who said Scott Peck was the boy who was always talking about things other people didn't. The boy who was 'always thinking too much' said in his thesis, 'How can I, far too young and uneducated to be considered an authority in any one small field, delve deeply into the material of many fields? Yet I must ask the age at which one is adequately prepared to tackle the molar task. Fifty? Sixty? Seventy? Certainly the sixty-year-old scholar is better prepared than I to take a molar approach to the problems of the world, but I wonder sometimes if he is not necessarily limited to the perspective of his own generation [and would] have difficulty in seeing the wood for the trees. Perhaps I seem here like a rebellious child whose eyes are bigger than his stomach.' Perhaps he was.

Two out of three Harvard professors accepted Peck's thesis so ardently they wanted to award it top honours, summa cum laude. One hated it, and failed it. Did the one who failed Peck realise that in the Introduction, Peck is playing more than a double game? First, he's doing what is required, producing a thesis. Next, he's producing an extremely interesting thesis and earning very high marks for it. But beyond that, in fine Marquand fashion, he's pricking the Establishment – only this time it's the educational Establishment and, in effect, professors who don't change their shirts or their minds. At heart, is this little boy Peck annoying the grown-ups, honing his skills for bigger things later? When Peck needles the 'sixty-year-old scholar' in his Introduction, was it the same Peck who cried out across the wedding banquet room that the wine was lousy: to see what sort of response he'd get? Like most of the people at the wedding, the third professor didn't like what Peck had said or how he'd said it.

What Peck finessed beautifully at Harvard, of course, was that what he wrote wasn't academic research and a thesis but a lengthy, speculative essay based on little other than his personal observations and reactions to the thoughts of others. As fascinating as it was, his main critic said scholarship it wasn't. As in his thesis, so with *The*

Road. The academics pointedly ignored it for its lack of footnotes and academic rigour. His books always generated a split decision, unevenly split – the majority of reviewers and readers were always on his side; just as happened with his thesis. With *The Road,* Peck is the first to say that he didn't invent anything new. He simply pulled together what already was in a different way.

Reflecting back on his thesis forty-five years later, Peck said, 'While I'm violently against post-modernism, oddly enough, as I look back on it, my college thesis was probably the ultimate unbeknownst post-modernist and deconstructionist piece. I took three ways of looking at the world and deconstructed each of them. None of them held water. Ever since, I've been answering my own thesis – the answer to the three ways of looking at the world is the Trinity.' But even in *The Road* Peck wasn't at the Trinity point. He was still three years away from being baptised.

When the ice froze in the winter of 1975, one evening just three years almost to the month after arriving in New Preston, inspiration hit. Whatever the level of friction in the family circle, this, for Peck, would be less a winter of internal discontent than one of inner, creative excitement. Late one evening, as he tells it and has done repeatedly, when he was stoned on home-grown pot and listening to Simon and Garfunkel, whatever he was wrestling with spiritually came encapsulated in three words: <u>discipline</u>, <u>love</u> and <u>grace.</u> 'The words were in my mind and wouldn't leave. I said, well, Scotty, you've had this idea for a book many times before and it's never turned out. Let's see how it floats in the morning when you're sober. And in the morning it looked good, and I said, well, let's look at it again in three weeks. I would keep saying yes, and let's wait another few days. At the end of those three weeks I felt as compelled to write it as I had the first morning after.'

Though Peck had recounted this scene myriad times, perhaps with great earnestness, for different audiences and interviewers, hearing it from him twice, it sounded slightly contrived – reality boiled down to a soundbite. It wasn't just pot, and Simon and Garfunkel, and three little words. It was the ponderings of an experienced psychiatrist who was, at base, the hurt, introspective child who never stopped being that, and the adolescent who'd written so extensively and clearly about Jonathan Edwards at Friends Seminary. *The Road Less Travelled* would emerge as Peck's version of Edwards' *A Faithful Narrative of the Surprising Work of God in the Conversion of Many Hundred Souls in Northampton, and Neighboring Towns and Villages* (1737). Peck was one of the souls. Not converted in public ceremony, but already deep into his own inner, Edwards-like 'wonderment'-filled conversion.

Decision made, Peck spent the next five or six weeks reorganising his schedule so that, starting in mid-January 1976 he'd cut his practice back to four days a week to allow three days a week for writing. 'I'd learned from Marquand that the way to write, for lots of people, was you did it as an eight-to-five job. For me it was eight-to-six. Back then I could write for ten-twelve hours with ease, for the most part in long hand on yellow pads, which were transcribed.' Seven days a week was a decision that meant a gruelling work life. The main burden, however, was really borne by the children, and Lily.

Peck's decision to write semi-full-time had been aided, psychologically at least, by an unexpected turn in his fortunes. His father had paid off Scott's mortgage, though Judge Peck later felt he'd made a mistake. As Peck single-mindedly settled into his book writing, Judge Peck would regularly chide, 'What are you doing writing a book? You know that books don't sell. You've got a good career going now and a shoemaker should stick to his last.' Peck said that at the time of his father's generosity, they were actually making more than they were spending. Within a few years, and before the financial bonanza from the success of *The Road*, with children in private schools and college when inflation hit, finances were tighter.

Peck stuck to his therapist's last *and* made a career shift. He had the dream, the theme, the determination, and a title: *Psychology of Human Spiritual Growth*. And while he didn't have a deadline, he did have a stark reminder that the years were pressing – in May, he'd turn forty. Peck kept up the brutal pace for a year, and in January, 1977, twelve months after he began, the first draft was done. This graduate of Harvard's social relations department, who referred to himself as 'an unusually socially conscious person', had packed his experiences together, 'and on some unconscious level all this stuff fed into, by the grace of God, my writing *The Road Less Travelled*.'

Writing a book is one thing, getting it published is another. Peck's is a cautionary tale for anyone thinking of a future in the writing business. He gave the book to Carl Brandt Junior, son of his mentor, Carol. Peck said Brandt called it 'sellable', and said, '"It will be sold." He took it to the top editor at Random House who called me and said, "You know, I've been going around telling everybody about this marvellous manuscript I've got and then I got to your third part, which is called 'Grace', and you just totally blew it. It was too 'Christ-y'." And I said I only quoted Christ a couple of times. We argued for a while and finally she said, "Well, I think you really ought to go looking for another publisher because I don't think we can resolve this." Carl Brandt then took it to Simon and Schuster, to Jonathan Dolger. He said it was a wonderful book, here's the contract.'

Dolger suggested to Peck that as Freud had intimated that faith in God was a neurosis, he thought Peck ought to address the issue. It was incorporated into part three, Grace, and Peck set about cutting part four which, by his own admission, was too long. Dolger also did not like the original title. Said Peck, 'I kept doing titles and they weren't pleasing to Simon and Schuster. Title number forty-seven was *The Road Less Travelled,* which Jonathan liked. I recognised it had a Frostian ring, so I didn't know whether I'd have to pay royalties or not.' He repaired to his Frost, he said, and saw that the words were not precisely as Frost had used them in his poem. Peck's original title was reworked into *The Road*'s subtitle: *A New Psychology of Love, Traditional Values and Spiritual Growth*. Shortly after the title change, Dolger left the publishing house. Several years later he became Peck's agent. In publishing parlance, Peck's manuscript was now 'orphaned to the trade' – a book without an editor, a literary sheep without a literate shepherd. It floated around and was taken up by editor Alice Mayhew. Simon and Schuster decided on a print run of 5,000 copies. Peck had achieved one thing: he now had a book that was going to be published. His private life in upheaval, Peck, undoubtedly on edge, waited for reviews. But, fuelled by the energy and ambition of completing one book, he had immediately started on the next. It would become *People of the Lie.*

For many writers, waiting for reviews is a soul-destroying time. Sometimes it brings redemption – a decent review. Sometimes damnation – a panning. Most often, for many writers, it brings the worst of all possible worlds, no reviews at all. Even a bad review is worse than none, for at least someone noticed. Peck's timing was unfortunate. The *New York Times* had gone on strike in August, an action that lasted eighty-eight days. Shortly after publication, a review of *The Road Less Travelled* surfaced for Peck in the *Washington Post*. Peck loves serendipity. Nothing and no-one in his writing life would ever be as serendipitous as Phyllis Theroux's decision to pop in on an editor at Simon and Schuster to discuss a book she was working on.

Theroux tells the story with ease, a sense of fun *and* in the full knowledge she launched the Peck phenomenon. 'All I did,' she said, 'was nudge the boulder and it began to roll.' She was just starting a writing career that would later include such books as *California and Other States of Grace: a Memoir* (1980), *Peripheral Visions* (1982) and *Night Lights: Bedtime Stories for Parents in the Dark* (1987). In 1978, at a time when her essays in the *New York Times* were attracting some attention, she called on Simon and Schuster editor Alice Mayhew. Though there was no meeting of the minds between the women regarding Theroux's book proposal, they did chat about their similarities, their Catholicism, their studies in philosophy at different Catholic universities. 'So,' said Theroux, 'I said goodbye, and that was that,' until a couple of months later when Mayhew sent her galleys of Peck's book with just a card. 'There was no letter, you know with, "We just love this book, blah, blah, blah",' said Theroux. 'Just a card.'

Theroux said that at the time, 'I was just divorced, it was early days, everyone was still bleeding, and I was figuring out how to support myself with my writing. I opened up the Simon and Schuster galleys. It said *The Road Less Travelled,* a guide to spiritual whatever, and I just thought, "Oh, really boring," put it down and didn't do anything. But a couple of weeks later I had a moment and came back to it, picked it up and read the first sentence, "Life is difficult. This is a great truth because once you acknowledge that life is difficult, life is no longer difficult," or words to that effect. I was hooked pretty early on. I got about halfway through and I thought well, if the rest of the book is horrible, it doesn't matter. The first half is worth it. So I called Brigitte Weeks, editor of Book World at the *Washington Post* at that time, and said, "Brigitte, I have a book I want to review."'

Weeks said give her the title, she probably had the review copy in her book pile and she'd see if she could find it. 'She called me back later that day or the next and said, "Well, there must be something going on between you and this book." I told her, "I just think it's an amazing book." She said to go ahead and review it.'

Theroux sat down and for the next two weeks spent all her time 'trying to write the most compelling review on the face of the earth so that people would be forced to read the book,' she said. It appeared on 29 September 1978. Even as the review was headed towards the presses, 'I couldn't keep my hands off it,' said Theroux. 'I called up Scotty. He was actually in the middle of a session, counselling somebody. I said to him, "You know, I'm breaking all the rules by calling you and telling you that I have reviewed this book. This is an amazing book," I said, "and I just want you to be prepared, it's going to be a big hit." It didn't happen my way. It became a bestseller in Washington, which was nice.'

The problem was she said, and Peck quickly noticed his dilemma, his publishers would neither publicise *The Road* nor commit themselves to another print run beyond the original 5,000. Theroux was also perturbed, she said, because 'in New York I would keep running into people like the number two at Simon and Schuster at the time. I remember specifically running into him at a book party and he gave me a ride home. I said, "You know, I want to talk to you about one of your books." And he said, "Which one?" And I said, *The Road Less Travelled.* He said, "Oh yes, it's kind of like an in-house discovery." I mean they never took it seriously. They never did anything for it even after it became a bestseller in Washington. Ho-hum.'

Simultaneously, Peck, knowing the book was selling out, was becoming increasingly anxious. At which point, Peck and Theroux, in a manner of speaking, joined forces. Said Theroux, 'My nature is such that I love promoting other people's books.' She called Peck and asked: 'Can you and Lily come down here, I'll give you a book party. All the people that already love the book can come and meet you.' It was at that point Theroux discovered Peck as micro-manager: 'No detail too small. By the time he got here I had gotten eighteen different letters from him [about plans for the party], and three different revisions of several,' she said. She kept telling him things such as, '"Scotty, this is going to have to wait, I haven't even thought about what I'm going to give people for hors d'oeuvres. You know, I don't do that until a couple of hours before the party." Anyway Scott and Lily came, and a lot of people came.' M. Scott Peck, author, was launched.

Theroux said that when Peck was leaving he told her, '"You know, I have to confess you weren't what I expected." I took it, rightly or wrongly, as a compliment, you know, he thought I was pretty?' The attractive-looking Theroux said, 'I don't know what he thought. I guess as a writer he'd probably created sort of a grim image of somebody. So I said, "Well, you were exactly what I expected." And he took that as a compliment,' said Theroux.

Peck couldn't help taking Theroux's remarks as a compliment, especially since she'd written the review: 'Books by psychiatrists on spiritual growth dot the ocean in great number these days. But *The Road Less Travelled* is a clipper ship among [motor boats], a magnificent boat of a book, and it is obviously written by a human being who, both in style and substance, leans toward the reader for the purposes of sharing something larger than himself, that one reads with the feeling that this is not just a book but a spontaneous act of generosity.'

By then, there was a second review, in the pages of the *National Catholic Reporter,* an independent newsweekly. Dr Gerald May, a psychiatrist with a fine reputation in the field, said bluntly, 'A book for our times. [Peck's] discussion of love is the freshest since Erich Fromm's, and his approach to spirituality is simultaneously honest and understandable. It meets our culture directly, encourages us to move forward, and points a trustworthy finger in the direction of wholeness.'

The next seven million copies of *The Road Less Travelled* had a brief excerpt from Theroux in the *Washington Post* on the front cover, and a slightly lengthier one from May in the *National Catholic Reporter* at the top of the back cover. But what Peck had already realised, given Simon and Schuster's ho-hum attitude, was that *The Road Less Travelled* would not bring success to M. Scott Peck unless Peck first brought success to *The Road Less Travelled.*

CHAPTER 8

THE ROAD LESS TRAVELLED

Two favourable reviews do not a best seller make, so newly minted author Peck was up against hard reality. 'My fantasy was it was going to be reviewed across country,' said Peck. 'It was on the *Washington Post* bestseller list and the local list in a week. In two weeks it was sold out. I called up my imperious editor and got her assistant. "When are you going to do another printing?" She said, "We haven't thought about that yet."'

The problem was that excellent reviews and strong local sales in Washington, D.C. made little impression up in magisterial Manhattan where Simon and Schuster – with no *New York Times* review to guide them – remained uncertain as to what they had on their hands. All this was as 1978 turned into 1979, and Peck's anticipations for the book were climbing exponentially. He needed more copies. His attack, he said, was he sought legal advice to see if his contract could force Simon and Schuster into a second printing. The book was selling.

Peck was creating a drumbeat, or 'buzz' through word of mouth, not least through Alcoholics Anonymous meetings and church reading groups, plus an increasing number of reviews. Sales literally began to double annually until, by 1984, he was on the *New York Times* bestseller list with 480,000 sales that year and almost one million sales since the book appeared. He remained there more or less for twelve years. Impressed, *Forbes* magazine wrote an article on Peck, the book and 'the glories of word of mouth' advertising.

Peck's initial publicity mill had limitations. At first there were but two reviews. Theroux's *Washington Post* rave was confined geographically to the Washington, D.C. area audience, while the *National Catholic Reporter* review had a national audience, a sophisticated, literate and highly educated Catholic readership, but limited to about 45,000 readers. Nonetheless, armed with the promise of another 2,500-book print run, self-publicist Peck hired a schoolteacher to mail out Theroux and May reviews in the hundreds. Throughout 1979 his packet was mailed out to anyone likely to have reviewing credentials in print, on the radio or in television. The package offer was simple – here's what others are saying, we can send you a review copy, too. It was a blitz. Peck was relentless in making himself available.

In three batches Simon and Schuster printed a further 4,500 hardback copies before releasing it as a Touchstone paperback, and sending Peck on a publicity tour that didn't provide opportunities to address people, just to sign books. 'A publicity tour which isn't a speaking tour. That was a laugh,' he said.

If newspaper editors glanced at the reviews they were likely to be impressed. Theroux was one of the few reviewers to mention what a fluid, engaging and persuasive writer Peck was. 'There is a logical order to Peck's thought, a careful progression of ideas that lap and overlap, like complementary waves, upon each other,' Theroux wrote. 'So the effect is of being borne, not bumped along, and given that Peck sets out to dignify mental illness, celebrate suffering, and demonstrate that "amazing grace" is not a figment of some revivalist's imagination, it is a miracle that he could pull the trip off.' Theroux had described it without saying it – as a writer, Peck at his best is an elegant stylist. Simple, clear, uncluttered.

'Peck begins with what we all know,' she writes, '"Life is difficult." Yet Peck the psychiatrist sees people every day who have not come to terms with this knowledge, or rather have come to terms with it, by developing neuroses and character disorders which are efforts of the conscious mind to avoid legitimate suffering. Most people, Peck contends, think life is difficult but do not accept it as a truth, but a terrible, possibly avoidable, state of affairs. "If there were not problems, we would never evolve from weakness into strength. If we do not grow into our full strength, we might as well not live at all. Real love," defines Peck, "is an act of the will to extend oneself for the purpose of nurturing one's own or another's spiritual growth."'

Without knowing of Peck's ongoing personal spiritual journey, Theroux identified him as moving along a God track on a journey that had a spiritual destination. She quoted Peck writing that '"most men and women are content to be ordinary people. The demands of consciousness, and the increased responsibility that greater knowledge entails, are too terrifying, and the evolution we seek is short-circuited by the way we are afraid to pay for it. We are, in a nutshell, unwilling to make God's work our own, which, as Teilhard de Chardin said, in *The Phenomenon of Man,* is what evolution is all about.'"

Psychiatrist Gerald May's *National Catholic Reporter* review followed Theroux's like the baton being passed in a relay race: 'This book insists that the path requires hard discipline, willful attentiveness, constant questioning, and responsible loving. Even then it is only through grace that true wholeness comes to us,' writes May. 'This is a refreshingly serious business, the more so because the author refuses to fall into pessimism or pietism about the heaviness of the struggle. In fact, the pages of this book express a bright and buoyant vision of hope.

'The early pages of the book,' notes May, 'are rooted in a solid understanding of traditional psychology and psychiatry. Sophisticated readers might be put off temporarily by the arbitrary labeling of personality styles and psychodynamics which occur here. There is no doubt that one hears a psychiatrist talking.' Continues May, 'His spirituality mixes traditionally non-threatening images of humanity with just enough gentle mysticism to keep one enticed and encouraged. He deals honestly and clearly with issues of evil and sinfulness, again from a metaphysical base which will be acceptable and understandable to most Western minds.

'Readers with a more contemplative bent may have mixed feelings about Peck's approach to mind and spirit,' said May, and 'they may wish he had gone further into the mystery and moved more closely to the simplicity which ultimately eradicates the struggles of discerning how one should try to live. But,' said May, 'they will celebrate the integration Peck has achieved between traditional psychological and spiritual insights.'

Peck had one comment in *The Road Less Travelled* – meant as an explanation – that quickly circulated to his disadvantage. He'd later say he wished he'd never written it because it was so easily mis-understood. Theroux had lighted on it in her review. Peck had written: 'Psychotherapy should be [must be, if successful] a process of genuine love, a somewhat heretical notion in traditional psychiatric circles.' Theroux, writing rhetorically, asked: 'Are there pitfalls to this commitment? Peck admits there are. "Were I ever to have a case in which I concluded after careful and judicious

consideration that my patient's spiritual growth would be sub-
stantially furthered by our having sexual relations, I would proceed
to have them. In fifteen years of practice, however, I have not yet
had such a case . . . It is out of love for their patients that therapists
do not allow themselves the indulgence of falling in love with
them.'"

Peck, as reviews increased in number, began on a small scale to
enter the public consciousness. He was still at some remove from
walking on to the national stage as a public figure, though he began
to realise that the true publicist might have to get out front for a
while. Peck's recollection was that even before publication, 'ninety
per cent of me felt the book wouldn't go anywhere, but ten per cent
of me had intimations not of immortality, but that it was going to be
quite an extraordinary book. I thought, if that should happen to be
the case, and it should become famous, how am I going to deal with
that fame? And the notion came to go into a monastery for a two-
week retreat.' Peck, ambitious but ambivalent about what lay ahead,
understood how the game might play out. The book was his entrée
to the public stage. He had his themes, those would be his topics. He
also had his hang-ups. He was painfully shy. He had absolutely no
capacity for small talk, and he had even less interest in extended
conversations he could not control and direct. He was in turmoil –
Peck was comfortable in control and uncomfortable when others
were. He needed help. He was already deeply into writing his
second book, *People of the Lie: the Hope for Healing Human Evil*, and
was coming face to face with the fact that he'd committed himself at
some level he could not yet fathom to becoming a Christian. To give
himself some space in a different environment, he decided to find a
monastery somewhere in the Hudson River Valley and go on a
silent retreat. There, he imagined, away from family, practice and
writing, he could gather his thoughts about possible fame in the
offing. His early intimations suggested to him he needed all the
guidance he could get.

'The Episcopalian Convent of Saint Helena, in Vails Gate,
seemed just right the moment I walked in,' he said. 'It has the most
beautiful chapels, the nuns made me feel very welcome. I had a
number of items on my agenda, one was to stop smoking, which I
managed to do for two days. But the major issue was how would I
deal with fame. Should I go public? Or, like J.D. Salinger [author of
The Catcher in the Rye], should I immediately get an unlisted number

and retire deeper into the woods? I didn't know which way I wanted to go. And I didn't know which way God wanted me to go.' While it is reasonably safe to comment that fame was not the initial spur for Peck, by this time it was certainly a lure. Fame holds an allure few authors want to resist, for the financial rewards are generally inseparable from the author's name.

He told the nuns he wanted to make a silent retreat. Sister Ellen Stephen, she likes to be known as 'ES', the person in charge of novices at the time, said the nuns were agreeable. Peck liked what he heard, liked what he saw, and soon returned to the convent, nestled in fifty acres of fields and woods with a backdrop of the river valley mountains. He returned for a ten-day silent retreat, his yellow Volkswagen Beetle packed with books. The nuns were surprised at this as the monastery had an excellent library. They were possibly even more surprised that Peck began talking to the sisters and more or less interviewing them. Silence was not a Peck strong point, though by the end of his stay, said ES, Peck 'seemed to have gotten what he wanted and became interested in us.' Peck had also become interested in walking around 'a sort of middle-class housing area' that bordered the convent. It would have some significance for him, shortly.

By day, alone whenever he chose, and by night, alone in bed, Peck had time to think, and thought about dreaming. 'Dreams can serve a revelatory function and I thought I would help old God out as much as I could and really pay attention to my dreams, which I hadn't been doing for years. Well, you can imagine what happened. For the most part I immediately stopped dreaming. There is a way around that, which is not advisable,' said Peck. 'That is, as you are falling asleep, you can, as an act of will, wake yourself up and capture images from your unconsciousness. I say it's not advisable because, if you get into the habit of waking yourself up every time you have a dream, you can get a profound case of insomnia. I thought the risk was worth it. So, in this way, I captured about a dozen images, all of which were very simple, but one. They were just images of gates and bridges, kinds of things. Which told me nothing that I didn't know, namely, that I was at a point of transition in my life. But one of these images was far more complex, a sort of cross between an image and a dream. I was an onlooker, in a middle-class home, like in this housing area. And in this home there was a boy, a seventeen-year-old boy, who was the kind of kid every parent would want. He was handsome, he was smart, he was athletic, captain of the high school football team, already scheduled to be class valedictorian at the end of the year, and president of the senior class. And if that wasn't enough, he had an after-school job that he worked at responsibly. If that wasn't enough, he had a girlfriend who was sweet and demure. He had his driver's licence, and he was a very responsible driver.'

Continued Peck, 'The only problem was, his father would not let him drive. The father insisted on driving this kid everywhere he needed to go, to football games, to proms, anything. It was really quite humiliating. Not only that, the father insisted the kid pay him five dollars a week out of his after-school earnings for the privilege of being driven around, which the kid was perfectly capable of doing himself. And I woke up from this image . . . woke with a sense of absolute outrage and fury at what an autocratic, over-controlling son of a bitch his father was. But I wrote it down, and was curious about it. Why did I have it? About the third day after I had it, looking at it, I realised that I had unconsciously capitalised the F in "father". Then I realised that I had had my revelation. Not a revelation I wanted. I had wanted a little bit of advice from God, like what one would get from his agent or accountant, which I was free to accept or reject. What God was saying to me, was, "Look, you just pay your dues and leave the driving up to me."' I had always thought of God as the ultimate good guy, and here I had cast Him in the role, or at least was responding to Him, as a horrible, autocratic villain.' The demanding father of Peck's childhood had been conjured up in yet another form.

Peck had approached God on a different path than most. 'I'm not sure I would ever have become a Christian had I not had some immersion in the paradox of Zen Buddhism. I don't know how else to put it except to say that God is truth and science is one of the best ways we get to truth.' It was typical that Peck searched not by going to the Old and New Testaments to read from the source, but by reading books by Christians and testing his views against theirs. Finally, he later told interviewer McNabb of *Door* magazine, he decided to 'check out the Gospels, so I read them for the first time at the age of thirty-nine.' (Peck's reaction was very different from that of another well-known man in his thirties who approached the Scriptures for the first time – Sir Winston Churchill's son, Randolph, on active duty in Yugoslavia in the Second World War. Randolph bet he could read the entire Bible, but gave up after a while, saying, 'God, God was such a shit, wasn't he?')

The Door quoted Peck saying, 'I had always believed in an historical Jesus who was a pretty wise cat.'

Expostulated interviewer McNabb, 'Cat? Cat? What is this, the fifties?'

'Do I have to take this kind of abuse?' retorted Peck, in jest.

'Yes,' replied McNabb.

Peck continued, 'Anyway, that is pretty much where I left Jesus. A nice guy who got shafted in the standard manner of the day.'

'And then,' McNabb asked him, 'you read the Gospels?'

'Yes,' said Peck, 'and when I finally read them I had already experienced a dozen years of trying in my own small way to be a teacher and a healer. I knew something about teaching and healing and with this knowledge under my belt, I was absolutely thunder-struck by the reality of the man I found in the Gospels. I found a man who was continually frustrated. It seeps out of every page. He says, "What do I have to say to you? How many times do I have to say it? What do I have to *do* to get through to you?" I found a man who was frequently angry, a man who was scared, a man who was terribly, terribly lonely. I realised that this Jesus was so real that no-one could have made him up. If the Gospel writers had been into myth-making and embellishing, as I assumed they had, they certainly would have tried to create the kind of Jesus that [Lily] calls "the wimpy Jesus". The Jesus who goes around with his sweet sickening smile that never leaves His face while He does nothing but pat little children on the head, the Jesus with His own highly developed Christ consciousness which causes him to achieve a mellow-yellow sort of nirvana and peace of mind. But the Jesus of the Gospel did not have peace of mind, and I began to suspect that the Gospel writers, instead of being embellishers, were in fact extremely accurate and conservative reporters.'

This was the nub of Peck's Christianity: the unwavering belief in Jesus who, despite Peck's wavering journey, never left Peck and whom Peck never again doubted. During the period before his baptism, with no thought of publication in mind, Peck would also write occasional 'position papers' on topics he saw as a blend of religion and psychiatry, such as 'religious ecstasy' (as any form of ecstasy can fall into the purview of psychiatry).

Lily's role in Peck's Christian search has not been explored, but it was likely significant. Not only because she was baptised and a believer, but she was the daughter of a fundamentalist preacher and pastor, and undoubtedly well versed in conservative Christianity's teaching tenets. If Peck had a relevant question about Christianity, Lily had more knowledge than he did. Their son, Christopher, said that for a period prior to Scott's baptism, his parents were Anabaptists. Anabaptists do not hold with infant baptism, and believe in the re-baptism of baptised believing adults. The Mennonites and Amish are among those groups that can trace their roots to Anabaptism. The Episcopalian nun Sister ES, who later became her order's provincial, said she did not talk to Peck about his Christianity or his exploratory reading. 'Scotty was a mystic in his approach,' she said. 'It was always the personal with God he was interested in, not philosophical proof. I think his reading was maybe C.S. Lewis.' The nuns invited Peck to receive the sacrament of the Eucharist with them.

In 1980, two-and-a-half years after he'd first entertained the possibility of baptism, Peck returned again to the Episcopalian Convent of St Helena and was baptised in its chapel by a Methodist minister from North Carolina. 'God kept tugging, pushing, kicking, prodding, and pulling,' he said. It was a joyful family affair, Lily and the children were present. An Episcopalian priest celebrated the communion, 'and afterwards,' Sister Ellen Stephen recalled, 'we had a jolly reception with some wine, and Scotty led us in *Amazing Grace*.' After that time, Peck referred to ES as his 'spiritual director'. She said she did not much like the term: 'He didn't check with me whether I wanted to be called a spiritual director. I like to think I [was] there for him sometimes, and he [was] there for me sometimes.' Members of his nationwide audiences had their varied assessments of this new Christian. At one gathering Peck addressed, the poet Maya Angelou, seated next to Lily, 'nudged Lily,' said Peck, 'and whispered to her, "He ain't no white boy. He's a black Southern preacher."'

Psychotherapist Peck understood that as readers tackled *The Road*, they would interpret his statements, his narrated incidents, patient case studies and observations to fit their own lives and needs. They would place themselves at the author's scene, as most people do when they read. It was the fact Peck made it so easy, so natural for them to walk beside him as fellow observer as he proceeded with his travelogue, that they gained insight into the predicaments of their own lives, insight they welcomed even though Peck offered no panaceas. By aiding so many people through the book, he was becoming aware he'd also inadvertently fashioned a role for himself that he genuinely did not want – that of 'guru'. He desired to be no-one's personal saviour. A Detroit newspaper headline called him 'The Reluctant Messiah'.

If Peck described his readers' lives by describing his own and those of his patients, if he gave them the essential feeling of verisimilitude, of being there, Peck's literary mentor, Marquand, without touching on the spiritual, had done no less in describing the social minutiae of Boston's prominent. Marquand dealt in social appearances, the exterior. Peck delved into everyone's interior, into the psychological morass of individuals coping with their confusion and shattered lives, and described the grit required to find a way out. What Peck wanted to do, perhaps all he wanted to do – he could not say – was to use the glare of reality as a lamp shining ahead, so the readers could see their own way forward. He hadn't really foreseen a hand-holding role for himself, and always shrank back when people tried to force it on him.

The Road has four sections: Discipline, Love, Growth and Religion, and Grace. There is no intention here to study *The Road*'s anatomy beyond repeating the wise words of the Rev. John W. Donohue, SJ, reviewing it in the Jesuit-run *America* magazine. 'It would not be far off to describe *The Road* as a set of practical directives drawn up with the perspective of a twentieth-century psychiatrist, for overcoming those natural obstacles to spiritual growth. Peck was writing as the experienced psychologist rather than as an amateur philosopher or theologian.' Father Donohue found 'the voice in these pages attractive – calm and kind, assured and reassuring. Even when he is admonishing he is rather hearten-ing: "We all have a sick self and a healthy self." Nice to know that one is not singular.' The Jesuit priest said Peck 'writes not as a remote Olympian but as a counsellor everywhere present in the book. He certainly tells his readers enough about himself to make his personality felt and to render those readers benevolent. His recognition of a natural resistance to spiritual growth agrees with a commonplace of Christian preachers.'

In essence, then, Peck's authorial success in *The Road* rested on the fact he writes what he knows, and he writes well. Certainly in the first two-thirds of the book he lays out the actuality as he has experienced

it. It rings true because he writes with such authority and assurance
the readers can peer through their own clouds of unknowing to see
into their own past experiences and current dilemmas with a clear,
cold, stark perspective. Because Peck's assurance contains re-
assurance, they can keep on reading, and – many millions of them,
in time – could move on more boldly with their lives.

There had been plenty of dilemmas for Peck to wrestle with
within the peaceful confines of convent walls. Now success was an
actuality. '*The Road Less Travelled* was being hailed as the great self-
help book,' he said. 'I may not have known why I wrote it, but it
was fairly clear to me at the time I was not writing it to be a self-help
book.' The readers – not surprisingly – were making their own
presumptions about that. One former Nixon aide (Peck declined to
name him), a man 'who got saved by religion,' said Peck, 'said to
me, "Scotty, it was just so clever of you the way you disguised your
Christianity in *The Road Less Travelled* so as to get the message across
to people." I said, "No, it wasn't clever of me at all. I wasn't a
Christian."'

If it wasn't a self-help book, and wasn't a low-key evangelising
tool, what was it, people wondered. Essentially, *The Road* is a
psycho/spiritual travelogue with Peck mapping the journey and
acting as a Canterbury Tales-like narrator, as he takes the readers
along the paths and through the labyrinths of their own social and
familial relationships. The labyrinthian emotional and psychological
landscapes he depicts have an almost Dickensian foreboding to
them, because he found them forbidding on his own journey. Yet
just as the pain of the telling might become unbearable, Peck pulls
aside a curtain, and illustrates another reality to banish those
particular shadows. He determinedly moves on to the pilgrimage's
destination, the shrine where people can lay their personal hearts of
darkness. He plays the roles of every pilgrim on the journey, he gets
the reader to the shrine. Peck, in addition, is a physician and
psychotherapist and they are all the more assured.

In Britain's *Baptist Times,* Gay Pilgrim saw Peck deftly utilising 'his
psychiatric practice as the vehicle through which he expounds his
theology, his understanding of what God calls us to become, and his
theories as to how we may achieve this. Much of what he says has
strong resonances with the Hebrew Scriptures and the Gospels.' As
Pilgrim suggests, Peck is at his best as a writer in the ease with which
he is also the skilled psychotherapist, as convincing and as capable

on the printed page as he would be in his office. In print he was actually very much more accessible to the 'patient' – for he holds little in reserve. His enthusiasm and brightness cheers the reader on. He's not a conjuror, not a charlatan, there's no sleight-of-hand palming a dark heart for a light one. He genuinely believes what he says and writes so well. Consequently, the overwhelming majority of readers apparently are convinced they can continue the trip on their own. More than that, they can make it with lighter hearts and brighter futures for having relived their pain on the pilgrimage and seen it as part of the human condition. Not every reader benefited, but readers benefited in sufficient numbers they encouraged others to find consolation on this Peckian journey.

Not everyone loved the book. Not everyone who loved the book loved all of it. Not everyone who picked up the book read all of it. Peck tells of a bookstore owner who had sold 600 hardback copies of *The Road Less Travelled* and had tried seven or eight times to read it. Though she'd made a lot of money from it, she could tell him, 'I'm glad to sell it to people but I can't get past the first page.' *Forbes* told of another bookseller who was selling the book and hadn't read it, read it and then sold hundreds more. 'Then, of course,' said Peck, 'there's a huge number of people who said they had the book and looked at it, read a page or two, and decided they didn't know why someone had given it to them. Seven years later they're walking into their library, the book falls out of the shelf and they pick it up and it's just what they wanted when they needed it.'

The Road Less Travelled was M. Scott Peck, and he, however much he detested some aspects of its success, was *The Road Less Travelled*. He was like a popular singer known for one song, the hit that never faded in the listeners' ears, but which the singer came to detest. Away from the book, away from *The Road Less Travelled*, Scott Peck was still himself, given to fits of great understanding and particularly inappropriate outbursts. During this decade his mother died; later his father remarried. The new wife was Judge Peck's childhood sweetheart, Gladys. Nephew David said he and his siblings rather liked her. Scott Peck declared he liked her at first before deciding she was 'one of the most evil women I ever met'. Peck in person was prone to making the exact sort of judgemental sweeping statement that he so carefully avoided as an author.

Magazine writer Gary Dorsey was one reader who enjoyed some of *The Road Less Travelled*, not all of it, and provided a reason filled with canny observation. Dorsey, writing in the *Hartford Courant*'s magazine, *Northeast*, said, 'Surprisingly, the first two thirds appeal to me as a journalist because of its tough-minded insistence that people question everything, never shrink from doubt, from dedication to the truth. Values such as discipline, delayed gratification, personal responsibility and truth are carried like banners through these pages. At the same time, just as he describes them as tools to holiness, Peck reminds that if used properly they will unlatch pain and emotional suffering. What bothered me was the section entitled, "Grace". Here his theory makes gargantuan leaps . . . "be ready to accept ethereal gifts that are unsought and inexplicable" . . . the very guy who had pledged an allegiance to scepticism and the scientific method was now asking me to have faith that he was right.'

Overall, the 316-page *The Road* was a book like his Harvard thesis – no index, no bibliography and barely a handful of footnotes. Peck, cleanly, cleverly, possibly unwittingly, had put himself forward as – in his own words – 'the nation's shrink'. It was a tag he later detested, but that doesn't mean he didn't take advantage of it – any self-publicist has to have a handy soundbite or two ready. Peck, at the end of his first draft of *The Road*, had a sense of the extent and weight of what he had written yet was, like most authors, unable to fully gauge its potential impact. Whatever he'd meant to say or thought he'd said, it is instructive to read what his readers thought he'd said. For years Peck included his home address in his books. The result of doing that, he said, finally, was in excess of 22,000 letters, at which point he halted the practice. (There are only several hundred letters in his archives. At the time of his death the two barns on the property contained much overflow from his office.) Excerpts of those letters given below, in the interests of privacy, are offered without direct identification except in a few cases where the identification adds to the authority of the writer. Rarely do Peck's correspondents confine themselves to jotting down a few paragraphs, some write five and six pages. Their response is an almost universal sense of relief and gratitude. There are uninhibited comments, many quibbles and critiques, along with penetrating questions and well-reasoned differing. The major chorus is wholehearted recognition of a fine undertaking, well written.

'The mail you get can tell you a lot about the book,' Peck said, 'and I knew within two-three months of publication that I had a good-selling book on my hands. My first fan letter, from Washington, D.C., began: "Dear Dr Peck, you must be an alcoholic." The writer couldn't believe I could have written this book without being humbled by alcoholism and having spent years in the programme. AA was terribly influential in *The Road*'s success, because AA is an ideal grapevine.'

Peck, who denied he was an alcoholic, was not an AA member and did not attend AA meetings in the United States. Peck in Okinawa had attended many AA meetings, 'not as a self-professed alcoholic, but to find out what it was about,' he said, and since then he'd been 'a great fan, teacher and promoter of AA and other twelve-step programmes.' *The Road Less Travelled* contained many elements that AA members would find bolstering – and familiar to the process of their meetings, for Peck made no secret of the fact that some twelve-step principles were woven through the book. As the AA membership includes people who are mobile professionally, and attend AA meetings wherever they travel, these AA members who liked the book were emissaries for it. 'It's all very quiet,' Peck said, 'and you don't know anything about it, but it was picked up by AA people and kind of zoomed through every AA meeting.'

Later, he said, 'one of my most popular lectures was really based on Genesis 3, after God kicked out Adam and Eve and the way was barred by two cherubim with flaming swords. Well, that's just an enormous truth saying you cannot get back to Eden. And in my experience, alcoholics and other addicts – just about all of them I've known – have had an intense desire, sometimes unconscious, to get back to Eden. Perhaps alcoholics and drug addicts are people with a greater thirst for the spiritual than other people. It's no accident that alcohol is an addiction to a spirit. I think it's a spiritual disorder.'

The Road has its hesitations, dry spots and flights into nowhere, but Peck at his best, which he is most of the time, is clean, lean and organised. Fred Hills, Peck's future Simon and Schuster editor, commenting later on Peck's writing, said, 'All of his manuscripts are well written. He's a pretty clean writer. Occasionally a syntax could be strengthened, but whatever editing was done he always went over it again and often would rewrite in order to keep it absolutely in his own voice.'

A fellow psychotherapist noted, as had Theroux, the nature of Peck's writing. He wrote: 'I especially enjoyed the flow of your text, transversing the delicate connections of psychotherapy, love, evolution, and spiritual growth. It often seems to me courageous to speak of soul and spirituality, without apology, in the field of psychology. Missing for me in your synthesis was a differentiation of the masculine and feminine elements in oneself, one's growth, and in our culture . . . Choosing to use non-sexist language is difficult and cumbersome, and I think it a very loving act. I challenge you to engage in a loving dialogue with a committed feminist regarding this issue.'

A man in Britain wrote: 'I was walking down Glastonbury High Street, shoulders hunched, peripheral vision gone, a picture of misery when I nearly tripped over a little blackboard outside a bookshop which simply said, "We also sell books on love." I went in and almost immediately found *The Road Less Travelled*. It touched me to the depths of my soul. That night, lying awake and in a spiritual agony which seemed to be driving me mad, I thought about what I had read.' The upshot was that the reader was soon volunteering in a Salvation Army home for people with learning difficulties, washing dishes and waiting table. He found he loved the residents, and 'to my surprise, discovered that the residents were equally capable of love.' His personal life continued downhill, but he nonetheless, with his 'little Jack Russell terrier, Spottie', walked on a pilgrimage to the Shrine of Julian of Norwich. The next stage was to go to university, and from there into a wider life.

From Llandudno, Cape Town, a reader wrote that *The Road Less Travelled* 'has just entered my being, thanks to you. Not only do you understand,' she said, 'you have found deeper echoes in the farthest reaches of me.' For a *Times of India* writer: 'Each time I pick up the book I go back to the first page. Each reading has a different revelation. The book teaches maturity.'

In many letters, sex quickly reared its controversial head. 'I found myself disagreeing with your characterisation of what you term "romantic love",' one woman wrote. 'I couldn't tell whether you thought this kind of love identical with sexual infatuation. I don't, incidentally. The characterisation struck me as too easily dismissive of something that has acted historically as a substantial force in human affairs; as internally somewhat inconsistent with other views you expressed; and, finally, as at odds with my own experience. I do think you might want to be a little more cautious about the equating of "falling in love" with "a genetically determined instinctual component of mating behaviour". You describe a very real phenomenon – people imposing their needs on other people in the name of romantic love – but ignore another very real phenomenon – people experiencing joy in each other precisely because of the suspension of need.'

To some of his readers, Peck's confliction was more apparent than he realised. While some letter writers poured out their own sexual experience woes, others asked for advice, for a chance to talk on the telephone. Many were highly literate – an indication of the type of reader he attracted.

On sex in marriage there was his attitude towards open marriage, disagreement with his notion that romantic love was really just the sexual drive disguised with lilacs and poetry, and sticking points around the statement Peck wished he'd never included in *The Road*. This is his remark that a therapist might consider sexual relations with a patient – though, he said, he never had – if, under circumstances he could not imagine, the diagnosis called for it. There were other therapist-client sticking points. Wrote a woman from California: 'The confusion I had dealt mainly with your theory about the relationship between a therapist and the patient. In fact at times I think you forgot entirely about the "patient" in this process of psychotherapy. Take, for instance, the ego boundaries and love. The professional was told to let go of the ego boundaries. But what about the patient? The patient wouldn't be there if a problem didn't already exist. Is the patient supposed to read between the lines at this point? Don't you think you leave the poor patient hanging in mid-air? To my way of thinking, now would have been the time for the patient to be told that the therapist is to be looked at like a loving parent figure. My psychologist recommended *The Road Less Travelled*, and I did receive a lot of insight as to what "love", "grace", and "lazy" meant.'

'Would you be so kind as to indulge my confusion,' wrote one man, 'by offering an explanation of the last sentence in the section of Love and Psychotherapy. What is meant by "they are content to be ordinary men and women and do not strive to be God"?' Despite the criticisms, the letters were overwhelmingly grateful, quick to point to personal growth that had resulted from reading the book, and appreciative of Peck's tentative, but quite apparent, belief: 'It took my breath away,' one woman wrote, 'to read about "recognising", to be confirmed that what I feel and have felt about God being me – my unconscious – that amorphous, ephemeral "something" within me that I can feel but which hasn't, up till now, seemed to fit in the world in which I live.' More tellingly, a woman in Charlotte, NC commented: 'There are many case histories where "the Church" has laid a real number on the young mind – taking [them] some time to get out from under.' Then she asked: 'What "formal religious training", if any, did you allow your own children to be exposed to?' The answer, of course, was not much.

Others he confused, not only on sex, but on God, contended Dr Wayne House, later president of Oregon Theological University. He said, 'Peck wrote *The Road Less Travelled* at a propitious time. Whereas psychotherapy stood at a distance from the average person – wrapped in scientific jargon and devoid of spiritual dimension – Peck offered solutions in a non-scientific and easy-reading style. He addressed the spiritual cravings of Americans who apparently were not being satisfied through the Church or their culture.' However, summarised House, 'Peck denies practically every major doctrine of Christianity while advocating an unbiblical morality.'

While the file drawers in Peck archives at Fuller Theological Seminary have many such letters to Peck, the last letter quoted touched on a thorny topic for scholars – that of the blended frontier where psychology, psychiatry and religion meet, and Peck's contribution, if any. Peck admitted he wrote first and researched later, consequently he'd probably little knowledge of the depth and width of the academic arena he'd entered. He'd soon begin to hear.

Peck gambled with *The Road* in the same manner he had gambled with his thesis, that he could say what he wanted how he wanted – provided he said it well enough. Where his thesis was concerned, two out of three Harvard professors agreed with him. With *The Road*, so did better than two out of three reviewers, plus the over-whelming majority of his readers and listeners. Those who didn't agree could disagree strongly. The *PsychoHeresy Awareness Newsletter* lambasted Peck for a lack of clear standards concerning the nature of truth, for viewing Scripture more or less as mythology, for denying God as sovereign. Peck's reliance on evolution and the evolving nature of man came in for a drubbing, as did his views on salvation, resurrection, heaven and hell. The coup de grace was that 'Peck's erroneous theology appears repeatedly throughout all of his books'.

Peck had dared to be different in order to care for the individual reader as warmly, though as disinterestedly, as if the reader were in his consulting room. He was telling them that if they were in

therapy, their assessments of their condition or situation were probably correct, as long as their assessments were honestly, candidly
arrived at. Readers could detect the difference in what this man was
saying from what they'd previously heard or thought. They could
not always describe what they now detected, but accepted Peck's
presentation because it was so reassuring. As for his 'erroneous
theology', Peck was genuinely unconcerned about what the religious
or psychiatric professionals might say. He would have liked their
endorsement, but he didn't crave it.

There was a tendency among some of his devout readers and
listeners to ask, as is posed in the Scriptures, 'From where does he
draw his authority?' and to listen to what he had said and how it had
touched them, and conclude he drew it from God. However one
explains or describes it, Peck drew his authority from within. *The
Road* is Peck. *The Road* is Buddhism ('you are your own refuge')
morphing into Christianity ('God is our refuge'). It metamorphoses
without losing the Buddhist injunction entirely. To the Christian and
many other believers, creative abilities are God-given. The believer
does not necessarily separate out personal creativity from God's gift.
Peck was comfortable describing his relationship with a giving God,
and a forgiving God, and a God creating through human agency.

Given that he'd travelled through Zen Buddhism and his flirtation
with Sufism on his track towards Christianity, it is scarcely surprising
that in Peck, to whatever limited extent, a modicum of Eastern
mysticism actually meets Western psychology. Mysticism and
psychology are not one and the same; East might need West quite as
much as West needs East, for mysticism and psychotherapy may
need each other. To explain: there was an English Benedictine
monk, Bede Griffiths (1906–1993), who became a Hindu sannyasi.
Dom Bede was an ascetic Christian who lived in the Saccidananda
ashram he had helped co-found on the banks of the River Kaveri in
Shantivarnum (Forest of Peace), in Tamil Nadu state, India. He lived
in the ashram for twenty-four years, and died there. He wrote, and
he travelled. One of the places he regularly gave retreats was at the
Osage Monastery in Oklahoma. And it was there that parish
counsellor Paula Sullivan and Dom Bede, in Sullivan's words, 'had
interesting exchanges about which should come first: was it healing
the mind through the human resources of therapists, and then going
on the spiritual path?' What Dom Bede replied was complementary
to what Peck was writing. The monk felt the ashram needed a good

psychotherapist on staff because so many deeply wounded people found their way there. Seen in that light, his burgeoning spiritual background meant that Peck, serendipitously, consciously or not, was operating at a higher level of spiritual integration than his readers, reviewers, critics, or he himself suspected. Yet he was totally down-to-earth about it. As was Dom Bede. A close friend of Bede's recalled there was a copy of *The Road Less Travelled* in the ashram.

To some Peck critics, all this smacked of the New Age movement. One article that listed New Age 'leading voices' placed Peck in a group that included the Jesuit philosopher Teilhard de Chardin, movie star Shirley MacLaine and former United Nations assistant general secretary Robert Muller. Peck was described by Drs John Ankerberg and John Weldon as an 'important' New Age voice, despite his lack of religious consistency (his claim he was a Christian who received divine help writing *The Road*). They missed perhaps, or did not like, that in *The Road* Peck is actually the practical amalgamator of psychotherapy and religion, so the everyday reader could pick up the book and benefit from it. *The Road* contains barely a nod to scientific method – despite Peck's declarations about being first and most of all a scientist. He isn't a scientist any more than he is a theologian. If his personal spirituality has a pick-and-choose quality to it his arguments on paper don't. He is what he has been all along: a writer.

Peck's cross in *The Road*, as in his own life, was that he could see what people needed to do, and describe how to do it, but scarcely practised what he preached regarding his own needs because of his narcissism. He became totally *self*-centred. His cross was not his weakness (in one sense it was his strength as a writer, in that his pain is a major element of the tension that sparked his creativity). His weaknesses were elsewhere. One continuing Peck flaw was the fact that he believed admission of a wrong was a form of exculpation. He lived as if admitting a wrong or a fault of itself brought forgiveness, that the admission obviated the need to express remorse, make amends, and seek a genuine reconciliation. Whatever this says about Peck the personality, none of this undermines what Peck the writer created in *The Road*. The other weakness was his inability to control some of his urges. For example, he had a tendency in recounting incidents from this period to paint the household scene of pot and alcohol in shades of genteel lack of restraint, a bit of naughtiness perhaps, but no more. Very much later, referring to some of his wilder New Preston behaviour, he said his success had a role in his behaviour getting out of hand: 'It happened so fast when it came,' he said. 'I was in over my head, I couldn't control it.' It released a genie Peck had kept in a bottle harking back to the time when the staid young man from the East Coast, in San Francisco doing his residency, witnessed the 1960s West Coast scene. He admitted, 'I was profoundly affected by the sixties in that first glorious year in San Francisco. It was one gigantic sort of love-in and it was spectacular.' He'd missed out on it then, but now, a decade later, successful and becoming wealthy, the worst part of him wanted some of it. And who was to say no? So he pleased himself.

He was already this split persona. He understood so much about a certain group of people hurting for an identifiable group of reasons, from childhood emotional abuse to later emotional betrayal, because he experienced – and indeed participated in his own life in – so much of what they had been through. Peck didn't necessarily hate all his aberrant behaviour, his narcissism allowed him to absorb much of it, but he certainly used the experience of it in his further writings and talks to provide the psychotherapeutic verisimilitude that resonated with his readers and listeners. Nor, as the Christian he became, could he totally suppress his knowledge of the outlandish, at times, life he led. And that did become his cross.

From his reviews, later confirmed by his on-the-road travels, Peck learned there were three groups of Christians that did not like him, he said, 'and they are very distinct. There's the real, hard-core fundamentalists. They don't like me because I am not a literalist – I do not believe the Bible is the directly transcribed word of God; there are places where it should be interpreted. The second group have been the New Agers. I have to acknowledge that they've been big attenders at my lectures, and that many have been supporters despite my criticism – and my biggest criticism is that they are total imminentists. They believe God dwells within them, not outside them. Therefore, any thought or feeling they have can assume the status of revelation, which is a very dangerous heresy. The others who haven't liked me have usually fallen into the Catholic camp, although they are a minority of Catholics. They're such trans- cendentalists they're into the authority and majesty of God to such a degree they can't deal with the fact that God can talk to the likes of Scott Peck – except through a priest, maybe.'

Truly not everyone admired Peck's book. It was liable to do more harm than good, wrote Roy H. Smith of Phillips Graduate Seminary in Enid, Oklahoma. Smith said Peck had taken the wrong road in claiming mental illness as a 'manifestation of grace', that this and his other errors would further afflict the afflicted.

Don Avirom wrote in *Aurora* magazine, that *The Road* 'seems to have struck a reawakened nerve of interest in looking at life from a spiritual point of view. Peck "attacks tunnel vision" – the pitfall of most religious revivals – while he simultaneously tills the all too neglected ground which separates psychology from religion.' *Campus Voice*'s Cynthia Lollar said *The Road* 'is a bold synthesis of psychological and spiritual insights into mental health that speaks to the modern American's alienation from a sense of higher good.' Peck would repeat in interviews that 'mental health is a process of dedication to reality at all costs. There are any number of fears people must face to reach that reality.' The *New Age Journal*'s Jeff Wagenheim spoke of Peck as 'spiritual therapist and psychological guru to the millions of lost souls he had led along *The Road Less Travelled*.' The same publication's Philip Bustil said the nerve Peck struck 'is a reawakened interest in looking at life from a spiritual point of view – a distinctly eighties blend of up-to-date psychology and down-to-earth religion. Peck in fact insists there is no difference between the two. He sees spiritual and psychological growth as intertwined; love, which he differentiates from romance and sexual attraction, for him is "the will to extend oneself for the purpose of nurturing one's own or another's spiritual growth." The rough road that must be tramped in the process of this spiritual and mental maturation is the road less travelled, and it is a long one.'

One mid-1980s reader of *The Road Less Travelled* was Omar Kahn, son of a Pakistani diplomat and today founder and senior partner in Sensei-International, a global management and business consultancy. Kahn attended high school in the United States and the Netherlands, where he was when he read *The Road*. 'I was intimate with it as I headed off to Oxford, and it has continued to be a seminal book for me at many levels.' Two decades later, Kahn recalled that 'what came through was the honesty of it, and the fact that this man had the ability and willingness to say things that I knew I had inescapably grappled with – even though parts of me didn't want to. Parts of me wanted an easier, simpler, fortune cookie remedy and the book wouldn't let me have it.'

Where did Peck find it all? A younger woman at a cocktail party remarked to his mother, 'You must be very proud of Scott and his book.' His mother replied, 'No, not particularly. I had nothing to do with it, really. It's his mind, you see. It's a gift.' True enough, the writing was a gift. What his mother could not sense – or did not care to – was that *The Road* also was a reaction to how he perceived his parents' behaviour towards him, and his retaliation against that parental treatment.

'The lessons Peck draws [from his psychiatric cases],' wrote Bustil, 'are scarcely original; often they seem a simple compound of courage and common sense.' Bustil quotes a Presbyterian minister and psychotherapist, Douglas Land, that [Peck] 'puts together a lot of things that a lot of people have been thinking. Peck happened to write a very helpful book at just the right time. It isn't just a self-help book – it's on its way to becoming a classic.'

Peck, meanwhile, was on his way to becoming more than mildly obsessed with evil. It was typical of his contrarian approach to life – he'd just spent two years writing about love, he said. Now he wanted to examine its opposite. At one level Peck believed in the possibility of possession by Satan, but more, that he was free to explore whatever he chose. He'd done four pages on evil in *The Road Less Travelled,* and, by December 1981, when he wrote to Rod Brownfield, editor of *Mission Ministries,* he'd expanded those pages into *People of the Lie,* nearly completed in first draft. Even that wasn't sufficient. This was the period when Peck undertook two exorcisms, and he wanted to institutionalise what he was discovering. In Georgia, the head of the psychiatric clinic was encouraging Peck to found an 'Institute for the Study of Deliverance' at his centre. Peck told Brownfield there'd be a triple focus, on the effectiveness of prayer and faith healing in physical disorders, on the 'effectiveness of combining Christian prayer ritual and techniques with intensive and confrontative psychiatric therapy in the treatment of people suffering from standard psychiatric disorders', and the questions of possession and exorcism. The institute did not come to pass. The clinic's professional staff balked. Ten years later, in a *Bloomsbury Review* interview, Peck was still talking about it, and the need for science to investigate. Nonetheless, Peck was adaptable. He filed away the 'intensive and confrontative psychiatric therapy' idea for later use. It would surface again in the early programmes of his and Lily's Foundation for Community Encouragement.

Peck told Brownfield in 1981 that 'life gets busier and more exciting each month. I am even, I think, beginning to become a decent speaker. [It] is an activist kind of ministry. All my talks tend to stir people up a bit and I am giving one which urges unilateral disarmament more and more frequently.' He was also in the middle of negotiations for his second book, *People of the Lie*.

CHAPTER 9

ON THE ROAD

Magazine writer Ben Yagoda was on the road with the now celebrated M. Scott Peck. Peck was stretched out on a bed in an Edison, New Jersey motel, nursing his perennially bad back, smoking the inevitable Camels and sipping his first of the evening's cocktails. The cocktail, wrote Yagoda, was made with "'Lake Waramaug gin", bought in his hometown liquor store' and packed in his case. Just in case. The motel scene and interview was one that could have been repeated hundreds of time over the decade of the 1980s once Peck decided to take his show on the road.

Not many writers, however, displayed Yagoda's wit. Seated by the side of Peck's bed, the writer listened to Peck recount his problems, and Yagoda decided, 'The scene isn't without irony, considering I'm not a psychiatrist and the prone fellow on the bed is.' Yagoda, a perceptive observer, described Peck ('pleasant face, graying, thinning, blond hair and horn-rimmed glasses'), and assessed *The Road* ('an attempt to combine more or less conventional ideas about psychotherapy with one of its traditional enemies, religion'). Later Yagoda went into the auditorium to catch part of the act and depicted Peck in front of his audience:

'People ask me [said Peck] if I was born again,' [Peck] pauses, then, with expert timing, 'It was a very protracted labour and difficult delivery.' *Laughter*. Peck [on the platform] is sitting in a large wing chair – his back again – a microphone in his hand, a carafe of coffee at his side. He waits out the laugh by slowly panning his head from left to right – another stand-up comic's move. He sounds like a cross between Garrison Keillor [an American radio personality] and [preacher] Billy Graham, with a dash of William F. Buckley [an ultra-WASP, right-wing

magazine publisher and television personality], especially in
the patrician pronunciation of words like '*littrachure*'.

Of the journey on the road and a later interview, Yagoda writes:
'It all sounds good. Actually a little *too* good, a little too smooth and
easy. I talk to Peck a few weeks later on the phone, and he tells me
he's had some trouble with his personal staff in New Preston and
they've had a retreat to try to iron out the problems. Another crisis.
He almost sounds relieved.' Two-plus decades later, Yagoda said he
never quite figured out Peck. —

The audiences were overwhelmingly female. Peck 'read' them as
closely as they were reading him. 'Towards the end of the
engagement, during the last question-and-answer period – it sort of
fit in nicely – I'd say, "Would you like to know about yourselves?
Would you like to know who you are?" And they'd say yes. And I
would say, all right, you are not an ordinary cross-section of
America, but there are some things you do have in common that
distinguish you. An extraordinarily high percentage of you either
had or are currently receiving psychotherapy, either through
traditional routes or twelve-step programmes.' And he'd ask those to
whom this applied to raise their hands, and 'Ninety-five per cent
would raise their hand.' They loved it. And him. He had a
particularly engaging manner when he chose to use it, which was
most of the time. 'The irony, of course,' said his nephew, David, 'is
how charming Scotty is/presents. He is every inch the WASP
(thoughtful and sensitive, but still a cultural type of the world in
which he was bred) that he often thinks he is not.'

On the road, Scott had it built into the contracts in advance that
he would do no cocktail parties, no social meetings with boards of
directors. He avoided cocktail parties, he explained, because he
never knew what to say. Nephew David gives one example, Peck
himself provides another. When nephew David worked at his
grandfather's old law firm, Sullivan & Cromwell, a partner told
nephew David 'what he thought was a funny joke about my father.'
But the partner had mistaken Scotty for the brother, David. The
incident occurred during the partner's college years when the future
partner met Scott (thinking he was David) at a cocktail party.
Everyone was well boozed up, the partner said, but Scotty (as
David) 'was going on and on with this philosophical bullshit that
everyone else was eating up. I couldn't take it. I had to run away,'

the partner said. 'I just wanted a good time and there he was, holding forth. O Christ, give me a break, I thought.' Added nephew David, 'and that would not have been a unique reaction to Scotty in that milieu.' Peck, during a *New Age Journal* interview, explained, 'I'm a very shy person and I've seldom been comfortable with informal communications. I have not been to a cocktail party for years. I occasionally *have* to go to a wedding, but I never know how honest or open to be; it's not an environment for listening. If I'm really open or honest, it can be threatening for people. If I'm with people I want to be all there, without having to figure out which level to operate on. I am all for being more formal, in terms of setting up definite parameters.'

Peck and his polished performance in New Jersey, was Peck the now-master of the public platform craft – a far cry from his first amateur sortie into the post-*The Road* spotlight, in Buffalo, in upper New York State, the home of Niagara Falls. 'It was in the fall of 1979,' he said, 'because a woman in Washington, D.C. had sent her college roommate a copy of *The Road*. They sold six hundred copies of the book in Buffalo. It was a remarkable speaking engagement because in the WASP enclave of Buffalo there's a large Episcopalian church and a large Presbyterian church.' Continued Peck (with one of his throwaway lines), 'They'd been arch-enemies forever. Somehow they decided to cooperate. I went for two days and I read my speeches. They paid me the vast sum of nine hundred dollars.' (A decade later he was charging $15,000 a workshop.) Whatever he'd anguished his way through at the convent, he was hooked: he'd taken *The Road* on the road. It was the first step from private person to public personality.

He offered his Buffalo audience his own angst and experiences, and the angst and experiences of his patients. It was the lecture circuit version of the book. In his book he wrote in declarative sentences. On stage he was the calm, mellow-voiced, reassuring and appealing psychiatrist declaring these things. In both he gave disguised examples from his psychotherapist's notebook that were direct, real, telling. His Buffalo performance, he said, 'was absolutely dreadful, but there was such a kind attitude dumped on me, such good feeling going around it overcame my reading my speeches. It was quite a happening, and then I also happened to give a good sermon.' He read it.

Peck was well read and well received in the South and the Bible

Belt. He felt he never got much of a reception in New York City. Fred Hills, his editor at Simon and Schuster, said, 'I think that's true. New York is a very tough town, a difficult town, for any speaker – speakers seem to be a dime a dozen. It's a major metropolis with a vast array of entertainment, intellectual or otherwise. Very few speakers find they get a great reception in New York. Often, speakers who come to the New York area do not speak in Manhattan or New York City. They speak in New Jersey or Long Island, where it's a much bigger event.' Hills heard Peck speak in Manhattan, in an auditorium in Paramount Pictures' local headquarters at a time when Simon and Schuster was owned by Paramount. Hills said that within a few years of the publication of *The Road Less Travelled,* Peck 'had become idolised by many, certainly of people in attendance at churches where he spoke.'

Peck did become a polished speaker, and a first-class extemporaneous one when, on a roll, he pontificated on a subject he enjoyed. He'd also tell his favourite jokes: 'Question: What's the last thing a co-dependent sees before she dies? Answer: Someone else's life flashing before her. How many Zen Buddhists does it take to screw in a light bulb? Two. One to screw in the bulb and one to not screw in the bulb.'

Early on, when he was still reading his talks, he was a tad preachy and could lapse into a sonorous, somewhat soporiferous style. That changed radically after an engagement in the American South. His host praised his presentation but quietly suggested he would have greater impact if he did not read it. Peck worked hard to alter his presentation method so he could operate from a few notes of key words and phrases. Reworked as a speaker he projected a convincing authority – one he always had when immersed in spontaneous, earnest pronouncements on topics of his own choosing. 'In my senior year in college,' he said, 'I took a course, run by Charlie Slack – the guy who found my thesis unacceptable – where we were actually given a patient in the state hospital. We ended the course with a kind of group therapy session going among us students. There was one student, who was an old man for people at Harvard, more like thirty when we were twenty-one or twenty-two, and he said, "Scotty, this is not meant as either praise or criticism. But whenever you open your mouth, it's like the voice of God." I did not know what to make of it at the time. I think part of it comes from my father who, at times, albeit rather rare times, spoke with the same kind of authority.' Recounting the incident thirty years later he added, 'Sometimes I think it comes from God.'

Said psychologist Guy, Peck *is* 'a kind of guru – but the title didn't quite fit him then, and still didn't later.' Said Guy, 'What's the source of his authority – he doesn't fall back on others writers and thinkers, not even the Bible. What I've seen, what I've heard, what I can measure, what I've detected is that he comes with a mighty message but the vehicle is that he's a human being. People want to be able to say the messenger is as mighty as the message – otherwise where's the message really coming from? You look at Peck, he's not so mighty. He's got all sorts of vices and quirks and he's as human as my neighbour. Yet he's the bearer of a message that helps people along the way.'

Peck would hear variations of such sentiments many times in the aftermath of his talks. Occasionally, the impression he gave brought more than just a comment. In the early years on the road he was in Jackson, Mississippi. Once more the venue was an Episcopal cathedral. And once more, in a group discussion, people really did ask among themselves, 'Where does he get his authority?' There was present a woman called Louise Mohr. She was sufficiently impressed with Peck, she told him, that she was conferring on him the mantle of Gert Behanna. Gert Behanna is the woman whose prayer opens this biography.

It's hard to imagine a Gert Behanna – or a Peck – surfacing in any country other than the United States. She was born to extreme wealth and raised in the old Waldorf Hotel in Manhattan by a series of governesses of doubtful ability or quality. Her father was a brilliant immigrant Scot who made an early fortune. His aim for Gertrude was education, education, education. Like Peck, Gert was a cosseted child of comfort who nonetheless felt smothered by her circumstances. She grew up extremely lonely. After her parents' divorce she was sent at age nine to school in Europe and was there until the onset of the First World War. She felt inadequate, a plain girl with a brilliant father and a beautiful mother, and at Smith College, an all-women's college in North Hampton, Massachusetts (Peck, a half century later, dated 'Smithies'), she broke loose. At Smith she a met a man 'who was silly enough to marry me the first night we met.' Gert Behanna's description of 'the bull and the virgin' on her wedding night in her autobiography, *The Late Liz: the Autobiography of an Ex-Pagan,* is an account of conjugal rape.

She had a child, and after four years of 'the nightmare, the contest macabre', she quit the marriage. It was back, with her young son, to the Waldorf and her father's 'I told you so.' From then on, for Gert, it was booze, men – 'I learned about men from men' – and the downward slide. There was a trail of three broken marriages, alcohol and drug addiction until, during a bedside moment confronting the loss of someone she truly loved, she heard 'the Voice' that led her, 'one climb up, one slip back', to Christianity. She was fifty-three. She became a preacher, with a cigarette dangling from her lip, a sassy, appealing Episcopalian evangelist. Her life was depicted in a 1971 movie, starring Anne Baxter. Louise Mohr knew Gert Behanna and Gert herself handed the mantle of her spiritual calling to Louise. That mantle Louise conferred on Peck.

By delivering an address in Buffalo, Scott Peck awakened in himself a powerful drive. He didn't know the depth of what he might achieve, but on a practical level he was sharp enough to see the financial advantages of selling his books at several levels; smart enough to know the consequences of boredom and isolation while travelling; and tart enough to demand his own way when people or a turn of events offered only obstruction.

Back in the Edison, New Jersey motel, magazine writer Yagoda did more than set the bedside scene. He penned a snapshot of Peck's operation. It was a three-day programme that cost those attending $95 a person, and brought Peck an $8,000 speaker's fee. The attendees got their money's worth. Peck always had interesting and stimulating things to say. He had a fine speaking voice. Frequently, towards the end of an appearance, he would read poetry, usually T. S. Eliot, infrequently one of his own poems. Towards the end of his lecture circuit career, he increasingly gave vent to what some described as an attractive singing voice, a singing voice which, when his housekeeper Valerie Duffy first heard it, prompted her remark to Peck to not give up writing books for a living. His preferred sacred song was *Amazing Grace*. But there was another side to all this, the gruelling aspects of constant travel.

Peck on the road would arrive, give his talk or conduct his workshop, and be out of there and off home – or on to the next appearance – as quickly as possible. Anyone who has travelled for a living, even business class and four-star hotels, knows how quickly, despite any momentary limelight, it turns into gruelling work. The lecture organisers, understandably, expecting nothing but a benign calm when Peck hit town, could sometimes find themselves considerably disconcerted by Peck's manner. A self-confessed control freak, he could utilise his skills to make people keep their distance, by being coolly unresponsive, or exercising other traits of WASP hauteur.

Equable of temper most of the time, Peck could burn with pure anger. Once, at the end of a speaking engagement in Virginia Beach, Virginia, he was driven to the airport by the sponsor who remarked what a gentle person Peck was, particularly in the gentle way he handled questions. They arrived at check-in about forty-five minutes before flight time, but stood in line to reach the counter for another fifteen minutes. Once there Peck produced his ticket for his seat, only to be told the flight was overbooked. He was informed he would be booked on the next flight and arrive four hours later than the current flight.

Peck remonstrated, 'I was here. I've got a ticket. I've got a reservation. And I'm going to get on that plane.' The counter agent told him, 'No, I'm sorry, sir, you can't get on the plane. It's overbooked.' Peck said, 'Let me talk to the manager.' The man replied, 'He's not available and he would just tell you the same thing.' The exchange escalated until Peck said, 'Then you'll just have to call the police, because I'm getting on that God-damn plane.' Then Peck turned to his sponsor and said, 'You see, I'm not always so mild.' And with that, he boarded the plane.

Of life on the circuit, Peck said, 'It was an exhausting schedule. I think that, as well as my cigarettes, is another reason I'm early old. I got to do all my writing on planes, a precious time for me. I'm a very shy person and don't like to talk to the person next to me, who's often intoxicated. I was riding on a plane to a speaking engagement in Minneapolis. The man sitting next to me was a man about my own age at the time. I gave this man my usual non-verbal messages that I was not interested in talking and he had absolutely no interest in talking to me, either. And so we sat there, me writing, and him reading a book, on an hour-long flight from Hartford [Connecticut] to Buffalo [New York]. We sat together in total silence in the lounge at Buffalo airport, then silently got back on the plane together. It wasn't until forty-five minutes west of Buffalo that, out of the clear blue sky, the first words passed between us. He looked up from the book he was reading and said, "Excuse me, I hate to bother you, but you don't happen, do you, to know the meaning of the word 'serendipity'?" And I said, well, it so happened that I was the only person I knew who had written a substantial portion of a book about serendipity. And that it was perhaps serendipity that, at the moment he wanted to know the meaning of the word, he happened to be seated in outer space next to the nation's authority on the subject. Serendipity is sort of my scientific code word for grace.'

This, of course, if the exchange went precisely as Peck described it, was Peck puffing himself up. While Peck might have regarded himself as the nation's authority on experiential serendipity, typically he hadn't bothered to research the word. He didn't know, when asked, that Serendip was a name for the island of Ceylon (now Sri Lanka) or that Horace Walpole coined the word 'serendipity' from the title of the fairy tale *The Three Princes of Serendip,* who, wrote Walpole, 'are always making discoveries by accident or sagacity, of things they were not in quest of.' Peck certainly made discoveries by accident.

Continuing his narrative about the exchange on the aircraft, Peck said, 'Well, when God comes in with one of his zingers, even I have to lay down my yellow pads. So we [he and his fellow passenger] got talking. He asked about the book, and I said it was a sort of an integration of religion and psychiatry. He said, "Well, I don't know about religion any more," that he was a Methodist boy from Iowa, but beginning to have some significant questions.' He spoke of his doubts and, said Peck, 'I told him that unlike what most Christians believe, in almost all instances, doubt is not a sin, but a virtue; that the path to holiness, as I'd said in that book, lies in questioning everything. And that I thought what he was doing was very holy. As we got off at the Minneapolis airport, he said, "Well, I have no idea what the hell this means, but maybe I don't have to leave Church after all." Moments of serendipity, moments of pure grace,' Peck concluded.

Two assessments of Peck's on-the-road personality can be drawn from a 1980s Baltimore, Maryland speaking engagement. Barbara Rich, a 'native Baltimorean' who had 'long loathed M. Scott Peck', said, 'He came – I believe in the early eighties – to deliver a talk at our local Thomas Jefferson Memorial Unitarian Universalist Church. The minister at the time, a man wedded to the art and non-science of New Ageism, was a keen admirer of Peck; hence, the invite, and the healthy cash paid out to the self-help guru of his time. I adhere to the principles of scepticism whenever faced with somewhat hysterical fervour about some new messiah.' Rich, a theatre critic for a newspaper in Virginia, takes herself seriously when she criticises. She once was quoted in the *Washington Post* as stating, 'I think irreverence is the greatest quality anyone can have.'

'I was in charge of greeting those who arrived for the event,' said Rich, 'and was told to do so to the speaker, who was sitting in a small anteroom, adjacent to the sanctuary. He was looking extremely bored, and when I approached him and held out my hand in welcome, Peck remained firmly seated, remained outwardly bored. Not having his divine insights I had no idea – to this very day – what was going on within his exquisitely sensitive self. I asked whether he'd like some water, and he refused. Anything else? I asked. He shook his head. So then, being me, I thanked him for his courtesy and walked away.' She continued that, 'Peck barely reacted to (I say this with pardonable pride) a small attractive woman not used to this kind of boorish behaviour.' She called his talk 'solipsistic' and Peck 'a fraud, and some of the stuff that's come out about the way his personal life has been conducted tends to bear that out.'

Paula Matuskey, later dean of Montgomery College in Takoma Park, Maryland, also heard Peck speak in Baltimore. 'I was reading Peck's book and was inspired to think more deeply about my life, beyond the day-to-day challenges and trials.' Presbyterian-raised Matuskey had been away from church attendance for fifteen years, and was thinking about returning when she read *The Road*, 'which really affected me. I subsequently purchased all of his later books, although I think the first was best. In a restaurant in California one time, reading one of his later books while waiting for my husband to meet me at the table, the waiter saw what I was reading and said, "His first book changed my life."' She later gave the waiter the one she was reading. In Baltimore, up close, she said, 'I found Dr Peck to be less engaging than I expected. He did not seem really approachable one-on-one, if you know what I mean. Yet I still got a great deal from his presentation. His lecture on death and meaning was particularly helpful to me when I lost four close family members and my best friend all in the course of three-and-a-half years.'

Business executive Ron Sharpe heard Peck speak 'three or four times, and I met him once.' At their meeting Sharpe offered Peck a paper he'd written. 'I can remember him snatching it like it was full of serendipity, like he would find something magical in it. I wonder sometimes if he ever did. Him I always actually trusted – for lack of a better word – to be unflinchingly honest. I tried to take apart his books to find any flaw. I could never understand how anyone could know so much [and] actually communicate it so simply and efficiently. The answer is obvious: God. Though he smoked, drank and had an affair, he let others know that he was not their hero – although a mentor – and that he was flawed. My background was a lot of business battles. The paradox is that it is in fighting the battles one learns the most about oneself and the ability to extend oneself, even without resources. I often tell people that *The Road*, and *People of the Lie* [1983], are the best "business" books ever written.'

However miffed some of his appointed minders might get at one of his appearances, the rewards for the majority of the attendees were genuine enough. For Peck on stage was genuine enough, master of the event and not so close his space could be invaded. He could sit in his armchair, bursting with a low-key fun and nonsense that smoothed the way for his palatable and unpalatable 'live life' prescriptions. He could be daring in what he said, witty along with the insights. In an audience of hundreds, people heard him talking to them individually. What resonated and struck a chord with one, did not necessarily do so for all, but the letters to him and comments in later interviews make it obvious that Peck was healer first, entertainer second. To his readers and listeners he resonated integrity. Rightly so, his skill in this healing art was a genuine gift. He cured. His public had every right to admire his strengths. Though his answers to questions could be plucked from his 'previously used' store, he was provocative and winning. It wasn't an act. Nor was the downside an act – the coldness, the disdain for those who wanted to get too close. The closer one got to Peck the person, attempting to penetrate the personality, the more prickly he reacted – unless one was hurting. If hurting, he was constant, he switched straight into psychotherapist and healer.

Christopher Peck praised his father's openness as a healer. 'His door was open to everyone – who was not delivering a court summons – on principle and in fact. It was his most noble stance, and perhaps the least discussed of his noble stances. Although he erected baffles to secure his safety and some privacy, and regardless of whether he was a quack who could do you more harm than good, anyone in the world could, with little effort, gain an audience with Dad at no charge. That was exceedingly brave and defies any question of motive.'

Peck the man in motion had a couple of phobias in his case along with the cigarettes and gin. One was he would never check luggage. His executive secretary Gail Puterbaugh said it was 'always the one time in twenty years they would lose it.' Travelling once with his then executive assistant, Mary Ann Schmidt, she reported that when he got in the car with the sponsor, the sponsor said to him, 'Oh my God, you've brought no luggage or extra clothes.' Kathy, Peck's second wife, said Scotty replied, 'I would rather stink than check luggage.' They were always amazed by his frankness.

Peck, constantly travelling, was experiencing a mid-life crisis. 'I had one of my God experiences that started me out of my mid-life crisis and depression. Again this funny voice came out of nowhere. I was tired and depressed and going up the stairs one night sort of feeling trapped – other people might not have felt trapped, but I was feeling trapped. About three stairs up I heard this voice say, "Take up music." I did my usual shaking of the head and said to the voice, "That's absurd," and continued up the stairs. And the voice said, "Take up music nonetheless." And I said well you're so damn smart, where would I begin. At which point the voice shut up. Then in the next month I had several patients who knew about music, and one of them was a musician, and I asked them where the beginning of music was. And they all became incredibly incoherent.' Every couple of years Peck would return to Harvard for an alumni college course. That year one of the two courses was 'The fundamentals of music'. 'I was forty-nine. I got several learning experiences from the course. One was a sense of how easy it is to become addicted to music and just forget about the rest of the world.' He'd obviously not been too traumatised musically by his failings as a child pianist, for Peck took up the violin. 'I had two experiences. I reached the point where I realised this was going to be a humungous amount of work but if I did it I could succeed at it. And with that came the decision that I didn't want to spend all that time and energy. So I gave it up. But oddly that was part of the reason that I exited my mid-life crisis, the sense I could do something else.'

It was while on the road that Peck initiated the longer of his two long-term affairs. It was with a Californian, Kathy Yeates. He told her that in the previous year during his travels he had slept with more than two dozen women, but that their arrangement could be monogamous, for he had an open marriage. That liaison lasted some six years. To psychologist Guy, he said, 'Since my libido dropped [when he was about fifty-one] and I stopped the infidelity, the relationship with Lily has been great. When I experienced [that] sudden, dramatic diminution of libido I happened to have an appointment with my local internist. I told him about it, and I said, "Don't you dare do anything about it. It's like a monkey off my back." It really has been a relief. I would say that ten per cent of me misses it, but ninety per cent of me thanks God almost daily for it.' Peck made jokes about his missing libido but didn't need to search far for its cause. His heavy gin intake probably led to a form of 'distiller's droop', and the strain of 200 days a year on the road did most of the rest.

Peck found regional variations in how audiences responded to him. 'I used to routinely get standing ovations when I spoke,' he said, 'except in the Midwest – finally after the longest time I got one in Chicago and once they started they couldn't stop. But I was aware how unresponsive Middle-western audiences are, how little feedback you get from them. I was even told there are some musical conductors that will not conduct in the Midwest. Finally, I was in Sioux City or Sioux Falls, one of them, and hit the absolutely deadest audience yet. Back in my hotel room I said, what is it with these people? It occurred to me that a hundred years earlier, these cities didn't exist. They hadn't time yet to form a culture. No-one wanted to be out of step. And the reason you get no standing ovations, of course, is that to start one, somebody has to stand. They don't know how to behave except to see what the next guy is doing.'

Peck never curried up to political figures. The closest he came in adult life to a major politician was writing a blurb for Vice President Al Gore's *Earth in the Balance: the Ecology of the Human Spirit.* Peck once nearly made it inside the Kennedy compound at Hyannisport, Massachusetts. He was contacted on one occasion by a member of the Kennedy clan, possibly, he thought, R. Sargent Shriver (the late President John F. Kennedy's brother-in-law and founder of the Peace Corps). 'There was a symposium of some sort on drugs at Hyannisport,' said Peck, 'and I was invited to speak.' Peck sent word he would do it for his usual fee (at the time somewhere in the $2,000-$3,000 range). Asking them for money, said Peck, 'was an absolute insult. They wrote to ask how could I possibly charge for this.' Peck's executive director replied for him and stated it was how Dr Peck normally operated, only to be countered with, 'If Dr Peck comes here for free, as he should, on Sunday morning he can go to mass with Mrs Rose Kennedy.' That week Peck missed mass.

After more than a decade on the road, and four more books, the reviewers and interviewers were still fascinated most by *The Road* and Peck's success. The March 1991 *Playboy* magazine said 'few books since the Bible' had more influence, this at a time when *The Road* was past the four million sales mark, was into its seventh year on the bestseller list, and had surpassed *The Joy of Sex* along the way. That same year, 1991, Peck spent part of August and September in Australia, once again dispensing with a refreshing seriousness his essential ingredient: hope presented in a quasi-spiritual format.

Everywhere that people paid attention, listeners, readers and reviewers could almost *feel* the strength Peck was giving them. Even though the word itself is laden with connotations unintended and apprehensions not easily allayed, most of Peck's readers were his *converts*. He converted them to believing what he wrote, and somewhere deep inside his soul he may have agonised at the purgatory-wide chasm between what he wrote and how he continued to live. Similarly, Peck frequently worked the same magic on his reviewers. He spoke to his readers conversationally, clearly and with genuine conviction. He wrote as he counselled. He was attentive to their needs, and was compassionate. The printed word did not run interference on the voice, it enhanced the message, for it was strengthened from the fact he did not have to deal with the reader in person, and to a greater degree than he imagined, that reality further freed him as a writer. The self-inflicted downside to all this for Peck comes from the same source. He uses the same candid, declarative and forceful statements to manipulate people by shading the facts a little when he begins to deal with his shortcomings, his failings, his affairs, his neglects. In print he describes these sadder attributes with the same elegance and economy he describes everything else.

With each succeeding book beyond *The Road Less Travelled*, his candour (he eschews the word guilt, and doesn't deal with the word remorse particularly well), has him revealing more and more 'between the book's covers'. He pounds his failings into his readers or listeners in the same manner he brings to his readers examples of reaching personal wholeness, of improving society's wholeness, of facing evil if it is Satan, of facing down evil if it is euthanasia, facing down self-centredness. 'Narcissists are people who can't think about others,' he said. 'I believe we are all born narcissists and it is a condition we grow out of. There's a strong element of narcissm in me.' Peck did not suggest he hadn't grown out of it, he was allowing his readers and listeners to presume he had. It is Peck's way with candour. His writings and talks – at their best – with their compelling conviction, their acceptable, magisterial and yet spiritual quality. With his failing she did leave himself naked to his observers, critics and enemies, if they could penetrate the fence he'd constructed around himself. The Episcopal nun, ES, said, 'I think Scotty has been more vulnerable than [many spiritual writers or gurus] because he is dedicated to the truth and humanity. Others [who transgress] make these great manifestations [regarding their fall from grace]. He doesn't. He doesn't beat his breast or anything. He says, I am a human being just like everybody else. I don't know of anything that Scotty has done to hurt anybody. I don't think he has done anything that most human beings haven't done.'

Within a few years Peck, 'sick and tired of the lecture circuit', was yearning for retirement. But with *The Road Less Travelled* behind him, yet working its acclaimed way towards bestsellerdom, Peck had discovered his next mission: community building. There was, however, an even larger event in his life: Peck was now a baptised Christian. And in his second book, *People of the Lie*, that was writ large and clear.

CHAPTER 10

PECK THE EXORCIST

There are probably not many exorcists who, having just made contact with Satan during an exorcism, leave the room to make a telephone call to ask what to do next. Not a bad idea when in doubt. Perhaps the problem lay in the man Peck telephoned, the Irish-born former Jesuit priest, the Rev. Malachi Martin.

Equally so, it's unlikely many exorcists grab a shot of bourbon on the way back to the room to help with the coming encounter. But Peck was convinced that the woman on the bed with the crucifix on her chest was possessed, and that the latest manifestations of her muttering and declamations meant he was facing either the anti-Christ, or Satan, or a combination of both. These details were not in Peck's next book, *People of the Lie: the Hope for Healing Human Evil* (1983). Indeed, Peck does not reveal he was the exorcist when he writes in *People of the Lie* that he'd witnessed exorcisms. He waited more than twenty years to unveil the fact. His 2005 book, *Glimpses of the Devil: a Psychiatrist's Personal Accounts of Possession, Exorcism, and Redemption,* is simply and complexly a detailed account of those two exorcisms.

Within the corpus of his works, *People of the Lie* takes on additional meaning as the moment he publicly announces his Christianity. He has been baptised. He uses that Christianity to effect in *People of the Lie* and his future books. His Christianity he employs as one half of a dual-validity authorial work permit that allows him to explore evil and all else, as both a psychiatrist and a believer. He wrestled with a sensitivity quandary in *People of the Lie* that surfaced again in *Glimpses of the Devil* – a patient's, any person's, right to privacy. Explained Peck, 'I was brought up to be a good little WASP boy and among the things that are drummed into you are you don't go into anybody's house uninvited. Right? And you don't ask certain questions, and you don't ask about their sex life. You don't ask about money, you don't ask how much they paid for their house. Right? Well, then I grew up to become a psychiatrist and had to do all those things I was taught not to do. And it was very difficult for me because I had to really fight against all my instincts, which are to not violate a person's right to privacy. Yet I learned to do it and do it fairly well.' He did not do it all the time, however, and did not probe as deeply as he might have in the first exorcism he conducted. 'The only thing I plead in self-defence is that there are certain moments in a person's life which are kind of such holy ground that it is theirs alone. It's hard for me to put into words that make sense. It's between them and God, and for you to step in, you're not really going to understand anyway. It's like people who, sometimes, you know, somebody has lost a husband or a wife and they say, "Oh, I know how you feel." And the person kind of looks at them blankly and in effect says, "Go away."'

People of the Lie opens with evil, and some excellent cameos of people whose behaviour he labels 'evil'. His passages on the Devil, exorcism, in fact prepare the way for *Glimpses of the Devil,* just as his four pages on evil in *The Road Less Travelled* paved the way for *People of the Lie.* This 'hope for curing human evil' was half completed in first draft even before *The Road Less Travelled* received its first review. He later praised his 'four extremely well done pages on evil' in *The Road,* 'for when I was writing it I hit on evil and I just took off. I wrote about fifty pages, and was still writing away when I said, this is ridiculous, you've got a totally unbalanced book, condense everything you know, Peck, into four pages. You can write about evil in your next book. And so, before I was even done with the final rewriting of *The Road Less Travelled* I knew that my next book would be *People of the Lie.* The other thing is, almost all heresy arises with somebody running with one side of the paradox. And so [having presented Good and Love at length in *The Road*] I just owed it to present the other side.'

Peck said that the first agent to whom he gave an initial chapter of *People of the Lie,* turned it down. 'She said, "It's probably a very good book but I can't represent it because it scares me too much." She did me a great favour though. She said, "Where you are [in terms of *The Road Less Travelled* selling well] I don't think you need an agent – agents are needed by people who are not yet published or don't have a reputation, or are too busy. You're sort of in-between." So that saved me a great deal of money, actually.' Peck might have been developing a reputation, but that didn't mean anyone wanted his next book. Simon and Schuster didn't, he said. They passed on it twice. Finally, Peck surmised, *The Road*'s rising sales convinced them otherwise.

People of the Lie, a 270-page book that would also become a best-seller, was received with accolades in the *Wall Street Journal* ('this is a ground-breaking book, the long overdue discussion between psychology and religion has begun, and nowhere does that beginning bear better fruit than in Dr M. Scott Peck's [book]'), to the *Charlotte Observer* ('so compelling in its exploration of the human psyche, it's as hard to put down as a thriller . . . such a force of energy, intensity and straightforwardness'). Readers coming to *People of the Lie* from *The Road Less Travelled* would, if not scared out of their wits facing up to evil in life, quickly settle into Peck's engaging style. He began with stories from his casebook designed – rightly so, given their content – to startle the reader into setting aside some reservations about even delving into the topic of evil. Storyteller Peck provides précised biographies of evil characters and evil couples, and surrounds them with Peckian analysis and commentary. These evil people in the everyday world are 'people of the lie', they lie to themselves about the evil they do. Peck's account of the couple who give their son for Christmas the rifle with which his brother committed suicide is an example of how Peck can startle and unsettle and keep the reader fascinated.

When his pen is at its best, in bursts of writing that hint at an unrealised novelist's skill, Peck attracts the reader deeper and deeper into the topic's abyss, luring her or him further along with tales that have mini-saga overtones as they detail acts conducted with a frightening ordinariness that lead to horrific consequences. Peck's goal appears to be to get the reader to the bedside of an exorcism. Some readers might say of *People of the Lie* what magazine writer Gary Dorsey said of *The Road Less Travelled* – that it switches at the two-thirds mark as it goes from cogent argument and declaration to asking the reader to suspend disbelief (or, rather, to accept Peck's version of belief in possession and exorcism). In *People of the Lie* there's a similar format twist: factual cases cogently discussed, then the switch from the everyday to the paranormal, to accepting that Satan exists, and that people can be physically possessed by the Devil.

In an attempt to return to the ordinary, *People of the Lie* ends with an account of 'group evil' using the massacre of Vietnamese civilians by US troops at My Lai as its example. One suspects, however, that very few of the readers disinclined to accept the existence of Satan made it as far as My Lai. However, Donald A. Klose, a California psychologist who reviewed *People of the Lie* for the *Journal of Humanistic Psychology* (and who blasted the *New York Times* for calling it a 'self-help' book), praised the strength of its arguments, said it needed no theological foundations to make its statements, and provided his own extensive analysis of Peck's treatment of group evil, which he found compelling.

And even those with an open mind regarding satanic possession might well take issue with Peck's seeming judgemental blanket use of the term 'evil' to cover a variety of aberrant behaviours and cruelties. The Dominican theologian the Rev. Richard Woods, said, 'In fairness, Peck was not a theologian. Technically he's right – that moral evil is still evil whether we call it sin or badness. My problem is when the language becomes used as a weapon – not that Peck did, but others might.' What the book did do in its first two thirds was attract an interested readership into the discussion of evil in ways to set them wondering. For that it was widely admired. Equally, whatever the percentage among Peck's readers, a significant percentage of US Christians does accept that Satan exists as a corollary to accepting the existence of God. And they were favourably impressed with Peck's dual grasp of both evil and Satan's presence in the world.

Peck owed his growing preoccupation with evil and satanic possession to an outside source, the Rev. Malachi Martin (1921–1999), a headline-grabbing, book-writing Irish-born priest. Martin had a reputation with many Catholic insiders as a troublemaker, a liar and a cuckolder. In the eyes of the exorcism crowd, Catholic and otherwise, Martin's reputation switches from infamy to fame. Peck was in the latter group. He dedicated his 2005 book, *Glimpses of the Devil: a Psychiatrist's Personal Accounts of Possession, Exorcism, and Redemption,* to Martin.

The two met through Simon and Schuster. Martin was one of the publishing company's authors, and when Simon and Schuster circulated copies of Peck's first book to its authors for publicity comments, Martin, the only one to reply, wrote 'a nice long comment,' said Peck, 'and I said, well, who's he? And I figured he must be a psychiatrist. I looked in my big tome of American psychiatrists. No Malachi Martin. So he might be an author, and in *Books in Print*, lo and behold, he had plenty, including his most recent, *Hostage to the Devil*, on a subject I was already interested in. I called him up, got through his formidable phone defences, and he was eager to meet me and have me down for lunch in New York, the first of four or five lunches we had.' *Hostage to the Devil* convinced Peck that Martin was the authority on exorcisms.

The Dominican priest Richard Woods, who at one point had interviewed Martin on television, said this about the Irish priest and his exorcising: 'It fell to my lot to conduct a pre-publication review of Martin's *Hostage*. I was allied in this with an internationally celebrated clinical psychologist. Working independently, our conclusion was the same: Martin's "five cases" were the fabrications of an inventive but disturbed mind, lacking all psychological, historical, theological and pastoral credibility.' When Woods interviewed Martin, he found him 'a clever, charming engaging Irish rogue who evaded every effort to document the instances of possession he so graphically described.' When Peck's *People of the Lie* appeared, Woods said he was 'appalled' that a newly committed Christian 'of a vaguely evangelical stripe had accepted and endorsed Martin's fictional ravings [about exorcism] as accurate and instructive.'

With *People of the Lie*, the reviews, and the related interviews he gave, Peck created a different sort of stir than he had with *The Road*. In *The Road*, folks read the book and looked into themselves. With *People* they looked out at others. Peck's friend, the psychologist Dr James Guy, said *People of the Lie* has 'something in there to bother everybody, to bother therapists, theologians, and churchmen. When I read it I said, "Ah this one's not going to help him," but he's telling the truth about how he feels about this.' Peck's Harvard roommate Jake Severance called the book, 'quite a different piece of work, but that was to be expected. I was fascinated with the discussion of evil. I'm not at all sure that I agreed with all of it but there were some fascinating takes on just what evil is and [that] the friendly postman on your block might also be an evil person, that sort of thing. But I didn't go as far as some of my relatives who said [of *People of the Lie*], "My God, it's Halloween." They thought he'd gone around the bend. I didn't think so.' Peck was concerned about evil taking others around a bend that psychiatry had been unable to fathom.

Peck did not consider himself particularly radical. 'I never thought,' he said, 'that I would become a middle-of-the-road anything, much less a middle-of-the-road Christian. I am damned orthodox in practice, with one exception, and that is during the Nicene Creed I fall silent when they say, "resurrection of the body". He had noticed, too, he said, that many others do not say that part of the Creed and speculated there may be 'a sort of little mini-revolution going on.' Peck obviously did not consider celebrating his own 'rogue' eucharists exceptional.

In the early 1980s, through the urging of his nun friend, ES, he said, Peck took to daily meditation, not a large leap for someone who'd begun his young adult belief life with Zen Buddhism. His prayer life, he said, was 'ninety-nine point nine per cent spontaneous, my own dialogue with God about what I'm feeling. Sometimes when I'm worried in particular about the state of the world, or a bunch of people, I will often pray over and over again, the *Agnus Dei*, "Lord God, Lamb of God, you take away the sins of the world . . ."'

Once *People of the Lie* was circulating Peck, psychiatrist and Christian, was soon hearing from his readers. As with *The Road Less Travelled,* his admirers were not hesitant to simultaneously admire and play critic.

Peck's regular lunches with Martin had sealed their pact. The psychiatrist's adulation of the priest-exorcist fairly drips off the *Glimpses of the Devil* pages. Peck was not, however, blind to Martin's failings. 'He was a bald-faced liar, and I believe that what Robert Kaiser wrote [see *Clerical Error: a True Story*, by Robert Blair Kaiser, 2002] was probably correct, and that Kaiser got him kicked out of the Jesuits for sexual activity. When I met Malachi he had this cover he was a plain clothes man for the Vatican, the Pope, to hold back the progress of Vatican II. It was all a bunch of bullshit. Malachi also had a good side and it, too, was of heroic proportions. As I say in the book [*Glimpses of the Devil*], that other than his identity, he never lied about anything important. I asked him at our first luncheon, "What is the effect upon an exorcist of doing an exorcism?" and he just looked at me and said, "It will give you greater authority and make you more lonely." And, of course, it was exactly correct. After I was baptised, Malachi Martin started sending me cases to evaluate for "possession" (by the Devil), and I got involved in the first exorcism, which was a profound spiritual experience and a profound teaching experience.'

In spite of Peck's claim to have been 'cured' in therapy of his attraction to and subsequent willing dependency on likeable father figures, it seems unlikely this was actually so. In San Francisco, even after he had been in therapy, resident Peck idolised the strong men on the Letterman faculty. His gushing comments on at least two military commanders he served under go far beyond mere admiration. He was in awe of his friend Tim Childs, to a degree that Mrs Childs found, if not unsettling, at least misplaced and somewhat naive. He met the Rev. Martin and came under his baleful influence. The priest was a fabulist. In person, he was an entertaining cross between a chameleon and a faun, a subspecies of Irish priests known for 'a charming variety . . . of larning and piety'. During the sessions of the Second Vatican Council (1962–1965) in Rome, the Jesuit not only cuckolded the *Time* magazine correspondent Robert Blair Kaiser by leaping into Kaiser's half of the marital bed during the writer's absence, but slept in the man's nightshirt and wrote a fallacious account of Vatican II on his unknowing host's Olivetti typewriter. Martin ruined the reputation of at least one fellow Jesuit by planting false stories about him and wrecked the marriage of at least one Irish couple with his cuckolding ways, 'the venal, vicious, unsinkable Malachi outwitting everyone – Kaiser, his Jesuit superiors, his publishers, other men's wives, while working his wiles on visiting French girls.' (The quote is from this writer's review of Kaiser's book.)

Glimpses of the Devil included Peck's strange and stark denial that Malachi Martin was a father figure to him. (See Appendix: *Peck and Jones*, page 281.) When Martin was old, Peck ignored his early mentor. He did much the same, apparently, with his own father. Peck's apparent disinterest in his own parent caused a serious rift between Scott and his brother David. David, said his son, nephew David, 'loathed Scott for many things [including] how unwilling [he was] to shoulder equal responsibility as their father was sick and dying, and just left my father to face the death and estate on his own, which certainly left my father saying Scotty's view was not much more than, "All I want is my half when it's over and you've worked it out."' Judge Peck died in 1990. Added nephew David, it was 'a really shitty and spoiled thing to leave someone with; but which I guess reflected the cocktail of real and imaginary anger and resentment and arrogance that the cultural extremes of early failure and later success would produce. It hurt my father deeply and fuelled the resentments and wildly complex issues that existed between the two brothers.' (Judge Peck's estate was just under 1.5 million dollars.) Now it was father figure Malachi Martin who, Scott Peck admitted, he neglected. 'A good decade after our work together . . . Malachi asked me to dinner . . . Malachi somehow embittered and slightly over the hill. This was during a lengthy period in which I had allowed myself to become inhumanely busy, and I made no effort whatsoever to reach out to him. I suppose one reason I dedicate *Glimpses of the Devil* to Malachi is [as] an act of contrition.'

A publicly guilt-stricken Peck was a rare sighting.

What Peck believed in was his right to explore whether indeed there was such a thing as evil. However, and despite his professional declarations and listings at the close of *Glimpses of the Devil* concerning what an exorcism is or ought to be, there's an air of ambivalence that creeps in. Defensive of what he'd learned, he seemed sorry he'd ever become involved.

Indeed, however intriguing the topic – and at his best in *People of the Lie* and *Glimpses of the Devil* Peck is pushing people to at least consider his arguments – there is little agreement about 'possession'. Peck's Anglican nun friend, ES, who was one of the team for the first exorcism – though she didn't stay until the end – said she had 'an open mind' on possession. Reviewers came to both books to praise or scoff, according to beliefs they already held, though in one case a Peck interviewer admitted the author had convinced him. 'The most exciting thing about my participation in these two exorcisms,' Peck said in an interview with *The Wittenburg Door*, 'was not meeting the Devil, instead it was sensing the palpable presence of God. That presence of God was not an accident because in both cases there were teams of people (seven in one and nine in another) that came to work with the patient. When you get seven people in a room at considerable personal sacrifice and risk who have come in love for the purpose of healing, it's not an accident that God is in the room.'

In its 'evil' and 'devil' interview with Peck, *The Door* reversed the type and had white type on a black page, with Peck's photograph altered to include horns and a pointed beard. *The Door* interviewer, W. 'Bill' McNabb, said it was on the strength of Peck's persuasiveness that he, previously open-minded on the topic, came to believe possession was possible.

In a comment that perhaps explains the ambivalence at the close of *Glimpses of the Devil,* Peck told McNabb that 'demon possession should really be called partial or imperfect possession because clearly in these two patients there was a struggle going on between the demonic and the soul. One of my theories is that good people are more prone to possession than bad people precisely because Satan, in accord with traditional Christian theology, is on the run and is trying to put out fires, so he goes where the action is. Possession is not an accident. You don't go walking down the street one day and all of a sudden a demon jumps out at you from behind a bush and penetrates you. Both patients I saw had very, very difficult childhoods. They were terribly lonely in one way or another, both of them repeatedly sold out to unreality. Their possession was a gradual phenomenon for which the individual has a considerable amount of responsibility.' [Or, other psychiatrists might suggest, in their bid to escape their sad realities, the patients were stricken with multiple personality disorders (MPDs), and not possession at all.]

As for a definition of evil, Peck told McNabb the best he'd heard 'came from my son when he was eight years old. I asked him what evil was and he said, "That's easy, Daddy, evil is 'live' spelled backwards."'

Not long after Peck's second exorcism, a man in Buffalo – perhaps taking his clue from Peck's brief assertions on evil in his first book – telephoned him to consult about his wife. The wife, he said, was a 'very sane and sober church-going, church-involved Presbyterian', who left that for a New Age church, and a year beyond that 'suddenly went crazy and had been hospitalised for three years. And nothing was working.' Peck told him 'one of the things that might have to be considered is the possibility that your wife is possessed.' And he said, 'Why do you think I'm calling you?' Peck, who had just finished the second exorcism, was exhausted and told the man he'd get back to him. Then, in tears, Peck called ES, he said, and complained, 'You know, God could have waited at least a week, couldn't He have? Just a week.' And she said, 'I have no doubt this timing is not accidental, but it does not mean God is calling you to do another exorcism. It is quite possible that what God is calling you to do is say no to another exorcism.' Peck did see the woman, eventually, in the hospital. 'The insurance was running out,' Peck said, consequently 'the issue about who was going to do any exorcism was taken out of my hands. During that time ES said, "You know, God never calls anyone to do something that doesn't feel right in his heart."' Peck commented, 'I think that's true even for Jesus. I am not into philosopher [Joseph] Campbell's "follow your bliss". I don't think Jesus went to the cross following his bliss. He went sweating blood.'

Peck's new income source permitted him to close his psychiatric practice to write full-time. He was not the first physician to permanently close his prescription pad in favour of writing lengthier pieces; A.J. Cronin and W. Somerset Maugham are but two. He never looked back at medicine or psychiatry except for cameo moments to drop into his storytelling, or as bona fides to enable him to argue his case. Quite simply, writing was his new day job.

In academic circles, Peck was pummelled for his 'highly narcissistic views of his contribution to psychiatry and religion – he often erroneously implied he was the first Christian psychiatrist,' said Dr Hendrika Vande Kempe, a psychotherapist in private practice in Virginia. She is a former member of the Fuller Theological Seminary faculty, and also a past president and Fellow of the Psychology of Religion and History of Psychology divisions of the American Psychological Association. Religion and psychology were once in harness, said Vande Kempe, in a chapter, 'Historical Perspectives: Religion and Clinical Psychology in America', in *Religion and the Clinical Practice of Psychology* (1995). She wrote that 'psychologists trained in the dominant historical tradition of the twentieth century may be startled to learn that psychology and religion have historically been intertwined . . . when the Latin term *psychologia* was first used around 1524 it referred to one of the subdivisions of pneumatology, the science of spiritual beings and substances. The term *anthropologia* [was coined later in the sixteenth century] for the science of persons, which was divided into *psychologia*, the doctrine of the human mind, and *somatologia*, the doctrine of the human body.'

Vande Kempe argues her case down to recent times. Leaning back in his wicker chair in the sunroom of his New Preston home, Peck, the consummate realist regarding his range of knowledge, said he made no claims to an extensive understanding of the existing and wide-ranging scholarship around psychology and religion that Vande Kempe ably marshalled. He was satisfied with reviewers' statements that positioned him as the interface between the two fields – psychiatry and religion – for the non-scholar. In effect, Peck leapfrogged over the back of the academic discussion to land on his feet in front of the popular audience. But then, had he done any less with his thesis at Harvard for an audience of three – his invigilators?

Stephen G. Post was actually reviewing a later Peck book, *Denial of the Soul,* for *The World and I* when he penned words that apply to almost everything Peck wrote. Post was arguing the need was not for more professional books on medical ethics (or evil), but books 'for the common man or woman. The issues have become so pressing and timely that we need more informed popular works from leading public intellectuals.' And that was the sort of writer Peck had transformed himself into. The readers were pleased he had. Peck's nephew, David, an ordained priest, returned to the eighteenth-century theologian Jonathan Edwards as key to getting Peck in historical perspective: Edwards is 'essential, I think, in seeing Scotty for the various contributions he made as theologian, psychiatrist, political theorist. Like the poet Auden, whose reputation is undermined by his fame, I think Scotty's could be undermined by his.' What Peck carried through his works – and his better interviews – was the same sort of exclamation of surprise at what God could get up to that resonates through Edwards' own writings. Peck's comment, that what he felt most during his exorcist experience was not the presence of Satan but the presence of God in the people in the team conducting the exorcism, falls easily into this category.

A troubled student wrote to say, at great length in tiny handwriting, that he thanked Peck for the book but was 'deeply troubled for it exacerbated my belief that something evil was influencing the course of my life.' A Texan reader said, 'I join with others in thanking you for naming "evil" a "religious" concept in the midst of a scientific profession. Almost a heresy, perhaps, for you! But as a person who is both a Christian and a believer in psychotherapy, I believe that this naming is crucial to a correct diagnosis and treatment.' A man with an apparent background in the Scriptures chided Peck 'in a book that deals insightfully and compassionately with the quality of evil and the nature of the lies that precipitate evil, a repetition of the *lie* that has caused more malevolence and suffering than any other . . . the allegation that "fat cat" Pharisees murdered Jesus.' The writer argues an historical context defence of the Pharisees and asks Peck, 'Was your intent evil? I more than doubt it . . . it suggests a lack of knowledge.'

In a typed, three-page single-spaced letter, another American wrote: '*People of the Lie* is interesting but also disturbing. It recognises evil because of your examples of bad parents and others. It is easier to see your evils in others than in yourself. But I thought you could have been a lot more effective if you had not labelled the parents as evil. If one of your readers has done or said some of the bad things you gave as examples, the reader, instead of seeing evil, will be tempted to get angry and close the book. But on the other hand, if you gave the parents the benefit of the doubt about whether their ruling loves were good or evil, but called [their] actions destructive and harmful, you would be less likely to lose your reader. In fact, this is what the Lord meant when He told us not to judge. We are not to judge the person but the words and acts. We can and should say, "This act is evil and it will hurt you and hurt others." But once we say, "You are evil," we totally antagonise that person. Men like Stalin and Hitler were pretty obviously evil and we can say, "if this man is what he appears to be, he is evil." Most people are not that easy to judge, although you would be in a better position than most.'

Peck wasn't done with another variation on the evil theme, the topic of group evil in any 'corporate' or group. He simply ran out of time. His readers were with him, however, in identifying the issue as germane. A Londoner, commenting on the upheavals that saw the disappearance of Fleet Street as the centre of Britain's working press, wrote, 'I saw what happened to individuals in a group under pressure, and how easy it is to make that one first step of disowning responsibility for one's actions. It is so easy to talk oneself into doing something to save one's skin. So easy to convince yourself there is nothing wrong in this. So easy to betray everything you thought you believed in until your position is threatened. I can say from experience that the only thing that prevented me from going against everything I was taught, the only thing that gave me the strength and support not to put myself first, was my Christian faith.' The Londoner continued, 'You give many reasons for group evil, but I do believe you missed out the most important of them all: self-knowledge. If we even have an idea of what we are capable, we are then on our guard when faced with certain situations. But if we truly believe, or talk ourselves into believing, that we are "good" people who aren't capable of those terrible deeds we read about – and most people feel this way – then when we are in a similar situation we will act similarly. We still may, but at least we will know we are wrong while we are doing it, we will at least have a conscience, and hopefully will be stronger the next time.'

The most compelling of the many letters was from a retired US Marine Corps pilot. He had napalmed My Lai, on orders, at the time of the massacre, and in a harrowingly emotional letter convincingly traced My Lai's evil effects into the broader reaches of the military and society. 'My wingman and I refused to be decorated for attacking the village for what then appeared to be no reason. My observation [is] there is more evil in this affair than has ever been imagined.' The writer believed that with the air attack, 'I think we covered up a massacre by killing the few survivors, but I cannot be certain. When I found out I had attacked and destroyed My Lai under dubious circumstances, I did report it a number of times and was told to stay out of it. I'm the last person alive to see My Lai, and may have killed hundreds of people and nobody cares.'

Peck cared, almost violently so, about the presence of 'group evil' in the world, and the lack of interest in seeing it explored and analysed scientifically. At the end of his life, in a desperate effort to have his say on the topic, he wrote a rambling coda to *Glimpses of the Devil* that was meant to deal with group evil. It was too late, too unfocused, and mercifully never published. There's a reasonable chance, however, had Peck lived another decade in decent health, he might have returned to the topic of group evil with all guns blazing, much as he had in his book on euthanasia, *Denial of the Soul*. A book on group evil could have been a first-class contribution to a needed popular discussion too long delayed.

Simon and Schuster editor Fred Hills, who came to the firm as *People of the Lie* was in final proofs, summed up Peck's first two books this way: 'I don't think *The Road Less Travelled* was written as a self-help book. It evolved to the extent that people – many readers – found it was a life-changing experience for them. Nor was *People of the Lie* written as a self-help book. I mean it doesn't have sections on how to apply it to your own life, but ironically, that book has sold just about a million copies.' Money wasn't the root of all evil in *People of the Lie*, but as a book it did rather well generating it. Almost twenty years later, it had a renaissance in Japan, where, said Peck, it became a bestseller and brought him a further several hundred thousand dollars.

People of the Lie might have followed *The Road Less Travelled*, but it was not a natural extension of it. Peck's executive secretary, Gail Puterbaugh, manager of those aspects of the Peck enterprise he didn't reserve for himself, was his reader of raw first drafts. To her, and the argument has great merit, *The Road's* true sequel is *Denial of the Soul: Spiritual and Medical Perspectives on Euthanasia and Mortality*

(1997), Peck's penetrating condemnation of the euthanasia movement and defence of end-of-life palliative care. Author Phyllis
Theroux, who gave Peck his first ever review in the *Washington Post*,
sides with Puterbaugh. She said she tends to think of *Denial of the
Soul* as '*The Road Less Travelled* for grown-ups'.

Peck was correct about one thing, however. Evil is never passé.

CHAPTER 11

COMMUNITY BUILDING

In November 1981, borne along on the currents of *The Road Less Travelled*'s success, Peck arrived at the George Washington University in Washington, D.C. as an all-day visitor to someone else's group. His task was to facilitate a spiritual growth workshop. Peck declares it 'the day I had a miracle happen to me. I was leading my first workshop, at the end of which sixty people were hugging and yelling and screaming and saying it was the best hundred and twenty dollars they ever spent and the best thing they'd ever done in their lives. I knew I'd be invited to do further workshops, yet I knew I could never do a workshop that would approach the success of this one.'

Here was the new venture, the fresh experience that, inevitably, would lead to another book, in this case, *The Different Drum: Community Making and Peace*. There's nothing timid about Peck: *The Different Drum*, from life lessons and psychotherapeutic practice, embellished by his explorations into learning what builds community, is extrapolated into a discussion of practical steps towards world peace, written when the Cold War between the Soviet Union and the West offered an instant destruction scenario. The geo-political scene may have shifted, but the common sense insights in the book still remain relevant.

Peck's readers liked to write to him and the aftermath of *The Different Drum* was no exception. 'I feel I know you so well I was close to addressing you as Scotty,' one reader, from Wimbledon Chase, London, began a three-page, single-spaced letter. 'I am very grateful to you for *The Road Less Travelled* and *The Different Drum*, both of which have moved, enlightened and educated me.' The writer then encouraged Peck to meet up with her group.

As always in writing to Peck, the readers say a great deal about their times and their own reaction to those times. 'I'm an atheist, a

WASP and a forty-one-year-old child of the Flower Child generation and locale, the San Francisco Bay area,' wrote a man in Nevada. Nevada told how he'd written to a friend for the return of some books he'd loaned him. The friend was sufficiently miffed to package up more books than he'd borrowed and one of those was *The Different Drum*. Said Nevada, 'Its title and outward image are not what I would pick off the shelf. I have a prejudicial vision which says, upon seeing the outward aspect of your book, here is another la-la book by a mindless peacenik whose naiveté will just cause my blood to boil. [I] scanned the Table of Contents. That didn't do much to change my mind, but on seeing a chapter entitled "Human Nature", I decided to kick the tires. I have not been able to put it down. I consider myself to be far more spiritual than those who consider themselves religious.' The writer took issue with Peck's critique of Ayn Rand's *Atlas Shrugged*, but continued nonetheless: 'I find your ideas to be so full of wisdom in so many ways that you have my adrenalin pumping. Community is important to individuals. It is something that it is to the advantage of the individual to cultivate, but just like love, you can't box it and sell it, you can't coerce it, it must come freely from the resources of willing participants. You created something very special and powerful. You are making money off this book, I hope, but that is not the reason you wrote it.' Consequently, Nevada suggested, Peck had sold Ayn Rand short. 'I suggest that had you been commanded to write it whatever would have resulted would have come far short of the gift that you have made the world. Only because you had the ownership of your own desires and choices could this book have resulted.'

Peck's desires were played out in a complicated arena. There was certainly no way the writer in Nevada could have known the extent to which Peck, also a WASP, was not so much 'a child of the Flower Child generation and locale, the San Francisco Bay area', as an adult adoptee of the Flower Child generation converted to it – by what he saw and experienced in San Francisco. From Kimberley, South Africa in 1988 came the comment that *The Different Drum* was 'thought-provoking and inspiring reading with particular application, of course, to our country's great need for reconciliation at this critically important time.'

As Peck set about trying to analyse what had happened at George Washington University to produce community, he knew he was already demolishing some of psychiatry's shibboleths. For one thing, he said, in psychotherapy training conventional wisdom held that 'the biggest group you could work with was maybe twenty, max. And that was really too big, and the ideal was ten to twelve. And yet in that first day-long workshop, by the end of the day, sixty people were all in community.' Next, Peck decided he 'could never do a workshop this powerful unless there were rules, and unless they were repeatable.'

Whether people wanted it or not, scientific researcher Peck now deliberately developed every future *Road* workshop into a how-does-it-happen community-building laboratory. 'I gave the workshops the title, "*The Road Less Travelled* and The Way of the Cross" ['The Way of the Cross' refers to the crucifixion of Jesus Christ]. I gave them a short blurb,' Peck said, and informed the potential workshop attendees that in 'this highly experiential, and at times, painful workshop people might have personal experience of the Way of the Cross (Jesus' Passion).' The 'painful, powerful workshop' meant that Peck could now implement the 'confrontational' psychiatric practices he'd wanted a setting for since the abortive 'Institute' dreams in Georgia in 1981. Some people found the experience more painful than therapeutic, or too high a price to pay for 'community'.

In relatively short order he'd conducted sufficient workshops, he said, that, 'I'd discovered the laws.' He next decided the laws were teachable. 'There's a motto in surgery,' said Peck, '"watch one, do one, teach one." Watch an appendectomy, do an appendectomy, then teach the next guy how to do it.' The dilemma was, where would he go with the new community-building information and skills at hand? By mid-1983, during a *Road Less Travelled* workshop at an Episcopal retreat centre in North Carolina, help was at hand to answer the question. 'A well-to-do businessman came up and said to me, "Look, I believe in what you're doing. I would like to help out in some way."' Peck explained he was himself uncertain which way to go, and wanted help in making his decision. 'I think it ought ultimately to be my decision but I need community advice, and I would like it to be international, totally ecumenical, interracial and so forth. Would you,' he asked the businessman, 'organise, pay for, such a group to meet and advise me what I would do in my life?' The man said he would. In late winter 1983, twenty-eight people gathered in Danbury, Connecticut. 'It succeeded in building community,' said Peck, sounding a mite sorry for himself, 'but by that time there was really no energy left or no time left to focus on me or anything that I fashioned. So it did not succeed in that sense. I did ask certain key people for advice.' Even so, the community building was so successful, so powerful in tearful terms, its attendees became known as the 'People of the Kleenex', Peck said. 'This was during that period I began to think seriously of running for the presidency. The fellow who'd organised the meeting was one of those who wanted me to run.' Given that the United States at that moment had a B-movie star as president, the idea of a popular author-psychologist campaigning for the office was not extreme.

Fifteen months prior to this, during the period Peck was still researching why the university workshop had produced community, the Rev. Stephen Bauman (now senior minister at New York's Christ Church on Park Avenue, where Peck's parents had attended services) was in his first church appointment, in Connecticut. He read *The Road Less Travelled* and 'on a lark,' he said, 'I picked up the Yellow Pages and in those days "M. Scott Peck, MD" was still listed. I thought, what the heck, I'll give a ring, thinking I'd get his secretary. He didn't have one, and he answered the phone. I tumbled out something like, "I sure liked your book . . ."' A week later, at Peck's invitation, Baumann went to see him and for the next eighteen months, Bauman said, 'We developed a short, therapeutic relationship. Scotty was clearly in a state of transitioning. By the end of our [therapeutic] period his life was radically changing course. The phenomenal success of his book was in the air catapulting him into very prominent places. At the time we were formally ending our relationship, in the psychotherapeutic sense, he mentioned to me a friend had volunteered to pay for assembling folks for a several-day retreat to consider issues of community. He asked if I was interested.' The Danbury conference, said Bauman, 'was the beginning of the rest of our friendship.' There were several more gatherings of theologians, businessmen, doctors, therapists and others from around the country in various locales, one of the more significant ones organisationally was at an Episcopal retreat house in Valle Crucis, North Carolina, in 1984. Those attendees became known as 'the People of the Balloons'. By that time, an organisational outline was taking shape in Peck's mind. But he still had caveats about getting too close to the potential throng.

His *Road Less Travelled* journeys and workshops had produced a strong reaction against those he described as 'wanting to touch the robe' – the groupies, and those who craved a guru. Janice Barfield, an Atlanta-based flight attendant for Delta Airlines, first saw Peck at a hospital workshop, and witnessed the tendency of some to want to 'touch the robe'. Barfield, who had read *The Road*, went with a friend to hear Peck at St Joseph's Hospital in Atlanta. The lecture was part of a three-day workshop, 'he was the facilitator and I was completely blown away. It was very profound for me, and life-changing – I had never experienced communication with a group to that degree. He was a wonderful facilitator because he listened so well. I was struck by so many things. He appeared to be a little nervous. He would say some outlandish things that I had trouble believing, you know, then he would just kind of zap me with something so profound. He was a very, very deep and very spiritual person. And because I myself am a spiritual person, I was very drawn to that part of him. It was easier for me to understand the spiritual part than a lot of the intellectual stuff he would say. One thing I was struck with in the workshop,' she said, 'was there were a lot of people – and I began to see this over the three days – that sort of had Scotty on a pedestal, their guru. I mean it's unbelievable. One of the things I liked about him was he said, "I'm not your saviour." I appreciated the fact of his honesty and candour in saying that I'm not going to be your salvation here.' I liked that because it was important to me not to follow a man. I did not want a saviour, I already had a Saviour. I didn't want a guru. I wanted somebody that would facilitate and lead. I was even more drawn to the work because I realised that the work he was talking about was a lot bigger than him.' Journalist Cindy Lollar, who'd attended a North Carolina workshop in order to interview Peck, also immediately had seen the problem for Peck. 'There was a lot of disciples, a lot of that weirdness of [people] kind of falling all over themselves [to get close to him]. There were a lot of young women about who hung around him.' (She also said, when interviewed, 'I hope you haven't found out he was sleeping with all his young acolytes. I hope he wasn't one of those who was a really good man who couldn't keep his pants zipped up.')

During the Atlanta workshop Barfield attended, Peck told the group that because of all the letters he'd been receiving, he and his staff were talking about forming some kind of foundation. Continued Barfield, 'And then he said, "If you're into prayer or meditation, I would appreciate your prayers or meditation." That's all he said, but I was hooked. I felt a great sense of I don't know what. So I wrote him a letter after this and he was kind enough to

write back personally. That was in the spring of '83, and he was
supposed to come back to the same place next year, but was very ill.
I got his number and called his wife, Lily, and told her that I would
keep him in my prayers. He did come back to St Joseph's in the first
part of '84 for another lecture, and of course I went up to see him.
He had still not formed FCE.' They later talked on the telephone
and Peck invited Barfield to Memphis. 'On my part,' she said, 'I was
more convinced than ever this was a calling for me, but I didn't
know to what.' She went to Memphis, Tennessee.

That assembly in the Peabody Hotel in 1984 was the group that
formally created the Foundation for Community Encouragement
(FCE) with offices in Knoxville, Tennessee, where its first president,
Patricia White, lived. (As hotels go, the Peabody is unique in one
respect. Daily, at 11 a.m., four ducks and a drake, accompanied by
the hotel's Official Duck Master, are escorted from the birds' rooftop
Duck Palace to an elevator which descends to the hotel lobby. The
ducks walk across a red carpet to frolic and feed in a hotel fountain
pond until 5 p.m. at which time they are escorted back to their
rooftop pad.)

Eleven people attended the Peabody Hotel meeting, a cross
section of society, from churchwomen to a Dallas lawyer to a
Catholic priest. It was interracial and interreligious, and the Dallas,
Texas lawyer, Vester Hughes, suggested the name, the Foundation
for Community Encouragement. For Peck, these gatherings leading
up to FCE's founding were a new world of open communication in
several ways. One was, he said, 'Until I started FCE, I generally
enjoyed communicating with black Americans more than I did with
whites.' Though Peck did not see it in these terms, he appeared
unduly prejudiced against whites in general as part of his reaction
against his class in particular. The fact was that except in the
military, Peck rarely dealt socially with whites outside his class until
after *The Road Less Travelled* put him on the road.

He could say he had to first 'penetrate' the African–American
façade, but, 'once that was broken they were remarkably honest.'
However, the community-building workshops enabled Peck to
penetrate white façades with pretty much the same result. As for the
FCE undertaking itself, 'I'd thought long and hard about what I
might invest in with philanthropic money that would have the
biggest payoff. By the time we started the foundation,' he said, 'I had
no question about that.' (Lily Peck once quipped that if the Pecks

were ever to create a second foundation, it ought to be for the preservation of WASP culture because Scott was so anti-WASP.)

In 1999, Peck said, 'Lily and I started the Foundation for Community Encouragement with a very large grant, and this is a very big piece of our lives. It was founded in 1984 and closed its office doors in 2002. We spent probably close to three million dollars that we donated, we were its largest donors but we got several other large donors, too. I think it was the best money we ever spent. We also donated an enormous amount of our time. It closed not quite knowing whether it had been a tremendous success or a failure.' FCE's mission statement is still on the foundation's website. It states:

The Foundation for Community Encouragement (FCE) empowers people, in a fragmented world, to discover new ways of being together. Living, learning, and teaching the principles of community, we serve as a catalyst for individuals, groups and organisations to:

- communicate with authenticity
- deal with difficult issues
- bridge differences with integrity
- relate with love and respect.

'FCE's approach encourages tolerance of ambiguity, the experience of discovery, and the tension between holding on and letting go. As we empower others so we are empowered by a Spirit beyond ourselves.'

Omar Kahn, introduced earlier, son of a Pakistan diplomat, had come within Peck's orbit when he and his wife, Leslie, were establishing their consultancy business in Pakistan and Sri Lanka. When Kahn read *The Different Drum*, he said, 'It occurred to me the community building described by Scotty could be of great value in those communities. I wrote an honest letter about my life and where his work had been of value to me – in community-building terms, "emptying". First I got a form letter back, the usual "Dr Peck doesn't correspond with members of the public", a week later I got a letter from the man himself saying he thought my letter was excellent, and he enclosed a copy of one of his speeches and that FCE would be happy to cooperate. So I brought FCE out to Pakistan and Sri Lanka and got to know ES, Sister Ellen Stephen, very well.'

Kahn explained that what an FCE community-building session actually did was 'put people through an experiential interaction comprised of two or three days in which a group of previous strangers would learn to pass through the four stages. Initially they would be facilitated to take their own leadership and move towards the first phase, pseudo-community, when everybody pretends to love each other already, and on to a secondary phase called chaos. Chaos happens when people start actually expressing what they think and feel rather than what would be politically correct to say.' At this point, said Kahn, the attendees 'hopefully, eventually move into a third phase called "emptiness", where people stop posturing, stop trying to heal and convert and fix everybody other than themselves.' (The nun, ES, one of the first FCE facilitators, says of the 'emptying' process, 'It's a letting-go of one's biases and fears, prejudices and defences, intellectualisation and all that kind of junk. The strength of it is it brings people into reality, it makes it safe. Without doing much talking at all, facilitators have to know how to guide these people into being who they really are instead of who they think they ought to be.') Continued Kahn, after 'emptiness', 'if the group were fortunate and the context and conditions were right, if there was enough honour and heroism and guts, they may reach community. Meaning,' he said, 'whether "community" actually arrives is really the choice of all the people there, and how far they're willing to take it. It's hard tension.'

As far as Janice Barfield was concerned, the strength in FCE 'was this incredible commitment to spread community.' Barfield, who over the years facilitated some thirty to forty workshops, with groups ranging from ten to forty people, said it worked 'because the facilitators were committed to authenticity, to following the guidelines. Usually you have community when there's some sort of chaos that brings people together. They rise above their differences. But with the FCE process we found a way to build community without the crises. It was very very powerful and, I might even say, very holy.' One essential to success in Barfield's view was that the facilitators themselves – there were always two, and occasionally three – be in community. The facilitators could more or less take it for granted that the attendees had read *The Road Less Travelled, People of the Lie* and *The Different Drum*. Consequently, one distraction at the workshops was Peck himself. 'People would fixate on him,' said Barfield. 'People would get past that if we stuck with it, but it could be a really sticky point sometimes – when even if he wasn't in the group, he was present.'

Most Americans are by nature a garrulous lot. The FCE stipulation that people attending the workshop not unnecessarily break the workshop's 'silence' – an element of FCE from Peck's Quaker experience – could lead to misunderstandings. Peck said attendees were informed they were to speak only when moved, and not speak when not moved. 'There was a Jewish-Christian-Muslim workshop in which the people could just not tolerate silence. We told them, "Listen, if you want to talk, raise your hand. But count to ten first." And some guy raises his hand and starts, "One, two, three, four . . ."' Worse than that, said Peck, and despite the advance notice, people would come to workshops 'and get from some "pseudo-community" to "chaos" to the beginnings of "emptiness", and then start complaining, "This isn't what I expected from this workshop at all. This is really painful. This is not, you know, the way a workshop should be."' Peck would ask if they'd read the description of the workshop before attending, and they'd say yes. So he'd ask if anyone had a copy, show it to the complainer, who'd usually remark, 'Well, I guess I didn't read it very carefully.'

Peck's posturing does not mean that people did not on occasion have a legitimate point or complaint to make. There are several letters in the Peck archives from attendees in America and Britain who complained of psychological or emotional harassment, or found the experience unsettling. One asked Peck if a community-building workshop could be 'evil'. Not everyone agreed with Peck, including other physicians. A doctor told a *Life* magazine interviewer the FCE was based on having to 'spill your guts out and have other people stomp on 'em. After you've emptied yourself you're ready to achieve a community state.' It was Peck's variation on the encounter session he'd suffered through when a Lieutenant Colonel.

FCE developed a flexible programme with two-, three- and four-day offerings. The two-day was a CBE, a community-building experience. The three-day, a CBW, a community-building workshop, how to take it home and use it; and the four-day had the added element of a group task to perform. Said Peck, 'Faced with a task – create a product, draft a proposal or whatnot – the group would fall apart.' That was the point, for out of that second wave of chaos could come what every organisation and community strives for: the integration of task and process, 'an experience of community so complete it's like watching a ballet. Everyone knows what the task is, and, fluid yet coordinated, everyone knows what needs to be done at any given moment and does it.' Peck had seen it happen, sometimes unexpectedly, and not of his doing. His favourite example, he said, was a restaurant in New Orleans where waiters did not operate at assigned tables but did what was necessary when necessary, and the operation flowed ceaselessly and easily.

Christopher Peck was a FCE co-facilitator for four workshops in the late 1980s. He said, 'FCE is an interesting matter. After much experimentation, the founders discovered that if you gather up to forty or so people into a room for a weekend, under circumstances [like these], they form a community of deeply touched, intimate, and almost ecstatic individuals. It generally happens on the last day and does not endure past the close of the workshop. FCE as an organisation was as demented as any I know of, but they hit on a novelty and shared it as broadly as they could.' That Christopher, barely out of his teens, could be a facilitator for mature adults, is simply another indicator of how flexible the organisation was, and how much FCE was Scotty's child, just as Christopher was his son.

Christopher continued, 'The difficulty of maintaining a community, in my opinion, lies in the crucial importance of mending fences. To my knowledge, the issue was never explored, no thanks to the fact that Scotty did not respect, or even notice at times, the boundaries of others. Scotty was fond of the poem, "Mending Wall" by Robert Frost, but sided with the frost heaves and the hunters and, perhaps, Frost himself.' Frost heaves will gradually break down a wall and reduce it to rubble. Breaking people down to their essentials, as Peck understood those essentials, was a component of FCE.

In FCE workshops, Peck used dreams as one unifying technique. All religions have a tradition of dream interpretation, he said. 'Dreams are an international language, and the workshops used dreams as a sort of Jungian contribution to the process. Using this common "dream language",' and working through interpreters, he said, FCE was able to conduct workshops with people of other cultures and languages. These community-building workshops were not an end in themselves. Peck believed FCE was in 'the process of forging the outlines of a new planetary culture. All culture is a set of usually unwritten, sometimes unconscious integration of rules and norms. What we were doing with these rules was teaching a culture, parts of which come from all over. I didn't invent any of the rules. The only thing I ever did was synthesise them so that some of the rules come from the Quakers, some from Alcoholics Anonymous, some from Christian monasticism. AA's twelve steps are absolutely extraordinary,' said Peck, 'but people have to be in a crisis to get to them. The first step is the hardest – simply to admit that I'm an alcoholic and admit that I'm powerless. One of the beautiful things about being a community-building leader is that you can have the experience of being totally powerless about once every two or three workshops. The fascinating thing about the emotion of hope [during an FCE workshop] is often when leaders just totally give up any hope that the workshop will come into community, and almost instantly thereafter the group will come into community. I saw it done as a participant rather than a leader during an Episcopal church workshop. Fascinating. Anyway, we integrated these rules and they work for people of all cultures. Not that everybody wants to buy into them, but we've never seen anybody who couldn't participate and benefit because of their race or their sex or the religion or whatnot. We've also seen some very sophisticated people who just don't follow the rules.'

Even so, a cursory glance at 'Peck's Principles of Straight Talk (and Listening)' suggests the 'sophisticated' had not forsaken their common sense:

1. Remember straight talk is difficult, and you won't do it perfectly. Just do your best, and better next time. Learn from your mistakes.
2. Set aside time for communication.
3. Increase your consciousness. Prepare.
4. Be honest with yourself and others.
5. Judge yourself first. Be introspective.
6. Take time in the midst of communication. Be thoughtful. Use silence. Don't feel you have to respond instantly.
7. Empty yourself to listen. This takes effort.
8. Be willing to be hurt.
9. Be willing to hurt.
10. Emotional fragility is cause for 'excommunication'.

11. Consult with superiors before attempting straight talk with someone you suspect is fragile.
12. Be gentle as possible within the constraints of not being devious. Get to the point. Don't try to be subtle.
13. No killer statements.
14. Speak personally. Don't generalise or otherwise rely on 'the system' or authority.
15. Be specific. Document.
16. Don't play psychiatrist or analyse others' motives.
17. Speak when you are moved. Don't cop out.
18. Remember straight talk is difficult, and you won't do it perfectly. Just do your best, and better next time. Learn from your mistakes.

Sojourners magazine reviewer Conrad Hoover, discussing *People of the Lie*, in passing commented that Peck 'clearly employs and calls for an overly rigorous mentality.' Peck's 'straight talk' prescription certainly confirms that. Writer Gary Dorsey went to a 1986 FCE workshop to scoff and stayed to weep. His account suggested tears were an integral part of the community building, for he described a veritable weep-a-thon at which he finally burst into tears himself. On his first full day, a Thursday, he announced he was a journalist writing a profile of Peck and that the profile might not be favourable. 'I heard one of the staff members gasp. By the time I finished,' Dorsey wrote, 'several people were in tears. Peck cried too.' That afternoon, as 'stories slowly began to bubble out of people about horrible incidents in their lives . . . each personal revelation triggered an unexpected sob and another sad tale. Some people choked on their own tears; others wept quietly . . . As people cried, others rushed to hold then, hugging them around the shoulders or at their knees, or simply clasping their hands.' On Friday morning, a minister present offered his night-before dream for interpretation, but that afternoon, said Dorsey, 'it was more of the same, tears, and hugs and reconciliation.' Dorsey by this time was having his own problems. He felt the group had closed him out. 'I needed to be accepted,' he wrote. Late on Friday afternoon, as Peck 'started to close the workshop,' Dorsey 'spilled out a rambling monologue' until he reached a point at which he said the word 'healing'. 'I broke down,' stated Dorsey. 'The man beside me put his head on my shoulder and sobbed with me. The man next to me was crying . . .

when I lifted my head, people all around the room were crying. When I stood up, there was a line of people waiting to hug to me. Scott Peck was one of them. That night we all went out for a big meal and celebrated. "We are a soft and wounded organisation," Peck said.'

Whatever Scott Peck's many FCE achievements, there is little doubt that the FCE period was a shining period for Mrs Peck. 'I trained with Lily,' said Kazimierz Gozdz, who first attended an FCE workshop in 1987 and later became an FCE facilitator. 'I went out on my first community-building experience with her as my co-facilitator – a lovely woman.' In Lily Peck, Gozdz, as a trainee FCE facilitator and later a friend, found 'a kind of introversion that was appealing. She had a good sense of humour and a capacity to move beyond herself. Scotty [was] a kind of egomaniac. He [had] a personal power to him, spiritual, social. She was the opposite. She was a person you could feel you fit in with comfortably. On the matter of her status, she seemed to present herself as a peer all the time while he – by the power of his ideas and experience – was kind of at the commander level of professional respect. Lily was a human being you could relate with and wonder how she could tolerate all of this sense in him. There wasn't the same kind of power and politics to it with Lily. She showed that the ordinary person could gain mastery in a domain. For a person like me it built confidence that she cared, [and I was] able to approach her comfortably.'

Janice Barfield saw Lily as 'very sensitive to people. I met her in Memphis. Scotty is strident; Lily is softer, but she's really very authentic, a good searcher, and judge of character. Quite shy and wonderful. She was very kind to me and consequently [as] I knew I was heart-to-heart with Scotty it was really important to me to be friends with her, too, because I'm a very faithful and honest person and didn't want to be misunderstood in any way. Lily and I did become very good friends. She has a real playful side to her, and she is incredibly patient and very, very kind.' Omar Kahn and his wife, Leslie, met Mrs Peck for the first time at the Peck home in New Preston. Lily, he said, 'was clearly a very private person. We never found her to be touchy. I could also tell that she sometimes would try to be helpful to make sure Scotty had heard something we said or that we had gotten enough air time for some of the things we wanted to talk about other than what he had in mind. And I could see that she perhaps played that role at other times in her life.'

Peck wrote this about Lily under one of his poems ('The Dambuilder', 1967): 'Both she and I are avid conservationists, but to me this sometimes gets rigidly worked out in a desire to keep everything the same, while Lily is more playful than I. It was at a moment when her playfulness annoyed, coming as it did during the often stressful earlier years of our now forty-year marriage.'

FCE developed an international presence and Kahn described the situation in Asia when he introduced FCE techniques. 'In Western culture,' he said, 'if people are silent for too long, somebody jumps in. In Asia people are very comfortable being silent, just happy to sit there and look around at each other – much to the discomfort of some of the facilitators.' Kahn said the facilitators in Asia learned to draw out the attendees and persuade them to be a little more forth-coming, to let them know their cultural reserve might not be appropriate in a context where they have come to be known, not hidden. Kahn said that in the decade and more following its establish-ment, the FCE process was successful in many contexts including, by working through interpreters, in the former Soviet Union.

For him, one marker of a major domestic success in the United States, he said, was when it melded a group of physicians in a large Texas medical practice into community. When the doctors initially asked Peck if he understood how difficult it was to get seventeen physicians together for two days, let alone three, all Peck replied was, 'Yup.' Under Peck's leadership, it happened. The group built in ways to sustain the community they achieved, but later, said Peck, 'fat and lazy', they let the whole thing disintegrate until they finally fell 'out of community'. The physician who felt 'stomped' on had a different perspective. That perhaps community-building was a temporary achievement.

It was apparent when Peck talked about the Foundation for Community Encouragement that his discovery of his community-building 'laws', and its consequences, gave him more satisfaction than practically any other non-writing undertaking in his life. He told a British journalist that FCE was 'the cutting edge of his life'. It also provided him with his greatest experience of control. He'd grown up as an introspective loner who was rarely one of the group. His position as a popular leader in elementary school had been usurped by a bigger boy, and his pattern in high school and college was to flee the institution for another at the halfway mark, behaviour scarcely conducive to forming intimate, lifelong friendships among peers. (The exception was with Tim Childs, his lifelong friend from Exeter.) Some men find lifetime friends during their military service.

Later, in Okinawa, medical director Peck did create a strong 'team', and in Washington, D.C., as a lieutenant-colonel sent to evaluate an encounter session, he was 'in community' after he'd cried, pummelled a pillow, and was comforted by people who days earlier had been strangers. But there were no lasting Army buddies down the years, just a few annual Christmas cards at first that gradually petered out. Professionally, as a psychiatrist in New Preston, Peck was a solo operator who went from one solitary and isolating career, psychotherapy, to another, writer. However much he might have yearned for the opposite, there is little doubt the lone operative role temperamentally suited Peck. Short, controlled bursts of 'community' were enough. In FCE workshops he would willingly yield leadership and control, he said, in order to get something rolling, so he could withdraw and watch. This discovery of what was possible with the group opened up a new period for Peck, he had to reveal himself more clearly.

Peck was living a hectic life that included very little presence for his children: 'Mary Ann Schmidt, who worked for me in the position Gail Puterbaugh today holds, was leaving my employ,' he said. 'We had a kind of mutual session of what do we want to say to each other. One thing she said was, "You know what, Scotty, you never miss an opportunity. You never let an opportunity go by." Well, I wasn't seeing stopping to play with my children as an opportunity. I was seeing all these invitations as an opportunity, and not doing the ordinary stuff. For all of my life I've been very much an agenda person.' Even the family as community was not a priority for him.

There is no written history of FCE. Peck said he gave some thought to one, but held back. 'I've been terribly hurtful to a lot of people. One of the things I got in touch with after years of helping to manage FCE was the incredible amount of what I call "organisational pain". People you thought were absolutely wonderful and right for the job turned out to be just the wrong person – the pain they caused. To write a history it would have no colour unless I said who and what the brouhahas were about and that would be too personal.' Were there a history, Community Building in Britain (CBiB) would warrant its own chapter. He said, 'The people in Britain wanted us to establish a branch of FCE in Britain,' but, he said, he hesitated to develop an entity that might be known 'as FCUK.')

CBiB came about when a group of people in Britain contacted FCE to see if Peck would establish a British offshoot. 'We [at FCE] were having enough trouble communicating with ourselves,' said Peck, 'communicating with people running a group over there would have been a stupid idea. What we offered to do was nurture them insofar as we could to develop their own organisation. Which they did. These were all people who had been burned by organisations, terrified of organisations, and we tried to hold their hand as they organised. They were a very different kind of organisation than FCE, and somewhat better. About three times a year FCE put out a newsletter, so bland and corporate I used to scream and yell. I couldn't read it. Whereas CBiB put out a rather exciting newsletter about ten times a year.' By coincidence and good fortune, Peck's friend, ES, the Anglican nun, was headed to England, as, also on business, was William Thatcher, a future FCE president. The two agreed to meet with the British inquirers. They did, at St James' Church in Piccadilly, a location famous historically for its society weddings. Once CBiB was functioning, Sister Ellen Stephen several times conducted workshops for the organisation.

'FCE has been a painful institutional mentor for me,' said Peck. 'When we started I thought that the Church would be a natural client for our services – the Church talks about "community" and "early Christian community" and whatnot. As far as I can ascertain there's no real community in any of the local churches I've checked out. As a matter of fact, at one church that had maybe three hundred members, I volunteered for free to lead a community-building workshop for the church as long as ten people signed up. The minister, his wife, and one parishioner signed. A lot of people who came to FCE couldn't bear to go back to their churches because they were so sterile by comparison with community. FCE was deliberately non-sectarian. It was not specifically a Christian organisation, though it was definitely a spiritual organisation with a strange mission statement, the last line of which is, "In our efforts to encourage others, we rely upon the Spirit both within and beyond ourselves."'

He told *The Door* magazine editors, 'I am a nut about community, and what is missing in the Church for me is any realness between people. So many churches want pseudo-community and are not willing to do the work to have real community. They don't want authenticity and reality. They want to hear a sermon that is going to make them feel better, but they don't want to get real with each other and hear each other's pain and talk about that kind of thing. They don't want to talk about the real stuff of life. That is very sad. Jesus said, "I am come that they may have life and have it more abundantly." Many churches I go to are not very lively places. You get the feeling that, beneath the smiles and the singing and clapping, there is no real life underneath.'

He was a Christian who wrote an excoriating critique of Christian churches in *The Different Drum.* Gay Pilgrim, an associate tutor at Woodbrooke Quaker Study Centre, Birmingham, commented in a review that 'the importance of the Church as a body of people striving to live faithfully and drawing support from one another is nowhere acknowledged by Peck.' She was correct. Peck had no extended experience of belonging to a church community, he had never committed himself to one long enough to either know the people in it or help build it.

'The places we generally did business – with the exception of the churches – was wherever there was a crisis,' he said. 'We'd do it for town leaders in towns facing poverty. We did an increasing amount of work with businesses. The reason we could get away with doing this highly spiritual work in business is, somebody once said, "Religion has to do with answers, spirituality with questions."' One business to embrace FCE was a Florida car dealership, one of the country's largest, 'and our first fairly significant corporate client. They underwent a significant shift – they decided not to bargain any more.' Following the workshop, Peck said, the dealership 'lost probably close to half its salesmen who couldn't imagine selling without bargaining. But because of the morale at the company, they had a line twenty blocks long of people wanting to be salespeople there.'

During an interview with *Aurora* magazine, Peck said that at FCE he had tried to establish 'a scientific department' to delve more thoroughly into FCE's work and its results. 'To my amazement,' he said, 'I realised that about half the board didn't know what research was. Although they were college graduates they had never had to take anything which would really teach them what scientific research was.' The only 'solid piece of research' on FCE, Peck said, was a PhD dissertation prepared for the Palo Alto-based Institute for Transpersonal Psychology. The thesis, he said, compared the responses of people who had attended a three-day FCE workshop to

dozens who had attended a Joanna Macy 'Despair and Empower-
ment' workshop of the same duration. Macy, who describes herself
as an eco-philosopher and authority on Buddhism, was one more
among many in the 'self-help' and motivational pantheon.
Commented Peck, 'What struck me was that one hundred per cent
of the control group, the Joanna Macy workshop participants, said
that they had experienced a strong sense of community at the
workshop, whereas only seventy per cent of FCE attendees did.
What makes it worthwhile, however,' said Peck, 'is that every one of
the FCE respondents reported that the workshop had increased
their appreciation of interpersonal differences. And not one of the
Macy participants.'

Year-in, year-out, Peck was now on the road more than 200 days
a year. It was an enormous strain on a man frequently plagued by ill
health. Earlier in the decade, between the 'People of the Kleenex'
gathering and the meeting in the Peabody Hotel, he was seriously ill.
On 6 March 1984 he was admitted to New Milford, Connecticut
hospital with life-threatening pneumonia. He spent seventeen days
there, most of them in intensive care, as his doctors battled the three
different organisms that had settled in his lungs. Confined to bed,
Peck found himself obsessing about his possible presidential run,
until he was visited by a Baltimorean, Fred Clifton, a supportive
attendee at pre-FCE gatherings. 'Fred was the head of a sort-of
Hindu cult in Baltimore. He visited me and told me I didn't need to
make a decision about the presidency yet, and it kind of lifted a
great burden from me. A couple of months later I learned he had
cancer of the lung. He'd been a coal miner when young. I visited
him as he had visited me – the day he learned he had metastasis
from his lung to his thigh. He died, I think in November, with the
metastasis to the brain. If you have to die it's probably the single
most pleasant way. People that have it just gradually drift into a nice
coma. He was a remarkable man. A wise man, a holy man, truly. A
very good consultant, therapist. His bi-racial organisation probably
had a hundred families, about fifty-fifty white and black. The trouble
was they were extremely dependent on him.' Peck made a special
note of that as a lesson he kept before him when people tried to
mould Peck into their personal leader.

As FCE prospered it also faltered. No longer involved in its day-to-
day affairs, and no longer facilitating workshops himself, Peck
watched with keen interest. 'As the organisation grew more sophis-

ticated,' he said, 'we had a lot of trouble with the leaders. There were some who didn't want to learn new things, some who didn't want to do organisational work, some who didn't want any teaching and just wanted to build community, some who wanted to use the work for their own practice, some who regarded their contributions to FCE as their own intellectual property.' He'd heard, he said in the late 1990s, that 'the new leader corps is much more organisationally competent than the original one. But the original one came into an organisation that didn't know how to be an organisation yet. You know, if you'd asked me when I started FCE what Strategic Planning was, I'd have said it was something the Air Force did over Cambodia.'

By the time Scott and Lily were the FCE's elders, still with strong feelings of the need to keep the foundation alive, Peck was finding the fund-raising wearing. 'I got tired of it. I'd started to deteriorate physically, I could feel it. As a matter of fact, it started, I would say, about the time my libido dramatically diminished. I read a murder mystery. One of the characters was dying, and it was a description of how I was feeling. That was in [the early 1990s] when I could still do a full day's work. The energy was flowing out of me. My dreams for FCE, other than that it survive somehow, has to do with a new planetary culture.' In 1999 he said, 'Lily and I, we're retired from the board, which is very nice. We can give advice, but we don't have to take responsibility.' FCE closed its office doors with 'the wake at Wake Forest', an honouring ceremony at Wake Forest University. Scott and Lily did not attend. Janice Barfield was present. 'I don't think FCE died because [something] went wrong,' she said, 'I think it was time for it to die. It was a process, just like anything else. I remember Scotty from the very beginning saying this is not going to last forever. But it lasts a lifetime for people who went through it,' she added, 'and there are thousands of them. It was phenomenal for me personally, very significant in my spiritual and intellectual life. I learned to build community with myself. I think I listen better. I'm really aware of how much I didn't listen, and I thought I was a good listener. I learned to reflect more, learned to love silence more.' The 'wake at Wake Forest' recalled the names of those who'd been in the FCE. 'It was very sad, very precious,' Barfield said, 'and I think reconciliations were made there.' What remained, apart from the network of facilitators, and a movement one person described as a 'viral gene' in the field of creating community, was Community Building in Britain (CBiB); Mouvement vers l'esprit communautaire,

Quebec, Canada; Kahn's adaptations for Asia; and interested though not always flourishing small groups in Denmark, the Netherlands, Spain and Taiwan.

In retrospect, said the Rev. Baumann, 'Community building is a very powerful human dynamic and Scotty had put his finger on a very powerful process. It was not completely original, it's a collection of learning he gleaned along the way.' Bauman understood Peck's skill, perhaps genius, for packaging the process 'so it worked. It doesn't work universally and there are certain constraints on it. Another strength: there were some really interesting, creative people attracted to it. It was a genuine learning community.' A decade and more later, Bauman believes FCE's methodologies, and the outcomes of those methodologies, would now have to be applied in different ways, given that society has shifted, technologies have changed and expectation levels are higher. Nonetheless, he said, 'I think the FCE methodologies and learning are bigger than its time frame.' If FCE had a weakness, said Bauman, 'it had the weakness of being founded on a charismatic founder and all that that entails. Scotty, in some ways, is a cipher. He has a capacity to see with a searing laser some distance from him. He has a difficult time seeing anything close up. Both these qualities, this ability to see far and not seeing near, are pronounced, they are exaggerated so that his strength is really, really strong, and his weakness is really quite weak. As you might imagine, that creates by definition a kind of unbalanced environment, unbalanced around a whole lot of things and issues.

'So, on the one hand Scott could be soaring the heights,' the minister said, 'and on the other hand be just dumbfounded or dumbstruck at something that's right there in front of everybody's eyes to see. As a loner seeking community he's a built-in paradox. And it's particularly paradoxical for the organisation,' Bauman said, 'because the organisation is a product of that person's personality. He's a phenomenal synthesiser of information into palpable and otherwise unseen truths. It's his strongest gift. There's both a boyishness and an innocence that goes along with that gift. There can also be a petulance and a self-centredness that goes along with the boyish innocence, sort of the dark side of the same thing.' Baumann said he had a great affection for Peck, and that he'd been an important mentor in many ways. 'But I don't have rose-coloured glasses about that.'

Nor does Kazimierz Gozdz, though Peck pays Gozdz the ultimate compliment. 'He is somebody I really worked at mentoring,' said Peck in 2005, 'and now he is becoming my mentor. Kaz is absolutely brilliant. He's been a researcher on the cutting edge of community, and has deep insights on the best and worst of FCE.' And into the best and worst of M. Scott Peck. Said management consultant Gozdz, who first heard Peck in 1987, 'I do now know Scott Peck. I know more than most about him, but we have had a series of relationships. He has played various roles in my life. I know him differently from each of these perspectives. He is a complex man of significant depth and breadth. Peck is inter-disciplinary and his work reflects it. My critique of his work is biased and I know it. [After almost two decades of acquaintanceship] I feel I got to know Scotty as a friend just recently. It was not something I pursued or expected. Something happened in our relationship. I stopped wanting or needing anything from him professionally or personally. I felt his mentorship of me was over. Our relationship was over. We stopped relating. I stopped using his theories and practices in my everyday work. Somewhere in that territory I discovered I loved him. I am not sure why. It was not important to me that he understand or knew that, I just did. At that point we met on some ground of humanity beyond our agendas, and I came to know him as a man. We had Eucharist together.'

As for FCE, as Gozdz tells it, 'Peck built a model of community in *The Different Drum* that was both focused on group dynamics and the developmental dimensions of community building. He deliberately reduced the concept of community to focus on psycho-social-spiritual development. It did not focus on professional, cognitive, economic and other lines of development classically associated with building community in society. Peck's theory and methodology was: teach anyone to experience community repeatedly and over time they make a developmental leap to a new stage of integration. His theory works, but not the way it was implemented at FCE, and not the way Peck envisioned it.'

Omar Kahn, who took FCE out to Pakistan and Sri Lanka, said: 'When Scotty decided to retire, I think the organisation took a tailspin. Though he doesn't like to admit it, most of it was, I believe, kept alive by his stewardship and to some extent by his charisma. One thing Scotty did, which was rather clever, was come up with a vision statement for FCE; what they alighted on after a lot of agony and soul-searching, was to be available. I think to that extent, FCE still exists. If we were able to marry ability with need, FCE could very quickly come out of hibernation because the people are still out there, the abilities are still out there, and really, the organisation was secondary. It's not like a brand, or as if it had some particular supply chain, it was more like a network.' As for Peck himself, said Kahn, 'I believe everyone who knows him would agree with this. I believe Scotty's universal appeal is that he's able to take his own failings and extract the universal value of them so that they can guide not only himself but the rest of us. I believe he has a remarkable honesty in terms of taking a look at issues we probably all thought about and putting them before us in an accessible way that we can all recognise and resonate with. His great gift is that rather than fleeing from the demons he has discovered inside himself – and I don't mean demons in the literal sense he's written about in his ultimate book – I mean the shadows he has discovered, he's been able to face [the shadows] and look beyond them and illuminate what was dark with direct reference to what he's lived through. It's not glib. It's not frothy. It feels real, and that's very captivating.' There's more, of course. Kahn said that when they first met, three things struck him about Peck. The fact that he was 'an extremely, extremely thoughtful person who takes his time processing things. He's not somebody who will leap to an answer. He's not necessarily the quickest with a riposte, so you have to slow down a little bit. But the interesting thing is that slowing down is worth doing because what seems to come out of his processing is well worth waiting for.'

There were a number of FCE people, like Kahn and Gozdz, who, in Gozdz' words, 'took community building as a discipline'. In building community, said Gozdz, 'there is a moment when a group comes to terms with the need to become more effective and it's after people have pretty much tried to be effective – but they can't control the group they're with. An insight is gained about what to do next. Something happens when other people gain the same insight.' It happens in some religious communities, in sports teams, he said, indeed 'I think the same thing happens when a woman gives birth and there's a bunch of people in that delivery room.'

It was because Peck was surrounded by community, by the 'People of the Kleenex', the 'People of the Balloons', the gatherers at the Peabody Hotel, and because he had Lily as the midwife, that he was able to give birth to FCE. From the outside, the Foundation for Community Encouragement appears to slip into history as an attempt to make a difference. It offered a framework for breaking down some of the barriers that prevent openness and which, when removed, encourage a mutuality of interests. Subject to personal interpretation and application, some individuals still use their own variation of the framework to conduct their own community building. But as an organisation in the United States, and though not a cult, it revolved around Scott Peck. And when he and Lily withdrew, it was like the walls in Robert Frost's poem, it crumbled.

CHAPTER 12

GOD AND BOOKS

Peck was on a collision course with himself. As the 1980s ended he was more visible, more active, more imaginative and more productive than ever. He was still learning – learning that fame was a curse.

Peck's original works following *The Road Less Travelled* (there were also anthologies and compilations) are *People of the Lie: the Hope for Healing Human Evil* (1983); *What Return Can I Make?: Dimensions of the Christian Experience* (1985), with Carmelite Sister Marilyn von Waldner's music and Patricia Kay's artwork; *The Different Drum: Community Making and Peace* (1987); *A Bed by the Window: A Novel of Mystery and Redemption* (1990); *The Friendly Snowflake: a Fable of Love, Faith and Family* (1992); *A World Waiting to Be Born: Rediscovering Civility* (1993); *In Search of Stones* (1995); *In Heaven as on Earth: A Vision of the Afterlife*, a novel about Purgatory (1996); *Denial of the Soul: Spiritual and Medical Perspectives on Euthanasia and Mortality* (1997); *The Road Less Travelled and Beyond: Spiritual Growth in an Age of Anxiety* (1997); *Golf and the Spirit: Lessons for the Journey* (1999), *Glimpses of the Devil: a Psychiatrist's Personal Accounts of Possession, Exorcism and Redemption* (2005). (*The Friendly Snowflake*, *In Search of Stones* and *Golf and the Spirit: Lessons for the Journey* were illustrated by his son, Christopher.)

If, as the 1990s approached, Peck felt vulnerable it was because, if the investigative media got too close, he indeed was vulnerable. His pre-emptive strike was to become increasingly candid in print and lecture and interview about the flaws and failings of his own life. He had pressure points on a couple of fronts, most particularly his attitude in his writings, or his offhand remarks, regarding women. For all his apparent growth since he'd revealed himself on an Okinawa military television show as a card-carrying 'male chauvinist pig', he still left a strong impression he saw women essentially as sex objects; and was not above using them as such.

209

He could talk about his male chauvinism with interviewers as if it had been set aside or had evaporated. Not in the opinion of *Los Angeles Times* reviewer Carolyn See, tackling *A Bed by the Window*, who found Peck's depictions of women 'offensively drawn'. Wendy Kaminer, in her book, *I'm Dysfunctional, You're Dysfunctional: the Recovery Movement and Other Self-Help Fashions*, was no less critical of Peck regarding his attitudes to sex and women. Peck would say he did not understand women, but then provide additional analysis of them, such as saying that while the word '"macho" applies to men, women have their own version of it – they won't talk about what's really hurting them.'

Here he is again, with phrases likely to set women's teeth on edge: 'I made a mistake in one of my early speaking engagements, in Charlottesville, Virginia. A cute, young chick reporter asked me how did I happen to write *The Road Less Travelled*. I was bored already with the question. And because she was a cute young chick, I said, "Well, keep this confidential, will you? It's off the record, but I was just sitting in my living room at home one night, stoned, and the three words came to my mind: discipline, love, grace. In that order." The headline the next day read: "Doctor's Pipe Dream Comes True." I learned never to say to a reporter that anything is off the record.' He'd have received many more letters of outrage had his 'cute chick' remarks been as widely circulated as his books.

And finally: 'When I was a young psychiatrist we didn't have the term "mid-life crisis" yet. We knew about it first in women, a lot of women really fall apart when they get to menopause. The women who would really fall apart and not adjust to their age, were those who would continue to harbour fantasies that the Hollywood talent scout, or whatnot, was still going to come around,' he contended. 'Empty nest, empty life, and no amount of make-up could any longer hide the wrinkles. The healthy women, even back in the 1940s and 50s, by the time they were twenty-eight, had noticed the little crow's feet at the corner of her eyes, and so forth, and accepted the talent scout wasn't going to come around, and when the youngest of her children got to be five or so she would start moving out to develop some sort of career or existence for herself outside the home. And then when menopause came, she'd sail right through it, with the exception of the hot flashes. And the reason was she'd had her [emotional-psychological] menopause between twenty-five and thirty-five.'

The paradox was it was women who had made him famous, the millions of women who, through *The Road Less Travelled,* he had genuinely helped. Many disputed with Peck over his open marriage attitudes, or claims that romantic love was simply thinly disguised sex on the prowl. But they understood his direction-changing contributions to their lives even though they were not taken in by everything he said. Scores of letters from women describe the strong and positive impact he had on them, and it never hurts to quote from one more. This from 1984:

'Over and over, as I read, I cried with relief,' his correspondent wrote. 'To have found someone who has struggled with the same things I have – I can't tell you how wonderful it feels to know I am not alone. I feel that I'm not just a misfit who couldn't accept the religion I grew up with. I finally had the courage to give up, to reject really, the religion of my parents – their understanding of God, anyway. I had been too afraid to say, "I don't believe" for many years. But finally I had come to accept the fact that I never have and never will understand God the way it seems the majority of others do. I know it isn't as simple as they see it. And then I read *The Road.* And it was like looking in a mirror. I feel so much less alone now.'

In the late 1980s, increasingly bored with routine, Peck decided on a vacation in Jamaica. His friend, the writer Madeleine L'Engle, suggested he take along some murder mysteries. Typically of Peck's fantasy building, he constructed a mini-saga around the fact he lay on the hotel bed and dictated his first novel, *A Bed by the Window,* into a tape recorder. God may have had a hand in the book, as Peck suggested, but the yen to turn to fiction is often acute in a writer who steadily grinds out non-fiction. True, non-fiction demands discipline, a degree of organisation, and a constant vigilance over the writing – so the reader doesn't become lost or, worse, bored. But it isn't as much creative fun as fiction. His non-fiction has certain strengths. When one reviewer, Stephen G. Post, writing in *The World and I,* addressed Peck's writing in general, he said, 'Peck sticks to his convictions with immense literary power.'

A Bed by the Window, completed as the 1980s came to a close, appeared in 1990. The novel was Peck's first book with Jonathan Dolger as his agent, the man who'd signed up *The Road Less Travelled* for Simon and Schuster more than a decade earlier. The nursing home setting for *A Bed by the Window,* while familiar territory for Peck, was less so for his readers and admirers. The tale is one of murder, spiced with a little sex and a hint of evil. Peck was sensible in picking a setting he knew. He had served as director of New Milford Hospital Mental Health Clinic. As he later told the *Los Angeles Times* (which panned the novel), he knew about placing people in nursing homes against their will. The *Los Angeles Times*' negative comments on his novel galled him. Even two decades later he could still describe himself as 'really hurt by that ghastly review.' But he perked up to add, 'Fortunately a day later the *New York Times* wrote one of the best two reviews I've ever gotten.' The book boasted excerpts from the *New York Times* on its back cover: 'Memorable scenes are powerfully drawn . . . a spiritual mystery . . . both moving and brave.'

Son Christopher Peck said that had his father kept at general fiction, like *A Bed by the Window*, 'He might have gotten pretty good, but his day job ruined whatever capacity he had to do so. He would never have been able to write the kind of classic dramatic fiction he respected. He kept his respect for it, although he'd stopped reading the stuff by the time I was old enough to read the titles of the books he did read. All of his writing, fiction and non-fiction, suffered from his disinterest in the god of little things. Dad habitually burrowed into the heart of matters, hunting out the great and most profound. Peppering his work with pretty nonsense, side plots, and surprising non-sequiturs that make up a rich and interesting world was drudgery to Scotty.'

His son said he'd not read *The Road Less Travelled* but listened to it on tape, and found it helpful. 'After that I only read books that we were working on together. He quoted himself a lot.' Regarding their collaboration on *The Friendly Snowflake* and *In Search of Stones*, the younger Peck said, 'I'm an illustrator, I realise I'm serving the author. Scotty might respect people at first, but then later? Dad had these weird personnel issues. If you go into management training you learn things, like you don't say, "You've got a nice tie but gosh, your work really sucks."' Peck would grade people to their face, 'not just me but other people. He would give them an A or B, which is not much help in improving one's work but also sort of demeaning.' His father 'never respected other people's skills.'

Peck had encouraged his son's career choice. Christopher said Peck had artistic ambitions, and Scott's letters home from Exeter occasionally mention what he is doing in art class. Said Christopher, 'I've never seen his drawings except for medical diagrams. He loved to do that to explain things to me, some of my warmest memories. I heard from others he did try his hand at painting. I took over his paintbox as a child. He was very encouraging in my line. I think he did want me to go to college [Christopher Peck instead went to a private technical college strong in graphic arts, strongly geared towards the commercial]. It wasn't that I was rebelling against the Harvard and Wabash aspect of my family,' he said, 'but I just had a really hard time being in a classroom setting. I just couldn't tolerate it.'

As for his father's later books, his son commented, 'Scotty's problem was he didn't really have editors. He really felt his power from the fact that *The Road* was a publishing legend. He was able to go up against the biggest, toughest editors in New York. And there was the other problem, that he'd rather have his way than sell a lot of books. There were always one or two pearls of wisdom in his books, but they were always clouded – I mean he wasn't writing to an editor, he was writing to himself.'

The West Coast panning of *A Bed by the Window* did not help Peck's other ambition, to sell it to Hollywood. There were no takers. '*A Bed by the Window* did poorly,' Peck said, 'with one exception. It's got a tiny cult following, a small number of people who literally said it was the best book they'd ever read. And they are enough just to keep it barely alive. While the upset is that Hollywood hadn't picked it up, we're going for a second try because I'd written it with the theatre in mind.' Fifteen years later, in 2005, *Bed* was again fleetingly a Hollywood possibility. Peck said the British director, Peter Kosminsky, who'd directed *The White Oleander* (from Janet Fitch's novel), had two name stars interested in the title roles, a production team in place, and Kosminsky was 'trolling for [production] money.'

Movie or not, there was more to *A Bed by the Window* than the readers or reviewers knew. His mother's personality made a major contribution to one of the book's strongest characters, a nursing home resident. In writing *A Bed by the Window*, Peck admitted, he wanted to give his mother 'a better ending to life than the one she had. One of my old psychiatry professors said everybody wants to change their parents. I myself wanted to change my parents. About the time we moved up here, to New Preston, I accepted I was not going to change them. I still made a few forays, like trying to get my mother into psychotherapy, and later, my father. But I went into the forays knowing they were more likely to be misadventures than good adventures. As soon as I gave up my notion I could change them, then, of course, my anger vanished.'

Peck drew from other sources, too, for *Window* characters. One was a former patient. It was 'a fascinating case of pseudo-senility of a woman on the verge of death, with bedsores, babbling, incontinent, no sense, couldn't walk, and I realised she was faking it all. It was a fascinating though not a happy situation. It was her ambition to get into a nursing home, and a particular one.' The paralysed young man in the nursing home was also plucked from Peck's own life. The model was the young man with multiple sclerosis in Okinawa whom the hospital commander asked Peck to meet. 'My characters in *Window* then took on a life of their own, and hence so did the plot. It was an exciting time when that happened,' Peck said.

Though *The Different Drum* didn't sell strongly, it and *A Bed by the Window* both made their advances. Peck was still doing well on the books front. *The Road* was still a weekly fixture on the *New York Times* bestseller list (and headed into the *Guinness Book of Records* as the longest bestseller by a still-living author). Peck himself was exhausted, but wouldn't quit. He described himself on one occasion as an addictive personality, and it is possible he'd become addicted to the routine, the way one can, doing something one increasingly dislikes simply because he relied on the security of it. In Peck's case, despite his demurrals, he was probably addicted to the prominence and the acclaim, and needed the positive reinforcement. After all, authors do write to be heard.

He next decided to write a children's tale. *The Friendly Snowflake: a Fable of Faith, Love and Family* (1992). Described in one review as a 'delightful story', it is one more charming small book for children. Harry the Snowflake is a conduit for Peckian wisdom about faith and love dispensed to the blizzard-bound family of a little girl called Jenny. She lives not far from a pond that could be Lake Waramaug, in a section of Connecticut that could be New Preston. When Peck's textual issues of God and life risk being too grown-up, his son Christopher's soft-toned illustrations keep the slim volume attuned to the younger reader. For much of the tale the father is absent.

What Snowflake reinforced, though reinforcement was scarcely necessary, was that since *People of the Lie,* Peck had indeed become a Christian writer on Christian issues. Perhaps contrarily, in 1986, he told writer Cindy Lollar of *Campus Voice* magazine that he didn't want to be thought of as a Christian psychotherapist. 'I'm a Christian and I'm a psychotherapist. Judiciously, and when appropriate, I do use religious concepts and images in the course of therapy, but I will not use only Christian ones.'

The major conviction now was his Christianity. Peck's declaration of Christianity in *People of the Lie* places any sceptic among his readers, reviewers or listeners at an interesting juncture. If the reader, interestedly or pruriently, accepts Peck's candid account that he cruised Manhattan as a teenager to pick up gay men for sex, accepts his claim that he was not always the world's best parent or most attentive husband, accepts his account of one-night stands and long-term affairs, accepts his claim that he is narcissistic and somewhat lazy, then the reader is more or less obliged to accept Peck's sincerity regarding his Christianity and its role as a prime motivation in his life after his baptism at age forty-three. In Christianity, said Peck, he'd found his ultimate paradox. 'What I suddenly discovered after being a mystic for years and years was the richness of Christ-ness. The central doctrine is Jesus is paradoxically both human and divine. Not fifty per cent one or the other, but fully human and fully divine. There's probably no more indigestible paradox than that.' There's no escaping Peck's evangelising edge. He declares his Christianity on the second page of the Introduction and reinforces it on the third page. But what was he declaring? Conrad Hoover, writing in *Sojourners,* declared Peck 'strangely mysterious about the circumstances of his initial conversion and affiliations.' John Donohue, the *America* reviewer, observed 'some stages of his journey are tantalisingly indistinct.'

There is a bias against personal religion in books. Too heavy on the God talk and any writer is no longer considered a serious writer for the general American public – by the critics, that is. With his 'My Lord' declaration in *People of the Lie,* Peck stepped sideways off the secular track on to a parallel one, marked 'mainly for Christians'. The reviewers noticed. A *New York Times* writer referred to *People of the Lie* as 'birdseed'. Peck the writer who'd mentioned Christ in passing in *The Road* was now too bold a Christian for mainstream American critics. The same fate had befallen the English novelist, Evelyn Waugh in America. The premier American reviewer, Edmund Wilson, who at one point labelled novelist Waugh as the 'greatest comic writer' since George Bernard Shaw, dismissed *Brideshead Revisited* as 'a Catholic tract'. Peck did not help himself with that audience in that his next work, *What Return Can I Make?* was, in fact, a Christian tract.

Secular publishers and reviewers, however, as one by one they faced Peck's stream of books, couldn't completely ignore *The Road*'s precedent-breaking sales success. He might just repeat it. The publishers had stopped looking at the content and docketed him in the self-help section. There was a partial break-out with *A Bed by the Window* – his novel was as fairly reviewed as any first-time novelist could hope for. Had he determined at that point to keep going with novels, he might in time have developed a more varied reputation. However, Peck had put his pen at the service of his 'Lord' much as Waugh had placed his at the service of his Catholicism. Each man knew what he was doing. Peck, in his twelfth book, *Golf and the Spirit*, admitted he would have liked to have written a book that wasn't about God, but found he couldn't.

By the time he wrote *The Different Drum* (1987), *A Bed by the Window* (1990), and *A World Waiting to be Born* (1993), Peck was more than just sprinkling God around the pages, like dressing in a literary salad bowl. In that regard, *A World Waiting to Be Born*, given its secular intent, is an example of a book a little too heavily flavoured with the God talk for a general audience. That said, *World Waiting* is an excellent challenge. This book is the 'life is difficult' concept of *The Road Less Travelled*, plus the community building of *The Different Drum,* taken into the lives of nations, with Peck leading the reader through the options for dealing with international and regional group tensions while he provides an array of sterling insights. Of *A World Waiting to be Born*, Peck told British interviewer Ros Miles, 'Read it, you'll be hooked from page one.' *World Waiting* is a plea for human understanding, the understanding that interdependence is as essential for nations as it is for groups, families and individuals. There's something else in *World Waiting*. Peck is beginning to bare his soul to the reader in a new way, though sparingly as far as the details were concerned. In his first six books, up to and including *The Friendly Snowflake*, Peck has allowed the impression to take hold that for all its ups and downs, his marriage was one not subject to much more than the customary vicissitudes of wedlock. Now he talks about a marriage that hit somewhere close to 'rock bottom', he said in print, just about the time *The Road Less Travelled* was taking its first steps towards stardom.

Peck said his favourite book was *In Search of Stones*. 'The first

chapter is terribly educational. I was doing a promotion on television, on *Good Morning America* or the *Today Show*, and the producer
said, "I like the book very much but it's a sort of nineteenth-century
book," and I said, "Yeah, because it's weaving in and out and sort of
like Dickens talking. That's also part of why it was not popular,'"
said Peck, partly by way of explaining its poor sales. Not that poor,
it managed three weeks on the *New York Times* bestseller list.

In segments of *In Search of Stones* (1995), Peck continued this
confessional approach. Peck said his mother's close friend, Edie
Hazard, 'gave me hell' for *Stones*. 'How could you?' she wrote. 'How
could you have done that to your father? How could you have done
that to Lily? How could you?' Yet this is Peck's favourite book and
in conversation he described it as 'a love letter to Lily' as, to his
nonplussed admirers, he revealed his extramarital affairs. He
implied in *Stones* that, with all its difficulties behind it, the thirty-six-
year-long marriage was finding new strengths in the couple's
maturing years. In conversation he insisted that Lily had seen the
book and approved of the revelations before publication. Perhaps.
Was Peck manipulating the situation to suit his needs? He needed to
tell the readers all was well with his world by telling them what was
wrong with it before he cured it. Subsequent events would show he
couldn't have been more off target with his optimistic assessments
regarding his marriage. His segments on his marital life, however,
are only a small part of the book. *In Search of Stones* is an entertaining
and informative 'ramble', a harking back to an era when many
columnists in magazines would pseudonymously sign themselves,
'The Rambler'. It was an earlier type of popular writing, the
narrated musing of a wanderer who'd set off on a journey with no
definite route. Scott and Lily had decided on a holiday in Britain
and found themselves occupied instead searching for 'stones',
megalithic tombs, miniature Stonehenges, standing stones, menhirs
and Celtic crosses.

The journey, which originates in Wales and reaches its denoue-
ment in the Hebrides, is punctuated with Peck's asides and
travelogue. *In Search of Stones* has its own little following as a travel
book. Clinical psychologist Dr Donald Moss, former president of the
Association for Psychophysiology and Biofeedback, interrupted
some remarks about *The Road Less Travelled* to insert an equally
favourable mention of Peck's *In Search of Stones*. Dr Moss said he and
his wife had used *In Search of Stones* to plan their own journeying to

the megaliths, and found it an entertaining and accurate guide. Throughout the book, yet with a lighter touch than on other occasions, Peck also conducts his customary seminar on life, with riffs and asides on topics that catch his fancy. In all, it is a satisfying, and at times extremely engaging, read. What outraged, or dismayed or disappointed his devoted followers was the admission of his adultery and affairs, and his seeming lack of remorse. On the printed page, he too quickly and easily forgave himself, and many admirers were quick enough to notice, and take offence.

As *Stones* was being published, societal change and debate intruded into Peck's world as a serious moral challenge from another direction. It was the legalisation of the 'assisted suicide' movement in the state of Oregon playing against Peck's intimations of mortality in wrestling with his Parkinson's. It spawned another book, one of his very best. Peck's rebuttal of 'assisted suicide' in *Denial of the Soul: Spiritual and Medical Perspectives on Euthanasia and Mortality* (1997) is Peck at his most passionate. Despite that, it is a most carefully modulated and reasoned work, and the essence of his writer's approach to life. *Denial of the Soul* is not simply a worthy successor to *The Road Less Travelled*, it is its culmination, its completion. The life he urged readers to live to the full in *The Road* came from a caring professional in the first flush of literary enthusiasm motivated to reveal his discoveries. Readers found him appealing and trust-worthy, and understood his desire to encourage, indeed to urge, cajole, stimulate, and reassure people, that getting on with their lives was not merely possible, but life's only option. If ever a man screamed 'seize the moment for living', it was Peck in *The Road*. Having encouraged millions of people to see that life was for the living, and knowing he had done so from the thousands of letters he received, Peck, exactly twenty years later, was not about to let them die needlessly, or wrongly, under the rubric of assisted suicide or euthanasia. His book came out in time for the debate over retired pathologist Dr Jack Kervorkian's decision to assist in the suicide of a fifty-three-year-old man with ALS, Lou Gehrig's disease. Kervorkian was convicted of second-degree murder and later sentenced to ten to twenty-five years in prison.

Denial is unique among Peck's books in that it contains a reason-ably comprehensive index. Dedicated to the hospice movement and those in it, Peck was able to correct an earlier wrong. British hospice founder Dame Cecily Saunders had written in 1994 'to make some correction to your comments on the origin of hospice in the United States' (in *Further Along the Road Less Travelled*). In *Denial of the Soul,* Peck paid tribute to Dame Cecily's work and laid out the development of hospice in America, with its origins in New Haven, Connecticut.

Coincidentally, the arguments in *Denial* regarding life link Peck's writing to his father's legal writing. Judge Peck's second book, *Decisions at Law,* which was in print for more than thirty years, dealt with twelve particularly critical cases. One – and this was in a book published years before the abortion debate began, was entitled 'When Life Begins'. The case explored whether a driver who'd rear-ended another car, causing that pregnant driver to lose her child, was guilty of murder.

Forty years earlier, as a medical resident in the US Army Medical Corps, Peck did 'pull the plug' on a dying soldier, he said. Had Peck been detected he would have been court martialled – by the standards of the mid-1960s. He describes the circumstances surrounding his decision in *Denial*. Four decades later, end-of-life standards and the frontiers of palliative care have been drastically revised, the discussion expanded, and the decisions once made by doctors alone now broadened to include the families. Peck wrote *Denial of the Soul,* he said, because he was fearful that the euthanasia movement growing up in the United States around 'assisted suicide' was going undebated and, indeed, was misunderstood. Cutting to the core of his argument regarding euthanasia and assisted suicide, Peck states, quite simply, that taking a life is not the same thing as allowing death, that there's a difference between hospice palliative care and active intervention hastening the end of life. To Peck, anti-life was anti-God. His well paced and tightly argued *Denial of the Soul* convinced one otherwise-inclined book reviewer, in the online magazine *Salon,* to publicly reverse his previously favourable views towards assisted suicide. Peck later said, 'The only reason I can figure the book didn't sell is purely that people don't want to look at the subject of [euthanasia and assisted suicide]. But it was a damn good book, if you don't mind me saying so.' He had reason to say so.

From FCE musings to his various books, Peck's God is never omitted from Peck's discussion of things. He describes the 'miracle' that inspired FCE as an example of God, or 'the voice of the Holy Spirit talking' and gradually being heard. Peck emphasised he did not take lightly nor accept as a given that every inspiration or event in his life came from the Holy Spirit, but he was curious about the Holy Spirit's role in people's lives. Before his baptism, he said he was 'in so many ways already converted. I was already a mystic, and I was a contemplative and I had a relationship going with God. Now I want to know about people hearing the Holy Spirit, the voice of the Holy Spirit talking to them. Am I the only one? No. How many are there that do? And how many that don't? I know most people don't. This ought to be researched.' He put the question to a fellow therapist: '"Margaret, do you ever have this still small voice inside you that you hear that isn't you?" And she said, "Oh yeah. Oh yeah. I mean not all the time. The last time was two months ago. I thought my father was really going to die and I was already in the process of parcelling out the little inheritance I would get. And all the voice in this instance said was, 'Margaret, you're thinking too much about money.'" And then she went on to recount other examples.' Peck said that when he prayed, he was talking to God 'and the Holy Spirit is God talking to me. It just never ceases to amaze me how frequently it or she speaks to me, and why am I so fortunate?'

Contrarily, Peck felt his message to readers in his books wasn't 'about God per se. What I am evangelistic about is saying [to the world], "Sorry guys, there is nothing beyond science and religion. There's no place to go beyond that." The answer does not lie in deconstructing Western civilisation in the hope there is something beyond, something other than science and religion to rely on, because there's not,' he said. 'Religion and science *at their best* are the best you are going to find. What is needed is to start integrating them. It means you religious folk are going to have to learn how to become good scientists. And you scientific folk are going to have to learn a lot about stuff like *kenosis* – a word I didn't even know when I wrote *The Road Less Travelled* – and *submission*, and waiting for God, and listening.'

Nephew David, when explaining that Scott Peck was in an American tradition that stretched from the eighteenth century (Jonathan Edwards) down through Norman Vincent Peale (who wrote *The Power of Positive Thinking*), to Jim Wallis (who works in Washington, D.C. and founded *Sojourners* magazine), continued that what was significant about his uncle in contrast to these men is that 'he was never a minister. He was a soldier and a medic. He could not appropriately have ever been a minister. He certainly had the professional weaknesses of a doctor – the macho, Lone Ranger saviour complex – and psychiatrist. He was a physician unable to heal vast tracts of himself.'

A Peck book in a different category from the others, an easy read for those who enjoy the quizzical theme, is Peck's novel on Purgatory, *In Heaven as on Earth*. Purgatory is that mythical place where souls are expected to redeem or purge themselves while awaiting entry into Heaven. Given the topic, the theme is surprisingly deftly handled in this, the lightest of Peck's books, and indeed he said it was the one that took the least time to write. Peck's imagery – Purgatory as a sort of sterile hospital waiting room – is only part of the fun. It is a very 'lonely' book. The soul awaiting entry into Heaven operates almost in isolation, and certainly not in community.

Obviously in a good mood when he wrote it, the tight tale has the hallmarks of a storyteller who was able to just sit down and crank this one out. A decade earlier Peck had admitted to journalist Lollar that he didn't know about Hell, and that scared him. 'I am this advanced spiritual soul, supposedly, but I'm scared of dying. In some ways as I get older, I look forward to it. But in some ways it scares the bejesus out of me because it is going into the unknown. I sort of hypothesise there is a Heaven and a Purgatory and a Hell. But I don't know how I am going to get there or which I'm going to go to. I suspect Purgatory is some kind of elegant psychiatric hospital.' In his book it was the hospital waiting room. The book contains sex of a sort, and evil – hell is the bottom of a garbage pail. Most of the people in hell are corporate executives. *In Heaven as on Earth* didn't sell particularly well.

His 1999 golfing book, *Golf and the Spirit*, was pure marketing in concept, and a very clever idea. As columnist Colman McCarthy wrote in the *Washington Post*, it was the book Thomas Merton would have written had he been a golfing Trappist monk. *Golf and the Spirit: Lessons for the Journey,* was a book cleverly intended to capitalise on the Peck name, linking it to an audience that didn't necessarily know much about him except his name and the title of his first book. As some 70 per cent of Americans believe in God, and almost 40 per cent go to church on Sunday, 70 per cent of America's 27 million golfers might buy the book. *Golf* is less a pilgrimage to Canterbury than Peck entertaining psycho-spiritual duffers and advanced foursomes all the way from the first tee to the nineteenth hole. Essential Peckisms abound with each swing of the club – at a time when his own golf swing was rapidly deteriorating. Sometime in 1993, though he did not immediately recognise it, Peck experienced the first flutterings of the tremors of Parkinson's disease. Since boyhood he'd had a slight tremor in one hand, but this was different, and by 1995 it was interfering with his golf. Peck could admit the interference, but not acknowledge what he now strongly suspected was the case – that he had Parkinson's disease. As for *Golf and the Spirit*, in a favourable *Time* magazine review, John Skow stood *The Road Less Travelled* on its head and said it's not life that's difficult, it's golf.

Even bestselling authors fight with their publishers. 'You know the way the publishing industry works,' said Peck, 'somebody writes a successful book and they think they've got a formula so they pay just extraordinary amounts of money for somebody to duplicate it or something. I'd gotten into the big advance business when Simon and Schuster threatened to kill my Christian evangelical book [*What Return Can I Make?*].'

The publishers may have been concerned about the overtly Christian and evangelising tone of the book destroying Peck's credibility as a 'secular' psychiatrist writing about matters that included but did not so overtly promote Christianity. *What Return* is a Christian prayer service with a series of sermons by Peck on cassette tape along with his text in the volume itself. Of *What Return,* one reviewer, a former Franciscan monk, Geoffrey Brooks, wondered, 'What kind of review can I write?' And proceeded in *Best Sellers* magazine to declare it an outstanding aid for anyone seeking God. And concluded, 'You don't even have to be Christian to enjoy it.'

Peck's assessment was 'that if they could kill a book [*What Return*] for which they'd paid me a $75,000 advance, the only way to prevent that was to get into the $300,000 to $500,000 advance price range.' Consequently, when Peck's golf book was sold it was for several hundred thousand dollars, he said. 'It still hasn't made the advance, but it was an absurd advance and I knew it wouldn't. I felt rather badly, the poor dears. I wrote one of my really better books, *Denial of the Soul,* for them [the publishers, Three Rivers Press], which didn't sell at all.' Said Peck of *Denial,* 'People who had dying parents have said the book just carried them through and said it ought to be mandatory reading for every divinity school student. The one on golf I wasn't quite as pleased with, but I think it was a pretty good book. It's one that is continuing to sell, and they may ultimately make their money.' Peck had another complaint about publishing houses. 'There's this anthology of quotes [from his writings] that I edited. All Andrews and McMeel could sell was 30,000 copies hardcover. Two months ago Borders [the bookstore chain] bought 20,000 at a ridiculously low price and the day before yesterday, after two months, they put in an order for 25,000 more.' *Further Along the Road Less Travelled: the Unending Journey Toward Spiritual Growth,* a 1994 collection of his lectures, was another compilation and bestseller.

His assessment of the likely reception for *Glimpses* was, 'I think it will make a great many people nervous and probably they won't want to read it. My audience now has the whole [exorcism] database I have, except with one crucial difference – I was there and they weren't. I do not expect many of them to be converted to a belief in Satan, but what I hope they might be converted to is greater open-mindedness. It was difficult for me at the time I wrote *People of the Lie* not to tell them about the two most extraordinary experiences of my life. And they are enthralling. It will be a page-turner. I have a feeling that Simon and Schuster is going to do this book,' he said, before his agent, Jonathan Dolger, had placed it, though Peck said he felt Simon and Schuster were 'not overly convinced' about its potential. He argued, 'Not only have all my [Simon and Schuster] books made their advance they've made quintuple their advance. They published six of my books and all made their advance, even the one they tried to kill, *What Return Can I Make?*, then republished by Harpers as *Gifts for the Journey.* The other five books, well, *The Road Less Travelled* was the most successful commercial book in history. *People of the Lie* sold well over a million copies. *A Different Drum* sold over 350,000 hardcover. *Further Along* sold 300,000 in hardcover, and I think that even *The Road and Beyond* sold 200,000 in hardcover.'

Peck said his fame never got him so much as a table in a restaurant, though by a fluke fax, it once got him a bedroom with a view at a hotel on the Isle of Skye, better accommodations than he and his wife, Lily, had been assigned. 'I still remember it smelled of lima beans. There were never any great perks of fame other than what money could buy,' he said. 'Fame gets very ambiguous, as does my ambition.' So did his love–hate relationship with the press. Peck wasn't sure what to do about reporters when they homed in on him, for he couldn't always say no. In Texas on one occasion, Peck participated in a conference on evil that was filmed by public television personality Bill Moyers' production team. Moyers, an ordained minister and President Lyndon Johnson's former press secretary, wasn't present but Peck, through a friend, sent Moyers a question. What, Peck asked Moyers, should he do about the 'publicity' business surrounding his success? Moyers sent back a note on the friend's note: 'Tell Scott Peck that either he will control the media or the media will control him. Period.' 'And that,' said Peck, 'was exactly what I wanted to hear.'

Peck did control the media, through the expedient of stock answers. He wanted the publicity of articles and media interviews and, for one level of journalists, stock answers were sufficient. Reporters and writers inclined to push Peck placed Peck at risk if he lapsed into garrulousness or self-justifying flights of fancy when he started showing off. On other occasions his candid answer was sufficient (see next chapter). In interviews with dozens of newspapers and magazines over the years, he recycled the familiar, and was diversionary when pressed with new lines of questioning. For example, Peck told *Playboy* that one way to maximise sexual experience – a craving he said was part of God's design – was extramarital liaisons with someone new for 'a day or two or a year or two'. When asked if he was a graduate of that school of thought, Peck changed the topic to paradox and game-playing. On some occasions the better insights were not from media sources – a minister, asked, 'What's Scott Peck like?' replied, 'He's the most self-centred and the most loving person I know.' Psychologist James Guy asked Peck if he saw himself 'as being narcissistic. What have you denied yourself?' Peck asked for time to think about it, talked about other matters, and finally said, 'I'm just not sure I have ever denied myself in any big way. I've denied myself in little ways all over the place.' He offered no specifics.

Even as his declining fame ebbed into the twenty-first-century, Peck's new books and statements and proposals continued to attract some attention. His one-time position on the *New York Times* bestseller list was still unassailable; magazines and newspapers still occasionally did none-too-critical interviews, or the rare one looked for chinks in the prophet's armour, flaws in the preacher's personal life. The *Guardian* headline in 2003 was 'Can a Guru Heal Himself?' continuing, 'When M. Scott Peck wrote *The Road Less Travelled* 25 years ago, he brought his self-help book into our lives and taught us all our problems were solvable. The book has been on the bestseller list ever since but how has Peck's own life matched up?' The writer found it hadn't quite matched up, but discovered Peck was a lot of 'fun'. Andrew Billen of *The Times* found Peck to be 'colossally self-deluded'. Billen's searing article (see next chapter), said Christopher Peck, eased a burden long resting on his own shoulders. 'Now I don't have to say anything unpleasant [about his father]; I can refer people to *The Times* of London article. That's a comfort because for the first half of my life no-one outside the family believed anything negative I said about him.'

Peck had admirers. He had critics. He had followers. He'd also had 'groupies', those who wanted to be hangers-on. By the twenty-first century, in his quasi-retirement, his groupies left Peck alone, though 'occasionally out here in the country I will find somebody wandering down the road looking for my house and perhaps wanting to come in.' Sometimes the request came by mail, as from an Italian priest who wrote and asked for a meeting, and Peck happily agreed. 'Groupies [he'd earlier referred to them as "ghouls" and "creeps"], I mean I've met a bunch, most of them, a lot of them, I don't like particularly. [Now] they leave me alone.' With his books, his memories, his demons.

Endearingly, Peck referred to Omar Kahn as one of his 'groupies. Omar's got a photographic memory and can tell you chapter and verse of what I've written, virtually what I said in what book.' Another who knew his work well, said Peck, was the Hollywood publicist Michael Levine, who dedicated his book *Lessons from the Halfway Point* to Peck. 'Michael's a weird guy, absolutely brilliant, can't even sit through a community-building workshop, writes about a book a year about public relations. *Guerrilla PR* is one of his works. He's been a groupie of mine and been helpful to me a couple of times. He had an idea which I heartily endorsed, which got nowhere: building in Los Angeles harbour "The Statue of Responsibility" to counter or balance out "The Statue of Liberty" on the other coast. Wonderful idea.'

By 2005, Peck wasn't exceedingly wealthy by current convoluted standards. In the final decade of the twentieth century, 'We were at the point of saying, "We need to make a major gift, or maybe give away a million of this," and then the stock market brought it down from $11.7 million to about $8.7 million. When Lily left me we split our accounts. I did very well in the market last year [2003], my equities were up sixty per cent for the year.' Given that Peck had pointedly focused at times on the idolatry of wealth, had he ever thought of walking away from it? 'I've not seen, not felt God requiring, suggesting, in any way, shape or form, that I put my entire monetary security at risk.' And then came Peck's sidestep of the question to prevent further delving: 'I'll tell you, I turned down a million dollars one luncheon. Peter Guber [*Rain Man, Clue, The Color Purple*], co-president with some other guy at Columbia Pictures, responsible for doing movies on Batman, was interested in maybe doing a movie out of *The Road Less Travelled*. Jonathan [Dolger, Peck's agent] said he couldn't imagine it. I couldn't imagine it. [Guber] wanted to talk about it personally so he flew Jonathan and me out first-class to Tinseltown for a power lunch in a movie-set trailer. I took an instant dislike to him which I think I hid, and he spun a few tales about how he might translate *The Road Less Travelled* into film. But they were sort of nonsensical.' Peck raised the issue of having artistic control; Guber said that 'was a total no-no and [they] needn't bother to talk further.' Guber's aide spoke up approvingly when Peck said he could write out five principles so he could do the film any way he chose as long as the film demonstrated those five principles. 'There had to be some way in which the film demonstrated that self-discipline paid off, demonstrate that there was something called grace, and three others. His assistant tried to encourage him, but [Guber] was adamant about it. [Guber] offered to throw in another $100,000 or $200,000 and make me, I guess, an associate producer. I figured out by the evening that all he was interested in was my name and the title.'

Back home Peck wrote to Guber and said that he and Dolger could not understand what Guber's intentions were for 'this non-fiction book. If you purchased *The Bed by the Window*, you could do whatever you wanted with it, and people would say, "Well, Hollywood fucked up another good book."' 'But,' said Peck, in conversation, '*The Road Less Travelled* is basically a book of principles, and if you changed it then people would correctly say that Peck sold out to Hollywood.'

He didn't sell out.

CHAPTER 13

ALONE – FOR A WHILE

The decade of the 1990s was Peck's peak. In 1997, a *Booklist* reviewer commented, 'Peck, very productive of late.' Eight books appeared in those years, an outburst of enthusiasms, all of them in the face of the barely tolerable, for Peck was battling Parkinson's disease. The onset of Parkinson's disease, or its first intimations, may have been present as early as 1993. Certainly Peck had known since 1994–1995, though he'd more or less denied or ignored it until it was confirmed in 1999. Four years later, in 2003, when Lily left the house and filed for divorce, he blamed her departure on his Parkinson's, 'and that's wrong. Definitely wrong,' said Valerie Duffy, the Pecks' housekeeper. 'She left him for her reasons.' Those included concerns about her health, and feeling stifled by Peck.

At the time she left, Lily's health was not good, said son Christopher, and this in addition to dealing with lupus, a form of arthritis, for more than a decade. (One form of lupus is life-threatening.) Said Gail Puterbaugh, Peck's full-time executive secretary, 'Lily told me once that she wanted to be happy. She realised she had fewer years ahead of her and she wanted to enjoy them and didn't feel she could in the marriage. I think it was easy. As in most marriages you're not in love you're in habit. For Lily I don't think she ever put behind her his infidelities and everything. He thought she did. He thought, "Oh well, it's over and done with. I've cleansed my soul. I'm being honest." He used honesty as a weapon.'

Lily's departure was an unlikely occurrence if played against the Pecks' life only a decade earlier, as somewhat glowingly described in *In Search of Stones* (1995). Her departure was understandable if measured against what she had endured over four decades, also revealed, if in brief, in the same volume. Despite her leaving, the household functioned smoothly, a tribute to Gail. Peck's one-page bow towards her at the end of *Glimpses of the Devil* is a platonic love letter. Puterbaugh had first met Peck in a doctor–patient role in the late 1970s. He was her therapist. She is a fair-haired, well-built woman with a ready smile, a winning greeting that suggests an ability to laugh at some of life's foibles. In the 1980s she joined the Peck enterprise as an assistant to Mary Ann Schmidt, who managed Peck's speaking engagements and travel, his business correspondence as an author with agents and publishers, collected monies and paid the bills, and kept the 'corporate' Peck operating smoothly. Peck handled the money management side of his life, investments and the like.

When Mary Ann Schmidt died, Gail took over her duties. Apparently those duties expanded exponentially and her eventual varied roles in the household made her a major part of the intimate social drama that began with Lily's departure and ebbed out in the months following Peck's September 2005 death and November 2005 memorial service. Puterbaugh was the indispensable factotum. Even before Lily left, Gail did the grocery shopping and arranged household maintenance. She paid herself and the housekeeper, and ordered whatever was needed for the home. She handled the correspondence, arranged schedules for weekend visitors, and shielded Peck from those he did not wish to see or talk to.

When Gail first joined the staff, she said, 'I thought Lily and Scott worked beautifully together. They were working on FCE; Lily was chairing different things and taking business management courses. They seemed to be very in synch, going in the same direction. The kids, well, when I came all three were just getting married. So there were weddings out of the house, there were weddings close by. It seemed to be on the surface what you would say a family is. I didn't see any stresses.'

Valerie Duffy, housekeeper for many years, kept doing the same once Lily left. She simply divided her time. She worked for Scott at the Bliss Road house, and a couple of days a week for Lily in her new home eight miles away. Fair-haired Duffy is diminutive, peppy and talkative in an entertainingly no-nonsense manner. She cleaned the house, attended to Peck's laundry, fetched and carried, all with the energy of a Scottish terrier, one that cheerily charged Peck a dollar a time for locating his errant car keys and mislaid reading glasses, and made him laugh by telling him the occasional dirty joke. She brought fun and laughter to the house on Bliss Road. Peck was cheap and kept the house cool in winter; Valerie complained but Peck ignored her. 'He used to like to keep the thermostat down, save on oil. One day it was cold and I was doing his laundry and he powered down for his boxer shorts and I said, "okay, I'll be right up." So I stuck his shorts in the freezer then I brought them upstairs. "What's this?" he said. I said, "That's what my ass feels like coming in here in a morning." That's the way we got along.'

In 1992, in a happier mood, Lily and Scott had bought a home on a golf course in Bodega, California and began to spend months at a time out on the Pacific Coast. They kept their western Connecticut house, their home for twenty years, and returned regularly. The 1990s California idyll turned into a working retirement. Peck was commissioned to write the spirituality book on golf, a sort of reciprocity book – golf as good for the soul, and vice versa. Back in New Preston, Gail Puterbaugh, his executive secretary, remained on duty, handling the mail, bills and correspondence. He'd give dictation over the phone. The California sojourn 'was actually a break for me,' Gail said, 'I'd still get to the house and all, managing the house, dealing with the subcontractors, but I didn't have to be there one hundred per cent, every day.'

Life on the edge of a California golf course was not bringing soul-peace to Peck. First, his game was deteriorating. Next, the major US magazines appeared to have declared an open season that decade on Peck, plus his misogynistic remarks increasingly drew the ire of women. The big magazines, to that point, had treated him gently. An October 1988 *Omni* magazine Q-and-A was mild, and the fourteen-page *Playboy* interview, December 1991, was softball treatment. A year later, in *Life* magazine in December 1992, he was carefully and effectively savaged. *Life* repeated the public claim by one woman, who identified herself, that Peck was 'a drunk and a womaniser' who'd led her into having an affair with him following a spiritual growth workshop. The phrase 'a drunk and a womaniser' gained some circulation, and not a little currency. A New York writer, Geoffrey N. Smith, heard a variation of it at a Manhattan gathering when a psychiatrist referred to Peck as a 'boozy womaniser'. To Smith, an author himself, the charges of 'booze' and 'womanising' were scarcely germane to the issue of Peck's qualities as a writer.

Peck's self-defence, quoted in the *Life* magazine article, was, 'People are flabbergasted that I should drink or smoke or that there might be some question about my fidelity, because they put me on such a pedestal. They're horrified that their idol has been broken, or they look at him and say, "Let's pull him down."'

Then *Time* magazine, in 1994, attributed *The Road Less Travelled*'s continuing sales not to the fact that people were helped by it, but they bought it as a gift for friends whose habits irritated them. No article irritated Peck more, however, than the October 1995 *Rolling Stone* article that revealed him on the road, and at his worst, hectoring the staff of a Boston hotel because his suite wasn't ready. The writer, John Colapinto, also visited Peck at home. Peck said the *Life* and *Rolling Stone* articles were the two worst ever written about him. *Rolling Stone*'s Colapinto, 'criticised my gin and my four cartons of Camels, but he didn't mention that he helped himself to the three packs he smoked while he was here. He ended with me sitting on my private golf course, but as a householder I owned one seven hundred and eightieth of it.' Of the incident at the reception desk of a luxury hotel in Boston, Peck contended he 'was generally very gracious to most people even at the very end when I was dead tired. What *Rolling Stone* picked up on still infuriates me. In that instance I'd arrived in Boston, one of two plenary speakers for an audience of over a thousand people. They made a mint off me. Well, I arrived at three to three-thirty in the afternoon to check in. At the registration desk I was told my room was not ready and they wouldn't even tell me when I'd have a room. So I went to the woman running the conference and said I would really appreciate it if she would damn well see to it I got a room, I was tired and needed to rest. And that was what it was all about. I made myself very nasty until about four-thirty when they had a room for me.'

Peck could argue it how he liked, Colapinto recorded what he witnessed. Not surprisingly, Peck was chagrined, aware his behaviour had been caught on the record, and how vulnerable he was becoming. He also was half aware, though not fully accepting the fact, that he was coping with the early stages of Parkinson's disease. By 1994, a year before the *Rolling Stone* article appeared, he could no longer compensate for the fact his left hand was 'cog-wheeling', twisting uncontrollably when he was teeing off. 'It's pretty diagnostic of Parkinson's,' he said, and he told himself, 'Oh, well, you've got Parkinson's, and I didn't pay any more attention. Except here I was writing this book about "you'll learn something about your soul every time you play and your game might just get better."'

After Boston, he made one trip to Canada then cancelled all his scheduled appearances, made no announcement, but ended his speaking career. 'I retired from speaking a year before I intended to,' he said later, 'almost on the heels of that Boston engagement, before the article came out. I just said, Christ, I quit.' Presciently, John Colapinto's article was headed, 'M. Scott Peck at the End of the Road'.

Done with the lecture circuit, Peck concentrated on his golf game. He'd never been a great golfer, only a reasonably good one, but he now started getting worse. He said, wryly, that Lily's game – and she had lupus – was improving as his deteriorated, and for the constantly competitive Peck, 'that made it worse.' He avoided looking more deeply into the physical difficulties he was experiencing even though 'I was lucky if I hit a decent shot any more.' He preferred to attribute his poor game to his bad back. By 1996, his game – and health – had deteriorated to the point that at the end of three holes he was exhausted and no longer interested. At that point also, he said, he went 'into a very, very dark period of about three years duration. About one-third of Parkinson's patients do before they are formally diagnosed. They have some sense that something is terribly wrong with them, but they have no idea what. For me that was one of the worse parts of Parkinson's disease. I used to have what I called death attacks at eight o'clock in the evening. I would suddenly feel like I was dying and it was all I could do to crawl up the stairs.'

During his training in neurology, he said, 'I don't remember seeing a Parkinson's patient. It's been amazing to me, in retrospect, that during my residency it was a disease in the closet. I had no idea what a devastating disease it can be. I also had no idea what a gentle disease it is, meaning it's slow, you have plenty of time to adjust to it, both physically and mentally.' In his late-1990s depths of depression – he was being increasingly handicapped by the Parkinson's disease he was still refusing to acknowledge – 'Lily kept wanting me to go see a psychiatrist, as did a couple of others. But I knew that what I was experiencing was not an ordinary depression.' ES, his spiritual director, who 'cared for me some years earlier when I'd gone through a mid-life crisis, a much more substantial depression,' thought he was perhaps going through a dark night of the soul. Said Peck, 'This wasn't that. While God didn't seem to be hopping around inside me, I didn't feel He'd deserted me. I emerged out of that terrible time about three years ago, let's say early 2000.'

Parkinson's disease and his declining fame were only two issues plaguing him. He had become estranged from his youngest daughter, Julia, and his relationship with his other two children, Belinda and Christopher, was emotionally fraught. When his Parkinson's disease was formally diagnosed in 1999, it could have been six years after its onset. At first the Parkinson's medicine nauseated him, 'but gradually I got into it and I came out of this dark period singing and incessantly humming, whistling or otherwise making a joyful noise unto the Lord. And that has been daily, nightly, for three years now.'

By the end of 2003, Peck also had this biography on him under way; it would simultaneously involve and tantalise him. Peck's letters and emails from December 2003 onward (see 'Peck and Jones') illustrate that whatever was occurring in the household and his private life, in terms of maintaining control, he was determined to continue to exercise as strong a hand as possible in shaping the biography, if he could. He eventually semi-capitulated in his efforts to force the book's development into an exercise in collaboration, a would-be collaboration he referred to as emerging 'out of community'.

Six weeks prior to any agreement to go ahead with the biography, he wrote (26 August 2003), 'contact my executive director (Gail), she has great expertise in setting up phone appointments, indeed she is an extraordinary person in almost every way and keeps me both alive and functioning.' By September, Peck was writing he was 'intrigued and excited' by the likely biography, later he would become alarmed and intermittently mildly combative. He continued, 'you requested me to put down on paper some restrictions were you to assume this labor. The first one is that you make no attempt to contact my children for the purpose of this biography. I made a firm promise to them a good twenty years ago, at their request, that I not involve them in my public life and have always considered that promise sacred. I think it highly likely that this off-limits restrictions will also apply to my wife, even though she has obviously been an extremely important figure in my life. At the current time however our relationship is in such a state of disarray for literally hundreds of reasons that it would not be fair to her (and I think would be a distraction as well).'

The following month (29 September 2003) Peck, in a letter,

recounted the anecdote of the neighbour who recalled Scott as 'that little boy who was always talking about the kind of things people shouldn't talk about.' Peck continued, 'I am still that little boy, and my outspokenness does upset some people. But it has also been a "gift" that has played such a large role in my books. Frankly I don't know of anything in this world that people can't talk to me about, and that becomes particularly important when talking about one's spiritual life and relationship to God. Back when I was a psycho-therapist I don't think I was all that great. But there were a number of people who found they could talk to me about God more openly and honestly than with anyone else, including almost all psycho-therapists, and these people seemed to get better just because they had the opportunity to talk about what was most important to them.

'Because I have been waiting for someone to do a biography, I have not taken the time to actually sit down and tease out of my work the most original and most influential contributions that I have made to the academic world of psychology and theology and to the larger world of intellectual thought and social action (see 'Peck and Jones'). This doesn't exactly sound modest, but there can be a kind of unrealistic modesty which I have had to learn to overcome in myself. I think most people in my position, and certainly those "spiritual soul mates" among them I have personally known, have had to continually exist in the tension between arrogance and humility.'

The letter stated, 'Even more important to me than my intellectual contributions is God. I think we need to have a serious conversation about how you would "handle" God in writing my biography and how you might allow yourself to be handled by Him. When I talk about God I am not talking about an intellectual construct or an idea or a belief; I am talking about a living being who has been my mentor, my companion, my lover, my tormentor – a being of such importance that relatively speaking all the other wonderful characters in my life have been but bit players.'

Peck's letters and emails written during this period, a time when he was completing *Glimpses of the Devil*, reveal he was still capable of enormous intellectual effort even as his Parkinson's disease rapidly worsened and cancer set in. There was will. And there was also wilfulness because he was forever angling for a collaborative effort on the book, though over the couple of years there was more cordiality than friction. In September 2003 he wanted 'more discussion with you as to precisely what an unauthorised biography might mean.' It meant he would not see any drafts or the final manuscript prior to publication, with which he had no quarrel, though he immediately began testing his ability to involve himself in the book's progress (2 October 2003), 'not seeing your early or final drafts doesn't bother me because I think I will have an idea of the tone of the book for the reasons you state. We will talk more about "community", I very much get the feeling that we will be able to be working "out of community".' (He was mistaken, but did not cease his efforts until the following year, when he wrote (29 June 2004), 'this is a formal letter of surrender. You commented not long ago that I seemed to like a good scrap. I have not liked scrapping with you; I have done so until now only on behalf of the biography you are writing. I have been scrappy only because most of the omens have seemed wrong. Although we have spent a great deal of time on the phone I do not yet feel that you understand me. You operate as close to the speed of light as any human I have ever met and seem totally determined to continue doing so. I admire the result you achieve thereby as a result of your extreme organisation and your loving intent. You do an enormous amount of very good work. But save for rare moments when I seem to have been taken over by the Holy Spirit, I am dedicated to operating as slowly as I can and am continually regretful I cannot operate more slowly yet.

'As far as I can ascertain,' he continued, 'there is no chance at all you will compromise. Consequently I will do what you ask and proceed ahead in our work with a kind of faith that does not come easily to me.' He said he was surrendering 'out of obedience' to Sister Ellen Stephen 'when she suggested the fact that I do like you so much should be taken very seriously as a very powerful omen.' That he may have discussed the matter with ES is likely, that he 'surrendered out of obedience' seems out of character, both his and ES's. 'I dare say it seems to you I am trying to write your book, and I apologise for that,' Peck wrote. 'On the other hand, if you let me (which you tend to discourage), I think there are ways I could help you write *your* book and make your difficult job easier for you. And while I commit myself to no longer scrap with you, I hope you won't mind if I tease you or toss you an occasional little barb.'

In this period Peck recorded his 'anti-secularist' CD, *Free Will*, in essence a stern chastisement, with some lighter asides, of those who deliberately close their minds and hearts to God's presence. It owed its appearance to Peck's friendship with the country music producer Kyle Lehning. As Lehning explains, it also reveals how quickly Peck's enthusiasms could sprout wings once he had an idea. Lehning was a person who saw Peck as artist first and all else a distant second. The country music producer addressed this in terms of Peck's ability to take the best of what he was thinking and hearing, use that as fuel to fire up his imagination, and then find phrasings for it and a rhythm to it in order to set it down for an audience, just as musicians do. Lehning came to know Peck through two of Peck's books and attending a community-building workshop. He was intrigued enough to train as a facilitator. Though FCE as an organisation had closed its doors, some in the movement, and Lehning was one, personally carried FCE into the twenty-first century and still conducted periodic workshops.

Lehning and Peck, therefore, had known and admired each since the 1980s, and Peck would regularly try to interest Lehning in different wisps of music he conjured up. Lehning never took the bait. Until 2003. 'I was on the cell phone with Scotty one day,' he said, 'and he sang me a song. You wish you could take things back – I said, "I think that song's pretty." I want to fast-forward – that the next thing we're working on is a musical.' Peck shifted into high gear. There was soon a Peck-hired graduate student doing research for the project's story line and, through Lehning, Michael Reid came up from Nashville with Kyle to lend a hand in the project. Lehning describes well-known pop song writer Reid, a classical pianist who has played with the Cincinnati Symphony, as a six-foot-four, 255-pound former all-pro American football tackle, whose country music includes dozens of number one hits in the 1980s and 1990s. Reid now met Peck. 'Scotty is playing Mike his ideas on the piano,' said Lehning. 'Scotty's so into it. They play, talk, develop ideas, and at the end of two days, Scotty, in all seriousness, says, "About a year from now I'm going to be renting an apartment in New York for when this opens on Broadway because there's going to be a lot for me to attend to there."' At which point Reid looks at Lehning and says, 'God, if I just had a little of that.'

Peck, speaking of coming out of his 1990s darkness 'incessantly happy, imperturbably joyous,' said, 'there are only two possible answers to that, either Parkinsonian brain damage or a kind of settled state. Take your pick.' There was another option, the answer he made with *Denial of the Soul* when he said that suicide was no way out of one's medical dilemma. He wrote his book about euthanasia, mercy killing and assisted suicide knowing he had Parkinson's disease. Did he delve into the topics such as assisted suicide in order to gauge his own feelings towards it, knowing that at some point he would be losing control over his daily living and personal functioning? It would be in keeping with his other explorations. Certainly he knew what was ahead, he said Parkinson's disease was 'a debilitating condition second only to ALS, Lou Gehrig's disease, which is worse.' This was the only time in conversation he gave an involuntary shudder at the thought.

Parkinson's gradually robs the afflicted of every aspect of his or her control. The individual becomes trapped in a body which responds less and less to the brain's instructions and has its own erratic behaviour. The intellectual faculties gradually follow a similar pattern of losing orderly control and all life's functional necessities – driving, balancing the chequebook, supervising one's medical services, are one by one stripped away. The sufferer's emotional anguish, from self-pitying to vicious outbursts of anger, are familiar to many spouses and companions of Parkinson's sufferers. Peck, to his credit, agreed to talk about many of these factors in depth, from the claustrophobia and loss of control that is genuinely threatening and frightening, to the physical weariness and unpredictability. He did not venture into interactions with care-givers, and in many Parkinson's situations, the spouse is the vulnerable recipient who bears the brunt of the outcry from an individual being gradually deprived of personality. In some cases the threats escalate, from accusations of abandonment and lack of caring, to cries of mishandling money or threats of divorce.

In some five hours of interviews specifically on the topic of his Parkinson's disease, Peck would discuss only the signs of physical deterioration he was witnessing. He would not venture into the psychological or emotional costs and challenges. All he finally said on these issues was, 'the emotional expenditure on accepting those things can be overdone.' In an email (23 December 2003) he wrote, 'I take my suffering for granted. You know: "Life is difficult." Ho-hum.'

Though Lily would have preferred to keep the California house, to meet the medical and external demands imposed by Parkinson's, the Pecks sold up on the West Coast and returned permanently to Connecticut. In Gail's view once Peck couldn't play golf he became paranoid about his health. 'I think Lily would probably have kept the [California] house, he lost interest in it,' she said. 'Looking back, I think Lily liked having it as a haven. It wasn't a major strain on them, the house was bought and paid for. When he came home he didn't want to go on the road any more. He really started – I've always thought of it as going into the castle and pulling up the drawbridge. He was just happy to stay where he was, very much more focused on his health. He didn't have a headache that it could be a brain tumour, kind of thing; his leg would bother him and he'd have bone cancer. I'd say to him, "You know, you're going to keep looking till you find something."'

Peck was also worried that in Bodega, California, Lily would not get the medical care she needed. In Connecticut, he had connections. He was a member of the local medical community and had watched it grow. 'I've a beloved internist friend [Dr Morris Clark] from the first day we moved here. So it's a superb medical community and one which I can manipulate to my heart's desire,' Peck said, adding, 'which is very, very nice because usually the medical establishment manipulates you.' As a patient, said Peck, there were both advantages and disadvantages to being a doctor. Being on the inside one knows what isn't being done. Being Peck, he had surfaced this disquiet into a chapter of his book, *Denial of the Soul.* He describes the chapter as 'a very good diatribe about pain mismanagement.' For Parkinson's sufferers, he said in 2003, 'It's terrible that people don't get the kind of treatment I can get with my doctor – because he knows me and will spend the kind of time it takes. Mo [Dr Clark] refuses to make any appointments for less than a half hour. I don't know how he manages to live financially because the insurance companies say no, no. And he's old-fashioned enough to just say, screw it.'

Continued Peck, 'As a neuro-psychiatrist I can't say that Parkinson's people should be treated this way or that, because it is just so individualised. But if I were a physician today facing someone with Parkinson's symptoms, I would schedule an initial two hours' appointment – this is me – to get to know that person. Because any advice that I might give him or her regarding Parkinson's, and my monitoring of him or her, should be tailored by my knowledge of the person as an individual.' He acknowledged that the chances of that happening today were slim to zero. 'In a back-ass way,' he said, 'that's the medical dilemma that the United States has come to.'

For Peck, the one physical resource that helped him combat Parkinson's, he said, was sitting in his garden. All who knew him well understood the spiritual and emotional tie Peck had to the 'little spot in the middle of the garden, where there's a tiny patio I call my anti-Calcutta spot. I'm a great admirer of Mother Theresa's work, there's been a beauty to that. But in Calcutta, to me, death was around every corner. And in this spot everything is growing, life-giving. I am content in this spot. Energised.' Peck was non-forthcoming regarding his emotions and concentrated on the body with 'a general message for Parkinson's patients. If the handwriting on the wall is extremely clear, read it. I mean that when my wife or my staff moved to make changes, like getting handles here or handles there, or a special chair to go upstairs, or a trapeze on my bed, they didn't move a moment too soon.' In his one allusion to deeper reactions, he played the stoic: 'It isn't, "Oh, I know now I'm going to die." But, as the neurologist who diagnosed me told me that first day, "Your first adjustment is to the disease's variability." That was very good advice. Parkinson's will not only vary from week to week, day to day, but hour to hour, minute to minute.'

He continued that he found his Parkinson's disease 'absolutely fascinating'. He said he watched his systems gradually shutting down. 'Because the brain controls everything through the nervous system,' he said, 'any muscle in your body can be affected as the brain function falters and different nerves fail. Swallowing, which relates to the voice problem, is a major difficulty.' Two prime causes of death from Parkinson's, he said, are pneumonia related to the loss of the swallowing function, or from choking. Peck told of the day his epiglottis 'hadn't woken up,' and he poured 'the whole slug of coffee straight down my windpipe. It was a little frightening.' It was more than an hour later before, considerably weary, he'd coughed it all out, he said.

Every Parkinson's patient, he said, battles with constipation and at least partial incontinence because the nerves are just not working right.

Unlike ALS (Lou Gehrig's disease), said Peck, 'with Parkinson's the brain, the thinking, is also affected – and that of course is a particularly fascinating thing for me. I have some very distinct brain dysfunction – not just outer nerves out of the brain – that I can identify. I don't know whether I could if I was not a psychiatrist and very accustomed to looking at myself.

'Memory loss first,' he said. 'It's not different than the memory loss that most people have as they get older except it's much worse than it should be for a sixty-seven-year-old. There's a nominal dysphasia, naming names or nouns. Probably at least every once a half hour I find myself searching for a word that I know, tip-of-my-tongue kind of things, which is a higher rate than one would ordinarily have at sixty-seven. I've gotten very adept,' he said, 'at asking people to tell me, you know, what is that word? That's the first and easiest to spot. Then there's expressive aphasia. Aphasia is a disorder of communication essentially. Expressive aphasia refers to a disorder in your speaking, communicating verbally, or sometimes emotionally. That's opposed to receptive aphasia, which is a difficulty understanding what is communicated. I seem to have no receptive aphasia, to date anyway. But I've definitely got a degree of expressive aphasia. I will speak the wrong word. It's sort of like a Freudian slip, only you know it isn't a Freudian slip. I was typing a letter to somebody about three or four months ago and I wrote aggravate and had meant anticipate. And it was not a slip. I can't prove it in court, again, but it feels different. The wrong word comes out. It's relatively mild, but it's definite.

'Not only the voice goes but the muscles – my lips are not working as well. So I can't pronounce words as precisely as I might like,' he said.

On the telephone Peck's enunciation was clear, his voice resonant. That, he said, was because the telephone masks how damaged the vocal cords are.

Is he sensitive to heat and cold still? 'I'm starting to have peripheral neuropathy [sensory loss rather than just motor loss]. My neurologist says, "Well, that's because you used to drink too much." Whether it's that or whether it is my Parkinson's, I don't know.'

'My drinking reached an absolute peak in the dark period,' he said, 'before I was diagnosed. The reason for it was that I had the shakes, the tremor, inside me. Among these other things I just felt very shaky inside me and drinking was magical relief for that. My brother and I were always heavy drinkers.' But, related to the pleasant state he entered three years previously, he said, alcohol wasn't doing much for him any more in terms of relaxation, and he had no trouble in stopping. 'Much less trouble than I thought I would,' he said. 'Before, I drank to calm down. What I miss now is just simply the taste. So I'm drinking nothing now except, occasionally, a sip of communion wine – because of the Eucharist, which is very meaningful to me, not for the wine.'

One loss of brain function due to the Parkinson's disease that particularly disturbed him, he said, was that he had lost his sense of time – not only how long ago things might have happened, but how long he had been talking. 'The only time my Parkinson's embarrasses me,' he said, 'is when I'm suddenly aware that I've talked too much. I ask people to tell me, to interrupt me. Friends will do that.'

Did it appear to him there is something of an epidemic or upswing in Parkinson's disease? If so, what might cause such a thing? 'I've wondered about that very question,' he said. 'It's not outside the realm of feasibility in medicine for a previously very late-in-life disease to suddenly start flourishing in younger people.' He said he'd had a hand tremor since his early teens. It all 'raises a fascinating question, though, which is the question of ageing and death and to what extent doctors can beat ageing and death. One of my little wonderings,' he continued, 'is "Gee, I wonder if this might have something to do with the body almost getting back at the capacity of modern medicine to keep it alive longer than it should?"' When asked if he was afraid of death, Peck replied, 'Less than I used to be, but yes, still afraid.' He admitted he was critical of people who won't face the fact that they're dying until the absolute end. 'Terrified they are, and still in denial – even intelligent people. The power of denial among people dying is unbelievable. I mean literally – a brilliant person, a previously introspective person, the body now down to a skeleton, but with a bloated belly, obviously dying and still just not dealing with it.'

He was concerned about the denial, he said, because it tends to make difficulties for those who would otherwise willingly or lovingly support the ailing person. He spoke of one woman who by her denial 'in the end had driven away all of her friends. If I'm dying,' he said, quoting the words of a friend, 'I'm going to want to talk about it, I'm going to grab the milkman, anybody. So that partly I can deal with my fears by talking about it.

'I also used to lecture people on dying – part of my missionary work,' he said. 'Parkinson's, in part, caused me to quit the lecture circuit.' The conversation shifted again. 'Everybody has got Parkinson's,' he said. Would he ever consider stem-cell implant? (Cell tissue implanted into the brain.) From the little he's read, no. Its success rate, he said, was too limited. But closer to the time when he might have to consider it, he might take another look. He had some very good moments, he said, 'moments of delight when my voice is somewhat functional.' And many moments of constant struggle. 'Reading is difficult after the first two pages,' he said. 'I lose track of the line. I'll find myself either reading it over or reading the previous line or going two lines down. The little tiny muscles that control your eye are activated by nerves. Difficulty with reading is another symptom.'

Not surprisingly, he added, 'I'll be bloody happy when I'm finished with this present book I'm writing. Can't drive, trouble reading, trouble sleeping, trouble everything, but still writing. Typing two fingers, slower than I would like, but faster than a real hunt and peck.' He was also tidying up the paperwork around his life, he said. The financial trust was signed and sealed. The advance medical directives completed. Extraordinary means of life support, such as a feeding tube, he could and would accept, provided he could still communicate. But once it was apparent that two-way communication had ceased, everything was to be withdrawn. When the Pecks returned permanently to Connecticut, housekeeper Valerie would help him pack his case if he was travelling. As he changed clothes she could see his physical condition deteriorating, his stomach extended and hard, 'his buttocks shrinking like an old corset. He had a fetish about his damn slippers, and I noticed they were not lasting, just flattening to one side.'

Peck was occupying his days by occupying his mind, thinking about music and reworking ideas for concluding the already overly long *Glimpses of the Devil*. There were guests some weekends, and occasional visitors during the week. Most evenings, however, found him disconsolate and moody, feeding his tendency to dramatise his slowly deteriorating physical condition as a signal of his impending death. Most of all he was bitter about Lily's departure. In conversation Peck could appear less concerned about the break-up of the four-decades-long marriage than the fact that one of his guaranteed 'care-givers', as it were, had deserted him. During this period Puterbaugh commented Peck would find someone else to take care of him.

In early May, 2003, several months after Lily's departure, Peck received a telephone call from his friend Kathleen Kline Yeates in California. When he told her, 'Lily's walked out on me,' Yeates replied, 'I'm happy for you both. Thank goodness.' Later, Kathy

Yeates commented, 'They had such a terrible marriage. I told Scotty, "There's a real opportunity for both of you to find some happiness." He said, "I'm not called to marriage." I said, "You don't have to get married, just have a good time."'

Yeates is a petite blonde, fourteen years younger than Scott Peck, divorced, highly energetic, intelligent, smartly dressed and direct-of-manner. She had worked for more than twenty-five years for the California State Department of Education, was a volunteer at a counselling centre and, with friends, owned and operated a bed-and-breakfast inn in Sacramento. Yeates and Peck first met in the mid-1980s when the counselling centre's administrator, impressed by Peck's *The Road Less Travelled,* decided to invite Peck as a speaker and use the occasion as a fundraiser, attracting both therapists and the general public. Because she owned a B&B, Yeates was asked to donate a room for Peck during his visit to help keep costs down, and she agreed. When he arrived she dropped him off at a restaurant so he could have dinner and he invited her to join him. 'He spent the night at the inn and did the show the next day,' she said. She was no Peck acolyte or groupie, and refused at dinner to be impressed by some of his more outlandish statements, she said, but he liked being challenged. As they talked they discovered they had a companionable ease with each other. And that developed into a fondness which in turn later on led to a long-term relationship. 'Scotty said he had an open marriage with Lily. I loved him for twenty years,' but for some fourteen of those, until 2004, it was at some remove. That was because, she said, she broke off their relationship after six years when she learned 'the magic was broken in our relationship because he slept with woman on a book tour in Canada, but he was miserable being on this book tour. It wasn't that he was playing the field.' At an earlier point, said Kathy, they'd had 'a serious talk, and I said, "How many women have you slept with in the previous year?" and he seriously looked at how many. And it was only twenty-five – and I know that may sound like a huge number to some people – he was looking at every woman with potential and fantasising about every woman.' The Canada incident was different. They'd been true to each other, she said, 'but with this Canadian woman – he didn't have intercourse with her, he couldn't get it up as it turned out – I just felt, you know, he was willing to go that far. He was filled with guilt and remorse, and called me to apologise and I said, "You know, Scotty, the spell's been broken – whatever was keeping us in a monogamous commitment to each other. I believed you were not sleeping with Lily, and I believed there was some magic in our relationship. But I don't believe we have it any more.'"

Though their relationship as lovers ended, the memory lingered on and the friendship prevailed. They would occasionally meet when Peck travelled, and call each other around their birthdays, his in May, hers in June. In 2005, Kathy said that twenty-one years earlier Scotty talked as if the Pecks were 'a happy family. I got, you know, what a great artist his son was and how proud he was of him, and how smart Julia was and she was going to Harvard and she was this and that. How wonderful Belinda was, I mean he talked about them in glowing terms. I don't know if it was pseudo-Scotty. I got the good Scotty, I got the romantic Scotty. He was totally romantic – as much as he fought against romantic love, he had to have romantic love in his life. The happy Scotty, the joking Scotty, the affectionate, the warm, the loving, and for six years he was – and he would talk about that he had an open marriage and a marriage that sounded screwy to me. And he was having an affair with a woman in town! All of this was so, like outside the realm of my imagination.'

When Yeates in 2003 made her annual 'Happy Birthday, Scotty' telephone call, health and death were much on his mind and a major part of his conversation. In addition to birthday greetings, Yeates needed a letter of recommendation for a new venture she was embarking on, and advice from physician Peck because 'my dad was very ill,' she said. They 'chatted about his divorce, and this, that and the other, and that was that.' A few days later Peck returned the call with his findings on her father's behalf, promised to look further into matters on her father's behalf, and they continued to stay in touch. In July she intended to fly to Ohio to see her father. Peck, who repeatedly told Kathy he was dying of Parkinson's disease, suggested she come visit him on the same trip. Which she did. 'We had a fun time,' recalled Kathy. 'I think Omar and Leslie Kahn were here on that occasion, or the next time.'

Kathy Yeates's father died in December 2003, and in the January 2004, still grieving, she made a second trip to Connecticut to see Scott Peck, who was still trying to convince all who would listen that he was dying. Even so, during those two visits, 'Scotty was charming, delightful, wonderful, it was the Scotty that I knew and he was terrific. We had fun, we laughed and all that. It [the potential relationship] was still turning, turning. By then we were talking on the phone every night.' A short time after her return to California, as she drove home on the highway from work, Peck called her on her cell phone. When she answered, they spoke for a moment and then he proposed to her. 'I can't remember precisely the date, but I remember I drove off the road, pulled over and caught my breath. I had to get home and we were still talking and I went four exits beyond my exit. He proposed. I said yes. And then I said but I've got to apply for a leave of absence. That's going to take a while. He said come for a year and let's see how it goes and then we'll get married. And I said okay, I'll get a leave of absence in case it doesn't work out, then I'll go back to California. And you know we talked about stuff and then the intensity upped because I was shocked that he had asked me. And I said, is this the same guy that said, "I'm not called to marriage"? And he said, "Well, now I'm called." He said, "I need someone to take of me." I told him he knew he wasn't dying.

'So I came again in the March, Easter time. We had a really nice time and he said, "Come, live here for a year, let's see, you know." So we talked and then while we were talking he said, "Oh, I didn't think my libido would be turned on again in my life. But since you've come back into it my libido is alive and well. You've awakened that part of me."'

One continuing link between them while they were apart was the newspaper cartoon strip 'Cathy', created by Cathy Guisewite. Cathy the cartoon character is a single woman in her forties with a frenetic, on again, off again love life. 'Scotty asked me to marry him right before [cartoon strip] Cathy got proposed to. I said to friends of mine I thought I was going to get married. And they said, of course you are, Cathy has been proposed to and, they said, your life always parallels hers.' The cartoon strip Cathy was to wed that February. Back in New Preston, Peck sat down Gail and Valerie for a talk about Kathy coming. Valerie said she thought, 'Three women in this house? Oh boy! I mean we've always been very protective of Scotty.'

This same spring, as he and Kathy Yeates were in regular telephone contact, Peck emailed to me the comments from his friend Jack Severance that, 'In my opinion a bio of M. Scott Peck would be no easy task: exasperating and even maddening; yet fascinating and ultimately rewarding. I hope your biographer has enough Dramamine to endure the rough seas of the voyage.' In a follow-up email Peck added, 'To your probable delight I'm seriously going to try to cut back on our emails. Three months to due date for *Glimpses*.' When, for a brief moment, it appeared work on the biography might not continue, Peck wrote, 'In our case, who has been the patient and who the psychiatrist?' The work did continue, and in the course of that year his comments ranged from, 'Sorry to have dumped on you the way I did last evening. Most of it you didn't deserve (I hope)' to 'Am I trying to write YOUR biography of me? In this instance, of course.' A much later email from Gail summed up the situation: 'I can only imagine that when a book is written about you that you would experience feelings of denial, anger, frustration, paranoia and even relief. So no matter what is put down you can never please everybody all the time. And you certainly sound prepared to handle it. It seems as if everyone knows a different Scotty, including Scotty himself. He truly can be a mystery.'

It was in spring, 2004, too, obviously with Kathy in mind, Peck emailed: 'Time to go courting, don't you think?' He did not expect an answer, his mind was shifting temporarily to matters other than books.

It may well have been during Kathy's third visit, said housekeeper Duffy, 'that Kathy and I were standing in the kitchen and I didn't really know her but I asked her age. She was four years older than I am. I said, "Can I honestly say something to you, woman to woman?" And I thought, I don't know if this is going to work, but it was really, honestly coming from my heart. I don't know her. I don't know if she's coming for the money – my initial thought was she's coming for the money. I don't know what happened [between Kathy and Peck] years ago and I don't really care. I said, "I really think you need to think about this. Really, really hard. You seem like a brilliant woman with a great job, coming from California to this tiny town [Peck's household]. You're giving up a lot, and if you married Scotty, you're not marrying Scotty, you're marrying Scotty and Gail." And she just said, "Thank you. Thank you very much." And I think she took it the right way. After I'd said it I thought, how could any woman understand that? One day, I don't know if she was already here, I said, "I don't know if you're coming for the money." I've seen the old Scotty. I didn't see anything appealing about Scotty other than I loved him to death and would have done anything for him. So obviously, she must have a whole different [view of him].' Gail's view was that once Lily left, Peck 'needed someone to take care of him and that someone was Kathy. It *was* because of his fears of his health.'

Duffy knew Peck was deteriorating from his Parkinson's disease and was concerned for his final care. She went to him, told him she didn't care who he brought into the house, how much money he had or who he gave it to, '"but you always told me that if you got sick and died there'd be enough money so you could die in your own house, enough for nurses around the clock, and we wouldn't have to stuff you in some home somewhere. That's the only promise I want from you." He told me how much he had and he promised me, and I took his word. And [as he was dying] it worked. He did that, and Kathy went above and beyond. But she and Gail, oh. Bad situation.' During the visit, said Kathy, 'Gail said, "When you come here you'll never be able to go to California again, you'll never be able to do anything." She said, "The drawbridge will be raised." She said, "Do you know what you're doing. You know you're crazy for coming here. You don't know what you're getting yourself into." She was very negative and tried to talk me out of coming.' Meanwhile, Peck told Kathy he intended to 'call some old friends, is that all right with you?' She said, 'Sure,' but was wary enough to ask if they were '"Just friends, or girlfriends?" He said, "Just old friends." And I said, sure, of course, that's fine. And so that was that.'

In California Kathy applied for a leave of absence, eventually granted effective the start of the September 2005 school year. Peck kept pressing her to come. 'I was working until August thirtieth. So it was very, very stressful because I said I wanted more time. And that's when the bad Scotty showed up. He called me, I was actually with my mother at the wedding of a family friend. He was very mad that I was with my mother and said that I should be there with him and not with my mother.' She told him it was ridiculous to be jealous of her mother and he was irate. He retorted he was going to call 'another friend'. When Kathy asked him if it was a girlfriend, he replied, '"Yes, she is, and you better like it." And I said, "Well, wait a minute, Scotty. Wait just a minute." I said, "Listen, you know I won't come if you want this other woman. You have her come, you be with her." I said, "You know, play the field. You don't need me, if you want somebody else."' Peck gave Kathy an ultimatum, to arrive in New Preston by an August date 'or don't come.' When she told him she couldn't leave work until her leave of absence started, he said, 'You better be here September first or don't bother coming.'

Kathy said she tried to probe what was unnerving Peck, and said, incredulously, 'You're mad about my mom?' He answered he'd had a friend visit for the weekend who said that if Kathy loved him she'd be in Connecticut. Kathy said she wondered if Peck was losing face with his friends because she was not there, and she wondered what the calls to this other woman meant. She agreed she'd arrive 1 September. 'For the next three weeks I pulled all-nighters to pack. I was wiped out by the time the moving truck came, packing at night and working during the day.' She arrived in New Preston at the beginning of September 2004.

Two months later, in November 2004, Kathy, asked why she would consider marrying a man already in the grip of Parkinson's disease, and whether she found an inevitable future geared to Peck's physical and emotional caretaking daunting, replied she could handle it. She loved Peck, she said, and had since they first met. She said that prior to the Connecticut move, 'I did a lot of research on Parkinson's. I did a lot of soul-searching of myself, and I'm not afraid of death or illness or my own death or illness. [I saw] my father die – it was a lovely time as well as a painful time. I had a fiancé who dropped dead of an aneurysm, alive one minute, dead the next. I didn't have a chance to say goodbye, or anything. I've had a lot of near and dear friends die, so I see death as something you can't avoid. Death is another adventure, another mystery. I have loved Scotty for twenty years, so it will be a privilege to be able to serve him and to love him.' Fifteen days later she was Mrs M. Scott Peck.

CHAPTER 14

A BOOK ON SALE, A SHIP AT SEA,
AND A HOUSEHOLD ON THE ROCKS

When Kathy Yeates arrived at the Springfield-Hartford, Connecticut airport in September 2004, Peck was there to meet her, 'all dressed up and had roses. A man from I'll Drive You car hire had brought him. It was very, very romantic.' But she soon had much to contend with. Peck told her that in the preceding months he'd been calling another woman friend (known here as R), who lived in the American Southwest.

Kathy said 'alarm bells' had gone off for her, 'but she'd rationalised his behaviour, for she had been talking to Peck only for 'maybe fifteen minutes in the morning on the way to work and fifteen minutes on the way home and he was lonely. So he would talk to [R] two and three hours at night. And I didn't realise that he was so lonely and in some ways it was my fault, because I didn't realise it.' Now permanently moved to Connecticut (or semi-permanently, for she did not unpack her boxes), she said, 'He didn't need to call R, but then he would obsess about her and about me. He wanted her to come so that I could meet her so that we could have a *ménage à trois*. I said, "I don't sleep with women and I don't sleep with people I don't love." He said, "Well then, maybe we can just get in our pyjamas and watch television." So he had this fantasy that was very upsetting to me. I thought, oh my God, what have I done. What have I gotten myself into?'

She dealt with the *ménage à trois* issue with humour. Kathy set up her camera in a bedroom and persuaded Gail and Valerie to climb into bed with her, all dressed, but with their shoulders above the covers bare. And that's what the photograph revealed. Kathy told Peck that was the only *ménage à trois* there'd be. It was a rare moment of all-around humour in a household becoming more tense with each passing day. As for R, the compromise Kathy and Scott made was that he'd just call R once every two months. 'I could tolerate that. And he kept to it,' she said.

'I came in to give him all this love,' she said, 'and I realised it was too much.' She said she was trying to gauge her next moves. 'Even though I had more love to give him – an abundance – I realised I'd have to step back because it was not comfortable for him to give him so much love – because he couldn't handle it. If I gave him too much love he would turn it against me. It was too scary for him. It was tragic. Even though he'd been in psychotherapy, I don't think he learned how to cope with it, hide it, manipulate it, explain it. Even with Lily and his kids and people that loved him, if they loved him it made him angry. The rage. I don't know whether we were all getting charged for what he didn't get as a child,' she said, 'still sitting on that rage that he didn't get that kind of love as a child. He was so angry. I mean I'm not enough of an analyst but it was very deep-seated. It's very hard to explain, but he didn't know how to give love, he didn't know how to get love.'

Asked months after her arrival – her boxes shipped from California still shoulder-high in downstairs rooms – if the unpacked boxes were a presentiment about their relationship's difficulties, Kathy smiled away the question. 'There were several things,' she said. 'One is unpacking is not fun. And there was no real room to put stuff in the house. There was also no time, you know, when you're really busy. I was doing things with him that were far more interesting. And there was no urgency. I would unpack quite a few boxes and be called away to do whatever. And then I would be like, where am I going to put this stuff, there was no place to put it. I was constantly trying to figure out what my role was. There were things that were set up before I arrived that Scotty didn't want changed. Lily didn't do grocery shopping,' Kathy said, 'Gail did the grocery shopping. But I did the cooking, so I wanted to do the grocery shopping and Gail was totally threatened that I was taking away her job. She was afraid that Scotty was going to fire her or limit her salary.'

Continued Kathy, 'Every time I tried to do something I was thwarted. I was either thwarted by Gail being insecure and, "We have to wait until Gail is more secure," and all that. Or I was thwarted by the fact that, "Oh, Lily spent too much money, so I'm going to give you an allowance." Or, "Lily did this so I'm going to punish you this way." And so I thought, okay, you know, he'll see in time. He'll see who I am, but for right now I'm going to have to pay the price that Lily didn't pay, and deal with this neurotic secretary that has all these phobias.'

Kathy said Peck didn't like change, yet he wouldn't handle his affairs himself. He'd turned most of it over to Gail, who was so familiar with everything he had to keep her. 'Gail took over,' said Kathy, 'and he let her. She thought she'd be with him at his death.' Day in, day out, life in the household was 'tense,' said Kathy, 'some of it was Gail's personality and my personality.' And practically all of it Peck's doing. There was another issue – Peck's predilection for walking around the house naked. It was not a recent habit. Kathy tackled him about it, asked him not to do it. He would say he was not ashamed of his body. 'I was trying to plead with him. Any kind of criticism he would not tolerate, and not tolerate it in a crazy way. I tried to explain it that this was a workplace, it was inappropriate [and, in the United States, against the law as sexual harassment].' Peck would repent, dress and the moment would pass. But if Kathy went to the grocery store, she said, when she returned he'd be naked again. Her decision was to step back and figure out how to deal with him. 'His narcissism did not allow him to tolerate any criticism. There had to be another way.'

It came one day when the yardmen were working in the garden and Kathy needed to talk to them about the work. The indomitable Ms Yeates told Peck, '"I'm going downstairs and talk to the men," and I started taking off my clothes. He said, "What are you doing?" I said, "I'm going to go downstairs and talk to them." I had my clothes off. And he said, "Naked?" And I said, "Yeah." And he said, "Why are you going down naked?" And I said, "Well, you have no concern about your body, I have no concerns about mine. I'm going." He stopped me and said, "Okay, put your clothes back on and I won't take my clothes off."' The matter was resolved. Asked if she felt she had to be a rather strong woman to deal with Peck, she replied, 'Well, I did because when I was taking off my clothes I thought, my gosh, what am I doing?' All this with a wedding in the offing, though the dates and the details were far from resolved.

Peck wanted to be married as soon as possible. He'd already booked the honeymoon, a fifty-eight-day luxury cruise around South America. He hoped and anticipated that his nephew David could marry them during an October visit, and when that proved impossible, Kathy suggested to Peck they go to England and be wed there. Peck demurred because he'd made a great fuss with relatives and friends for several years about his inability to travel any great distance, because of his Parkinson's disease, and felt the South America trip was test enough. The first search was for a minister, then a locale might suggest itself. They both wanted either an Episcopal or Catholic priest. Kathy enjoyed going to church on a Sunday, Peck didn't. He didn't like getting up in the morning for a church service and preferred what he called his own 'rogue' communion services: Peck as celebrant and preacher. The future Mrs Peck decided it was too exhausting to keep fighting him 'on the church thing' and instead attended Sunday services alone.

There were breaks in the wedding planning routine. Visitors came, including Kathy's mother, and California friends. There were Scott's friends, including, at Halloween, his back specialist Dr Cameron Brown and his wife, Jodi. Scott, Kathy and the Browns decided to work on a book together, *Psychosomatic Spiritual Illness.* With that and the South American honeymoon in mind, the Browns decided they would join Scott and Kathy on the Rio de Janeiro to Manoas segment of the planned South American cruise, and they could work on the book. But there was still the wedding to get to, and through.

On the marriage topic, Peck's next suggestion to Kathy was they could be wed in the church where his daughter Belinda was wed, with his friend, the Rev. Stephen Bauman, officiating. Peck also wanted Melissa Bauman, a superb soprano, to sing Mozart's *Alleluia,* as she had for the funeral of Peck's late executive assistant, Mary Ann Schmidt. Said Kathy, 'The moment Steve [the Rev. Bauman] found out we were getting married, he came up immediately, sort of blew by me and just talked to Scotty and said, "As your executor, as your trustee, you must get a pre-nup [a pre-nuptial financial settlement in the event of a divorce]."' When Peck told Kathy, she said, 'Fine.' But she was not fine with replicating Belinda's wedding or including Mozart's *Alleluia* from a funeral service.

She told Peck she wanted 'our wedding to be ours and not have previous attachments to compare it to.' When Peck asked Kathy where she wanted to get married, she suggested Peck's garden 'as the most spiritual place I've been here.' He agreed and suggested a Thanksgiving weekend (the fourth weekend in November) wedding, and 'we'll have to figure out a priest.' In telephone conversations at this time, Peck was happily anticipating the wedding and honey-moon. In the home, there was talk of Peck's daughter Belinda and family coming up for the wedding, but doubts that the pre-nup could be prepared by Thanksgiving. Early December seemed the most likely. There was an issue as to how many people to invite. According to Kathy, Peck said, 'If we have a big wedding I won't get to meet any of your friends, you won't meet any of mine. It will be a big bash and then we'll be exhausted, and I don't like to do that.' She suggested, 'Let's just make it a wedding full of love – a priest and you and me and two witnesses. And if you're worried about cost, we can bake the cake.' That much was set; all that was needed was a date, a minister and a bridal outfit. Scott Peck had never in his life been into a shopping mall, she said, but she 'dragged him to the mall anyway and made him sit outside the dressing room while I tried on wedding outfits. He was very sweet and did things like that. We were there for several hours until he was totally exhausted,' but she found a $300 white Liz Claiborne trouser suit she liked and put it on hold, and bought a matching scarf at another store.

Understandably, Kathy sought to experience some of the joy associated with wedding preparations, so the next day, with Jayne, a girlfriend, she went 'to these fancy shops and I tried on beaded dresses and formal wedding dresses and just got the girly bride out of my system. Beautiful dresses and it was just fun to be with Jayne to try on these dresses and get oos! and ahhs! and whatever.' They went to a second mall because Jayne wanted to purchase something from Filene's, a low-cost 'outlet' store. While there Kathy saw the same trouser suit she had on hold. 'It was only eighty-nine dollars, so I bought it, came home and said to Peck, "Honey, not only did I buy the suit that you like, I got it for two hundred dollars less." So he was very pleased.' For wedding slippers she wore white tennis shoes. Peck wore a navy blue suit with a pink tie with a wavy design on it.

As for a minister, he and Kathy both thought the chauffeur from I'll Drive You cars had seemed particularly spiritual; an enquiry revealed he was not ordained. Kathy said that as Scott knew many ministers they should go through his list, but that didn't produce an answer, either. When approached, a Catholic priest friend Kathy had on the West Coast said he would officiate and asked her to contact her local Catholic church. When she was told there'd have to be annulments, and that the time frame was impossible, her

Catholic priest friend said, 'Never mind. I like weddings, they're a holy time, a happy time. I will come and marry you.' A date was set, 3 December; only the matter of witnesses remained. When Peck suggested his executive assistant, Gail, and housekeeper Valerie, Kathy retorted, 'I only want people that have been supportive of us, and Gail has not. I mean Gail keeps questioning you and me and saying why do we have to get married. I said I don't want anybody that's questioning us. I want this wedding to be about God and about love, and that's all I want.' She was eager to please, but as relentless as Peck in not wanting to be steamrollered. 'When he suggested R as a witness I just looked at him. There was a part of me that wanted to fly off the handle, there was a part of me that was in disbelief. So again I kind of stepped outside myself. And I said, "Sweetheart, I don't know R, and I said it's really important that the witnesses really be supportive." He said, "I don't know this priest but I'm trusting you with this priest." And I said I know, but if you rather that we do someone else, I can understand. He said, "Okay we'll go with the priest." He was calm about it and later denied that he even mentioned R. He had no recollection of it. None. I don't know whether it was the [Parkinson's] medications or whether it was just his getting out of a conversation.'

The witnesses in the end were Peck's friend and personal physician, Dr Morris Clark, and his Anglican nun friend, Sister Ellen Stephen. Scott and Kathy baked the wedding cake together and 'had a wonderful time doing it.' Because Peck wasn't having a bachelor party, as a treat Kathy thought he might like to talk to R. She called R and said, 'Could you please call him as his bachelor party. I said I'd like to give him that. And she said, "You're not giving it." I said, "I didn't mean it that way, R, I just wanted . . ." so she snapped at me. I said, "I'm just trying to make Scotty happy and I think this would make him happy, and I think you want to make him happy." And she said, "Well, while I've got you on the phone," and then we started talking.'

Kathy said she told R that 'you know it hurts me when he talks to you, it hurts me when you call. I don't understand what this relationship is. And I said, you know, I don't know what your integrity is. I know that he flirts with you and it hurts me. I said woman-to-woman I don't know what you're getting out of this and it hurts.' Later, R did call Peck for his bachelor party as planned, and he was delighted to talk to her. She also 'told him what I'd said about her integrity level,' said Kathy. 'He got off the phone and was mad at me that I used that call to poison him right before the wedding.' Nonetheless, married or not, Peck and R continued to call each other once every two months. 'So for two months I was happy,' said Kathy, 'and then, right before he was due to call her, he'd start tormenting me [with it]. When once I said, "Yes, go ahead and call," and then he had no interest. I thought, gosh, I should have not gotten hooked, but I did, I mean it hurt my feelings.'

When she'd tackled him about it, he said, 'I'm from another planet' and he hoped she was 'from that planet too.' 'I said, "I'm from planet Earth." He wanted his way all the time,' said Kathy, 'and once he got it his own way, he didn't want it. But if he wanted to make me unhappy he would bring up R. It was silly because we would be ecstatically happy. He'd even talk about that he had no libido because that was a funny story. And he was wedded to his funny stories. But he got erections. It was not that his libido was dead. It was far from it. Far from it. He'd gotten rid of porn films, so we got more and so he was very sexual.' They were wed, on schedule, on 3 December 2004, and departed for South America on 15 January 2005, on the fifty-eight-day cruise. He had a pet name for her, 'Honey Bunny'.

As the new Dr and Mrs Peck set sail to circumnavigate South America, author Peck left behind his newest book to the untender mercies of reviewers. *Glimpses of the Devil: a Psychiatrist's Personal Account of Possession, Exorcism and Redemption* was his tale of serving as exorcist at two exorcisms in the mid-1980s. To the reviewers on the 'possession' wing of Christianity, this was Peck telling about Satan the way it is. *Christianity Today* magazine's reviewer said Peck's account corroborated his own observations at two exorcisms, and praised it as courageous, and valuable for 'theological reflection'. To others, there was little evidence in the book that that's the way it was. Satan was present because Peck said Satan was present. The book was precisely what Peck intended it to be, though general reviewers weren't much interested, it seems, in a blow-by-blow, or prayer-by-prayer account of two exorcisms.

Peck wasn't really done on the 'evil' topic. Had he lived for a decade more in reasonably good health, there's a good chance he'd have charged cuttingly into the assembled forces of 'group evil'. He talked about it, and gave hints in a *Glimpses of the Devil* interview with the online magazine *Salon*. His statement to *Salon* that an example of group evil at work was the US Supreme Court awarding the US presidency to George W. Bush over Al Gore created a media furore. The sad thing was Peck was no longer so adept at being interviewed that he was able to provide much context for his Supreme Court remarks. Consequently, if *Glimpses of the Devil* didn't get a lot of reviews, his 'evil' comment on Supreme Court certainly generated a great deal of comment from columnists and bloggers. One writer, radio personality Michael Medved, a former Hollywood columnist turned 'US cultural wars' commentator, called Peck 'an unhinged, best-selling' celebrity.

Prompted by the publication of *Glimpses of the Devil,* Andrew Billen of *The Times* of London called on Peck. He pressed Peck on his relations with his children and Lily, and the fact two of his three children no longer spoke to him. Peck replied as he had a dozen or two score times before, that he was 'less of a father than he should have been.' 'As for what kind of husband he made,' wrote Billen, 'it is for Lily to say and she seems to have voted with her feet.' Billen continued, 'I suppose, I say, women threw themselves at him on lecture tours. "I had opportunities, but it was not as many as you might think," he replies. "I used to protect myself very stringently."' At which point Billen recirculated the 'drunk and womaniser' charge against Peck. 'The paradox of this colossally self-deluded man,' wrote Billen, 'is that he is, on his better pages, a font, or conduit, of clear-headed advice.'

Dominican theologian Richard Woods closed his 800-word *National Catholic Reporter* review of *Glimpses* by stating: 'Dr Peck also seems to have transgressed the boundaries of professional ethics. But this is a matter for his peers to evaluate.' Woods said of Peck, quoting a remark attributed to Thomas Aquinas, '"Beware the man of one book." Here, clearly, it would have been wiser by far for Dr Peck to consult more widely than [Malachi Martin's one book on exorcism] *Hostage to the Devil.* And if one is tempted to read something by M. Scott Peck, choose *The Road Less Travelled.*'

Happily away from it all, though hoping for rave reviews he suspected would not be forthcoming, Peck and his new bride were on the high seas for two months of inescapable proximity to one another. 'It was glorious,' said Kathy, 'because there were no distractions or other people.' Peck didn't want to meet a lot of people on the ship, or, given his physical limitations due to Parkinson's, take many of the excursions. He was not about to let his control of the situation slip, however. Kathy said it was all 'very romantic, leading up to the cruise,' although once it was under way he was difficult. He said they were to use the time to work on their marriage. He told Kathy, '"I don't want you to be jealous of Lily, Gail or R," so we tackled each one,' she said. 'I wasn't jealous of Gail, although they had this strange relationship that I couldn't figure out. I wasn't jealous of Lily, although on the ship, in conversation with others, he kept saying, "We did this" and "We did that," and people would look at me and I would shake my head, "Not me, his first wife." I told him, "I'm not jealous of Lily, you just need to reference it. I talked about things I did with my first husband, but I say it was my ex-husband, or I don't even bring him up in it. It's fine. That doesn't bother me. As for R," I said, "it's not that I'm jealous of R, I don't even know the woman, but, you use her to torment me. It's not about R, it's about the way you do it." Criticism. He couldn't handle it. So we processed that.'

Peck began his shipboard day on the stateroom balcony, in contemplation, or having a cigarette. Kathy brought breakfast back to the suite, 'checked out the day's excursions and brought back information. He liked that.' He was content relaxing on the balcony looking at the sights, smoking; sending Kathy out to reconnoitre, and occasionally joining in at meals or shipboard events, such as art auctions. On the first leg of the voyage Peck contracted 'cruise ship flu' and 'was very ill with hints of pneumonia,' she said. 'That was because he'd keep going outside for a smoke on deck, despite the fact that he was stepping into the frigidity of a scenic beauty featuring fjords, glaciers and ice. For five days he was on antibiotics and used a nebuliser. It was the tangential stuff, pneumonia, that was very scary to me. He would sleep and send me off on an excursion to scout out the town.' She didn't take the trips to the hinterlands, but looked around, took some photographs, and returned to tell Scott what she'd seen. In all there were only two ports he did not visit himself, but he limited himself to two side excursions – one to visit volcanoes, the other to tour the Falkland Islands.

Otherwise, on board, Kathy said, 'I'd meet people – sometimes he would meet people while we were sitting in the lounge waiting for an excursion or something – he'd say, "Well, you're out here making friends." I'd say, "I'm not making friends. I was out doing stuff or listening to the lectures." They had wonderful lectures. I went to art auctions, by myself. He'd be in the cabin and I'd come back and report to him. And then sometimes I'd drag him along on something and he would gladly come and do it and stuff like that. The only friends we made were the two lovely Romanian women maids who cleaned our room.' Sometimes they attended art auctions together. 'There were some pieces that we liked in common. When we were on the Amazon I actually won a painting in the raffle. I was shocked and very happy about that. He was very happy when the picture came, he loved it and we hung it up. It looked like a lake scene, very colourful and happy.'

Towards the end of the cruise, when the vessel arrived at Rio de Janeiro, the Browns – Peck's orthopaedic doctor, Cameron, his wife, Jodi, his daughter and the couple's daughter – joined the ship. 'We went out for a lovely dinner and had a blast. Then they were with us. So every day we'd spend some hours on the boat. And then time exploring and whatever. When they left we had the last leg of the trip. Scotty was incredibly amorous and loving and very adventure-some and just terrific. And he had been terrific at various points but he was also difficult. Then, whatever the chemistry was, it shifted to amorous.'

In March 2005 the couple returned home to a New Preston house that was functioning on borderline civility, periodic confrontation, and not much fun. Valerie Duffy could recall only one day in the succeeding months when everything passed off pleasantly. Gail said she was in tears driving to work. It was dark clouds most days at the house across the road from Lake Waramaug. 'Valerie's got a great wit. She's very funny and Scotty loved her for it,' said Kathy. 'She remained helpful. Gail wanted to control and was going to leave Scotty. I mean she couldn't handle me any more. That was a big upset.' The issue was reasonably complicated. Just as Scott and Kathy were about to leave in January for their honeymoon, Kathy received notification from the State of California that as an employee in good standing she could 'buy' five years of retirement, which she decided to do, and withdrew money for it from a retirement account to pay for it. However, because of the imminent departure to South America, Peck persuaded Kathy to let Gail handle the paperwork. Kathy said she protested, but Peck said, '"Now you're going to have to trust me and trust Gail. Gail will have to do this for you because you can't do it on the ship. She'll be fine. If she doesn't do it right I'll cover the cost and make it right." Okay. So I had no choice. I turned it over to Gail and explained what needed to be done. Gail said she would do it, and that was fine.'

Many months later, with Kathy about to take Peck to the hospital in New Milford, Connecticut for exploratory gallbladder surgery, notification arrived from the State of California that Kathy's application had been denied because it had not been completed properly. Now there was a fresh point of contention between Kathy and Gail, though she decided not to say anything to Peck. 'Scotty sensed something wrong and said, "I'm your husband and I want to know what it is",' said Kathy. She told him. Once again it was Peck, unwittingly this time, who set the cauldron boiling. He'd told Gail she'd completed the application correctly.

Kathy was required by the State of California to return to her department to formally be reinstated in order to immediately apply for retirement in September 2005. Gail was aware of that, said Kathy, 'and the day I was trying to take Scotty to the hospital, Gail said, "When you come back [from California] I'm going to take another job." Gail was telling Scotty she couldn't stand to work in the house with me any more. Scotty was livid at me,' said Kathy. 'He was yelling and screaming. He was afraid he was going to lose Gail because Gail had so much information. I said to him, "Why should you be mad at me? My retirement's messed up and you said you'd make good on it" – which he never did. "If she wants to leave, fine."

'Scotty would complain about Gail, but I didn't dare because Scotty would get mad at me. He'd created this triangle. I mean he set up a triangle including Gail and myself. He would play us against each other and then say, "I hate it when you two fight."'

Gail said when she told Peck, '"I will stay with you until that woman comes back from California and then I'll leave you," he started crying and he kept saying, "You can't do this to me," and I said, "I cannot not do it." Kathy and I talked, later,' said Gail, 'and Kathy said they'd had a major fight about that, part of it instigated by him from the start. Kathy and I never stood a chance of getting along. Two women in the house with different parts of this man. She does not like me now. I don't like her. On some level if we could sit together in a room we'd start laughing at how we feel. But I don't see it happening.'

After the honeymoon, as before, Peck constantly added kindling to this incendiary situation between the two women, such as keeping Gail in charge of the household finances. He told Kathy that Gail would give her a cheque for her allowance once a month. That was her housekeeping money. Kathy protested. Peck would hear none of it. Kathy said, 'He put me on this allowance, he said, because of Lily's spending. He projected a lot of stuff he got mad at Lily for on to me: "You know, Lily had shoes she never wore." I'd just say, "Okay, someday you'll realise I'm Kathy, not Lily. I'm sure I've got flaws but I don't have the same faults that she had. And I'm not secretive." He was very tight. He was frugal. He loved counting his money on the stock market every day and didn't see any reason to spend money. He would spend a ton of money on a trip and then wouldn't spend any on stuff in the house that needed to be repaired.'

Within all this, and Kathy and Gail understood it well, Peck was tormented by his deteriorating health and inability to govern most aspects of his life. Parkinson's was now dominating the man. He could not leave the house alone, could not drive, could not stay on top of everything in the household. The deep-seated anger festered just below the surface, always ready to erupt. One day his friend Dr Cameron Brown visited with his wife. The doctor had been severely injured in an airplane crash. As Brown later recounted it at Peck's memorial service, 'I showed up at Scotty and Kathy's house, and my wife got out of the car and Scotty jumped into the car. He didn't drive much any more. He drove the car over the kerb and through some bushes and across the lawn to get me in front of the garden because he knew I could barely get out of the car. And he sat there and asked me questions about my jaw and about my lung. Then he stopped and did what he could do so easily, not with the hand he had been dealt in San Francisco [his training in psychiatry], but with the other hand [that Peck the man used to] pluck right into you.

'He said, "What do you have over me now?" And he knocked me out of kilter,' said Brown. 'All the time up the Amazon River and in the garden together we'd be duking it out and I'd be feeling pretty good about it.'

So he asked Peck, 'What do I have? Youth?'

'Exactly wrong,' Peck replied.

'Well, what is it?' Brown asked him.

'Wellness,' Peck told him. 'You're well.'

There was now a bitter edge to Peck, and he was less inclined to hide it. Christopher, asked about his father's seeming ability to be cruel in this period, and whether he'd witnessed any of it, said, 'I've seen lots of it. I've heard it said that people interviewing Nixon couldn't believe they were speaking with Nixon because it seemed like somebody doing an outrageous caricature of him. Scotty was now the same way. It just became more and more unfortunate. I saw the same qualities and cruelties very early in life. The difference was in degree – he lost his capacity to control. I don't think he was feeling differently about things, he just wasn't filtering, editing what he was saying. And he was never terribly good at it anyway. On principle he believed in being open and honest about certain things – he was just sticking by his guns.' Did his father ever apologise? Christopher said, 'Oh yeah, saying the words was not hard for him and sometimes I think he meant it.'

Added housekeeper Valerie, 'I saw the cruelty recently, but I have to be honest, I think it was Scotty losing control [of himself and everyday affairs] and knowing he was losing control.'

One way or another, everyone in the household who was close to Peck was lectured, or worse. He would lay people's faults bare, said Gail, 'tell them what they were really like, then back off and excuse himself by saying he was only telling the truth. He had no idea of how to be socially adept, not even little whites lies – I mean we all do them: "Oh, you look nice",' she said. 'Instead, Scotty would say, "Jesus Christ!" and take people apart. I said to Kathy, "I don't know why you don't go running and screaming into the night 'cause he's not going to change. That's not his goal. Everybody else grows and changes for the best, but Scotty doesn't have to." He was actually creating a worse situation with Kathy than he did with Lily.'

In conversation Scott Peck had described a much earlier incident where he had rebuked Christopher for been overbearing, and left a note on Christopher's bedroom door apologising for not being 'in community'. Christopher remembered it. He'd been about eighteen, and a potter, and was thinking of embarking on an extended hitchhiking trip. 'If you really had it out with him,' said Christopher, 'all out, it would very often result with some kind of peaceful resolution. My problem was there was only so much of that I could take. I'm not a confrontative person. It was a road to epiphany and calm waters he wanted from a lot of people. I just wasn't able to give that to him. He couldn't stand people walking out on him.'

Christopher Peck said, 'Scotty was always able to surprise us. I think a thing that surprised me about Scotty is that women found him attractive. I just couldn't understand it. Also, he had gotten out

of forty years of marriage, that he married so quickly. He explained
to me he wanted a nursemaid. He wanted to be babied. And by
golly, he got it in Kathy. Kathy was very strong, she had a year
where she always stood up to him on whatever. I would say that she
was thinking of leaving him from the moment she got to
Connecticut. But by the end, even before Scotty had been diagnosed
with whatever, I think she was starting to crumble. He was able to
give people the impression that they didn't really have a choice,
they had to be there to love him.'

Kathy put up with it all, she said, because 'there was something, I
don't mean this in an arrogant way, but there was a reason why he
chose me. I don't know if in the bigger scheme of things God knew
he was dying and wanted me to be with him because he knew I
would be steadfast and could handle it; would be there for his care
and his wishes about dying at home. There was a constant struggle
between the light side and the dark side of Scotty. I could see into
the light side but wouldn't tolerate the dark side. I mean I
challenged him on so much. Sometimes I feel guilty because I was
really challenging the dark side that he had used as a coping
mechanism for so long in his life. He realised I wouldn't roll over
the way Lily rolled over all those years. I wasn't going to roll over, I
mean we were either going to work or not.'

There was the complicated man and the simple good he had
done, she said. 'Scotty's writing was done in a beautiful, simple
ways. So many people that read his work felt they could have
written the book themselves. He resonated with something in their
own lives, they felt he was reading their minds. It rang so true that
they felt a closeness to him, that he was speaking for them, inspiring
them, challenging them.' Asked if she felt the same way, Kathy said
no, 'our very first time together, our first meal together, I was calling
him stuffy and pompous. He was used to people kissing up to him
and I didn't. I mean I wasn't rude, but I certainly disagreed. I spoke
my opinion and challenged him on some things. I'd met famous
people.'

Gail said, 'I mean I loved Scotty but I didn't deal with him.
Scotty, I think, for a long time had been *me, me, me*. Scotty would
give everyone their fifteen minutes and then they'd shut up. It was
definitely his ideas, his thoughts, and once you'd learned and
stopped being hurt by it, you knew he was listening but he wasn't.
He was definitely so focused he didn't even see what was going on

in his own home.' Asked about her relationship with Kathy, Gail said, 'It was hard for her to understand that Scotty did confide in me the way he did. I don't know if it was right or not, but that was the way we'd worked for years and years. I think one of the main problems between us [Gail and Kathy] is that I knew what their marriage was and she knew it. So I knew their fights, I knew every day of it. I know this, Scotty played us also. I don't know if Kathy mentioned that. He loved using us against each other. He liked having two women arguing over him.'

Gail, asked if she thought Peck was a spoiled brat, replied, 'Yeah, in a lot of ways he was. Yes.' As Gail perceived matters Peck hired people, 'he wanted what he wanted in his way. As boss he was entitled to it. He wanted Kathy to come from California under certain conditions. He brought someone to take care of him. I don't believe he was in love with Kathy.'

To Valerie, Peck 'loved control and in the end, after Lily left, Scotty gave up control, and he had no idea he'd done it. Gail controlled him and he allowed it. I never saw Scotty out of control when he was married to Lily. He was controlling, but he wasn't out-of-control mean. Scotty was a brilliant man but he had no common sense. He liked control, but he had this fear we used to talk about: 'When I die. When I die.' I'd always say, "Well, are you dying soon, because I have a schedule." I'd say, "Well, what's your worst fear?" He said, "That I won't have control of my life."'

He had preached about dying, given hope to thousands, but had become fixated on his own death and dying. Valerie said that years earlier, Peck lost a good friend who was on oxygen when Scotty went to see him. When Peck returned to the house, he took to his bed. 'That was it, the curtains were drawn, the whole bit,' she said, 'now he was going to die. Christopher came to see him and I can remember him having Christopher by his bedside saying his last goodbye. And I don't care how old Christopher is, you're still a child and this is your parent saying his last goodbye. And I was just so irritated. My God, he's going to be just like my father. He's going to curl up in a little ball and there's nothing really wrong with him. And I thought, Lily, if ever you're going to fire me, now would be the best time to do it. I opened up his bedroom door, the curtains were drawn and it was like a morgue in there. I whipped open the curtains and I pulled back the covers and I said, "Scotty, if you're going to die you can die on somebody's else shift. You're not dying on my goddamn time. There's nothing wrong with you." And I ran. I ran and hid in Lily's bathroom and I just looked at Lily and I went, "Oh my God, I can't believe I just did that." I thought I'd stepped way over the line, I might as well kiss this job goodbye. And he never said a word, but in a few days Scotty was up. When I would get him something, or say something to him, he wouldn't say a word to me. I'd be walking around for days thinking, OK, I'm going to be in that chair in his office, and the lecture is coming.'

Of Gail and Kathy's relationship, Valerie said, 'I don't like to hurt feelings, but [Gail] was jealous in her own way. Gail liked to plan things, so her life was planned that she was going to take care of Scotty and when he died we'd be at his deathbed and everything was going to be organised. When Kathy stepped in Gail was stripped of all those things. But Kathy was trying to be a wife, you know, do what we [Valerie and Gail] do, but as a wife. And was Gail quitting? Gail was going to quit. But then Scotty got sick.'

Gail explained, 'I worked with Scotty so many years when he had a wife who wasn't interested [in managing the Peck household], then all in a sudden there's someone in the picture who does care and does resent my being there and being such a part of it. He certainly pushed buttons in Kathy and me.' Finally Gail had had enough. When she told Peck she was leaving after Kathy returned from California, it was because, she said, 'I had no more endurance. No more. I just couldn't do it. I said to him, "I come to work crying every day. I hate being here." And I'm sure Kathy felt the same way. So we were locked in a terrible battle.'

Said Valerie, 'Scotty had no common sense. He just knew how to put money here and money there and yes how to write books and yes he knew all this. As he got older it had to be hard. So many people put him on a pedestal, so to speak, because he had saved so many lives. So many people who were down read *The Road Less Travelled* and were brought back up. As he got older he wasn't that important. He wasn't the young, the spunky, the good-looking man wanted by every woman that he thought he was. And maybe was, I don't know that. I didn't see that side of him. It had to be a letdown, not to be so important. Not to be special. To have new people coming up and being the new un-Scott Peck. Had to be a letdown.' Kathy said as much: 'He's still being quoted, but he was feeling like a has-been.'

'There were two Scott Pecks,' said Kathy, 'Scotty was just a residual-like dry drunk. The personality was already created from the alcohol and the drugs, then the combination of them. He prided himself that he went through therapy and talked about how he'd been cured. I think he just learned how to drive his neuroses deeper underground and how to control them. He could – because he was so intelligent he looked sane. And so these insane things. The good Scotty was really, really good. The good Scotty was so much more intelligent, insightful, brilliant – more so than anybody. Most of his friends got the good Scotty. He kept the bad Scotty for the people closest to him, whether it was to test them, or because he couldn't keep that Scotty in the box all the time. I mean he'd be screaming at me and then the phone would ring and he'd be all sweetness and light. He could definitely bracket in – most of his friends had no idea of the dark Scotty. They got someone who was charming, intelligent – all those things, you couldn't find anybody better. He would challenge you with thoughts and conversation and delight you with stories and make you laugh, challenge your thinking and it was wonderful. They got a wonderful friend.'

Then Peck became ill.

It started simply enough. His skin was yellowing with jaundice, his stools were light, and he was diagnosing himself, convinced it was the gallbladder, and he was not in pain. His blood sugar was extremely high, but he ate a lot of sweets, really craved them. Finally he called his physician, Dr Clark, who admitted Peck to the nearby hospital for tests. Peck was buoyant, said Kathy, so she went to the airport to collect her mother, arriving for a visit. There was an MRI that showed nothing, more tests, Peck accused the staff of withholding information, Kathy said. There appeared to be a blockage in the liver, and a stent was inserted and within a couple of days he was back home. There was much discussion with his physician friends regarding where Peck should go for more comprehensive testing, and finally, on the advice of his endocrinologist friend Dr Robert Hatcher, he decided on the Mayo Clinic, in Rochester, Minnesota. On the Friday he was released from the local hospital, he and Kathy and her mother went to see the play *Equus* at an outdoor theatre and picnicked on the grass.

By the Sunday he was complaining of feeling unwell, but refused to return to the hospital. On Monday he was in such pain he had to be admitted, and his condition was rapidly worsening. 'Lily showed up at the hospital,' Kathy said, 'and he didn't recognise her and said,

"Who are you?" She said, "I'm Lily."' Kathy left them alone and went for a forty-five-minute walk. When she returned, she said, they were just 'talking about this and that'. The hospital was waiting for the ambulance that would take Peck to the Mayo jet waiting at a nearby airport. It was late arriving. With more delays, Peck was going into shock, said Kathy. The flight was hampered by thunderstorms and rerouted, 'his blood pressure was forty over thirty,' she said, and on arrival at Rochester airport Peck was transferred from aircraft to ambulance and from ambulance straight into the intensive care unit for the next week. He had pancreatic cancer. It was one day up and one day down until the Sunday, at which point Peck was not expected to live. His son Christopher arrived. Said Kathy, 'Chris was nonchalant, he said, "He's been at death's door many times."'

Scotty asked that his daughter, Belinda, come to the Minnesota hospital from Texas, Kathy said. Belinda wanted to know how seriously ill or close to death Peck was. She said Christopher, when their father was transferred out of the intensive care unit, had told her, 'See, I told you he wouldn't die.' Kathy said Belinda was reluctant to make the journey, for it was her children's first day back to school, nonetheless the family took a plane to Rochester, Minnesota. By the time they arrived, Peck had rallied, his temperature had broken and an excruciatingly painful sensation he felt in one leg no longer hurt. Once he was further stabilised he'd be able to return home to die. As Kathy described it, the meeting of father and daughter 'was an opportunity to reconcile, and Belinda sincerely tried. Scotty, because of his narcissism, just could not admit he was wrong. He said to her he would apologise to her for all the sexual things that had gone on, but I couldn't understand what he meant actually, whether it was back in the New Preston wild days, or the reputation of having had affairs.'

'Belinda did tear up and look at [her husband] Paul,' Kathy continued, 'because she had legitimately tried to say some things that were of real concern to her in a sincere way. Scotty wouldn't take responsibility and started talking about totally inappropriate things, totally inappropriate. So Belinda and Paul left, and when they left, they said, "This is it."'

Peck was sick and confused, and perhaps still being wilful. Because Christopher had made the trip to Minnesota, he told Kathy he and Christopher had reconciled, and that now Christopher would come to visit them. When Kathy responded he ought not to count on it, Peck became angry with her and accused Kathy of trying to drive a wedge between him and his son, whereas, she said, she'd worked for two weeks to persuade Christopher to visit his father.

'If there was one thing I perhaps should have said to him,' Christopher said, 'it is that I found him intolerable but that he shouldn't take it personally. It just doesn't sound right and would not have held sway with him. I myself forgave him years ago, and have said as much. I forgive easily.' Christopher said the problem was he could no longer stand to be in the same room as his father. 'His past behaviour I did not hold against him; I just found him insufferably annoying. He couldn't manage to put a sentence together that wasn't like nails on a blackboard to me. That's my fault. I have an obsessive-compulsive disorder, which may have something to do with it. Valerie rightly says I need to let things roll off me like water off a duck's back,' he added, 'but I haven't learned that trick. I had held out hope for years that he would change just a little so I could make a visit once in a while, but all his letters and emails rubbed me the wrong way, and I just couldn't manage a visit and stay sane.'

Six months earlier, Dr Gerald May, the psychiatrist who gave Peck's *The Road Less Travelled* its second review, in the *National Catholic Reporter*, had died. Peck was writing an introduction to May's book, *Dark Night of the Soul: A Psychiatrist Explores the Connection Between Darkness and Spiritual Growth.* Kathy said that when, following May's death, Betty May wrote to Peck, 'I could see in the way she was talking about their children, and the relationship they had as a family, that it moved Scotty and it hurt him. He said, "I wish I had that kind of relationship with my children." It hit him very deeply. He really did tear up because he really envied people when families had a good relationship, but he was his own worst enemy with his family. I mean it was with the people that loved him most he showed his darkest side, and that was very hard on him.'

'Scotty never knew how to be a father,' Valerie said. 'I judge that because I had a wonderful father. I think kids need to be patted on the back. Kids do things we don't like. Kids do things that we don't want for them. I felt very sorry for Christopher. In a way I think Christopher always tried. I think Scotty liked to play games and analyse. You may be a psychiatrist but you can't get inside your kids' heads because a part of it is your own head and you don't even realise it. I really don't know much about Belinda and Julia. Belinda has been back and forth and Belinda to me is the good daughter. How she handled it really, I don't know. Christopher had cut off communications [with his father] for a while. I said to Scotty, this was after Lily left, and he was writing to Christopher, "Scotty, if [for] Christopher to survive it means cutting off communications with you, you have to accept it. I mean kids do things we don't like all the time. But Scotty, you have to learn how to be a father and it's kind of late." I got the silent treatment, which means I hit a sore spot.'

Peck was indeed deeply regretting his extremely troubled relationships with his three children. Perversely, he couldn't, or rather wouldn't, admit the extent to which he was responsible for the fissures and faults that had caused the breech. An unparalleled wordsmith in conversation, he was unable or unwilling to express remorse sufficient to the damage done, in words that sincerely conveyed what he felt. Or ought to have felt.

CHAPTER 15

THE HOMECOMING

Peck returned home to New Preston, to a hospital bed in an upstairs bedroom with plenty of windows. A good friend to his friends, Peck was soon seeing them all as visitors flocked in. The calendar on the kitchen wall filled with entries, two days marked, 'Guy, Guy' (psychologist Jim Guy from California), 'Kaz, Kaz' (Kazimierz Gozdz from California), or 'ES' (Sister Ellen Stephen from the convent). There was a constant, organised flow of well-wishers and those coming to say what they knew were final goodbyes. As far as unconditional love from friends was concerned, Peck was having a reassuring several weeks, though his condition was still deteriorating.

Said Kathy, 'He didn't have pain, he had nausea so he would throw up a lot, bile, all of his stomach. And as he was in bed, his lungs of course were filling with fluid because he wasn't able to exercise. I was afraid he was either going to aspirate vomit or get into a coughing spell and drown, the way a friend of mine did from pneumonia. He was gasping for air and desperate.' The inevitable deterioration continued, visitors coming now were finding a Scotty who could no longer hold a conversation, though he'd occasionally say things. Kathy was with him most of the time, often saying prayers aloud. If she squeezed his hand, he'd squeeze hers in return. There'd be bursts of talking, isolated, spiritual perhaps, talk of letting go though no talk of God unless Kathy mentioned God. He'd groan. If Kathy asked him if was he in pain, Peck would reply, 'No, I'm just letting go.' Was he then in that deep private discussion held only by those who see the end is near? The discussion too private to share?

Peck could still get furious. A few days after his return from the Mayo Clinic, Kathy and a visitor from California were in Peck's room. The visitor said to Kathy he would give Peck some marijuana to help combat his nausea. Kathy said to wait until she telephoned

269

Dr Clark to see if the pot might adversely potentiate some of the drugs Peck was on. Peck became furious, yelling at Kathy for daring to interfere with his medical care. She, equally tartly and emotionally, retorted she'd been taking responsibility for his medical care day and night for the past two months, and it was because she was there she'd break the Peck family spell of the men never having their wives by their bedside when they died. They were yelling and screaming at each other, she said. She was crying even as she recalled the evening.

Peck would have bursts of good humour, and, if provoked, recall. Kathy said that at one point Peck 'was trying to tell one of the nurses a joke. It was close to his death. He could still understand what was being said to him, but his mind had a loose wire and wasn't connecting – so he had trouble maintaining the length of the joke, and I would prompt him by saying a line.' But Kathy's line was not verbatim, 'and then he would correct me with the verbatim version,' she said.

There were major household tremors and tremblers still. At one point Peck had written a codicil to his will giving Kathy an additional bequest, a codicil he later revoked. He was ratcheting higher his bid to control, and didn't care who was hurt. At the Mayo Clinic, said Gail, Peck told her he intended to divorce Kathy when he returned home. Once home, it appears he was telling Kathy he really did want her better provided for while insisting to Gail he was going ahead with the divorce. The final bitter details around this, and the mutual recriminations and antagonisms Peck viciously fanned to a great heat between the two women, can be charitably attributed to the dying Peck struggling in a fog of pain and fear and morphine derivatives. Uncharitably, it could be considered he knew precisely what he was doing as he tried to exert his power one last time. 'On the [final] day he was really lucid,' Kathy said. 'Gail and I were in there – and I think he realised he was losing it as far as mental cognition. He said, "Gail, I have put Kathy through more in one year than I have put you through in nineteen." He said, "I had to test her love and she loves me and I love her."' But even then the issue of divorce versus adequate coverage swirled around his bed, spilling over into yet more dissension throughout the house. The point became moot as Peck slipped further towards coma leaving a bitter interpersonal bequest of his own deliberate fashioning.

It is impossible to know in those final few weeks what he really

wrestled with. He did not talk of God. Kathy said that in the period
when Peck was still communicating fully, his endocrinologist friend
Dr Robert Hatcher told Scotty he needed to cut down on the
number of visitors: 'You need to have a quiet time.' Out of the blue
Scotty said, 'I want to be Catholic.' 'Bob and I both said, "It's fine
with me",' Kathy recalled.

Two years earlier, asked which denomination he'd choose if he
joined one, Peck said that in 'a gun in the back situation, "join a
denomination or die," I would become a Catholic.' Now he'd
returned to the topic. His interest in Catholicism was piqued by,
though not limited to, the concept of confession. He twice spoke of
his wish to make a general confession, though on the second
occasion quickly added that his adultery would be pretty far down
the list. (A general confession is that in which the penitent reveals
and repents all the sins he or she can recall from across the span of
life after the age of innocence.)

With Catholicism in the air as a dying wish, Kathy suggested to
Peck that as there were no visitors on the calendar for the following
day, they should pray over it and then he could make a decision.
And they could call a priest. But Peck declined to pray over it, 'said
"unh, unh," so he didn't really mean it,' said Kathy. 'I was shocked
because I was turning to God the whole time. There were so many
times he was sleeping I was in prayer because I had no choice. It
was the only place I could go for comfort. I don't know if he was
angry at God, he never expressed that.'

Or had he, in a 1993 poem, 'Slip-Up'.

> I am sorry, saith the Lord.
> I assumed.
> I breathed into you Life.
> I created you in My image.
> And gave you freedom,
> Freedom to choose.
> Assuming you would know
> To choose the balance:
> The yes and no,
> The no and yes.
> Instead,
> You chose the heart
> Over the mind,

Or the mind
Over the heart.
You choose this
And not that;
To open or close,
And it seems to be beyond your comprehension
To be both –
To be both simultaneously –
To hold on and to let go.
I failed to teach you
My holy injunction 'and'
I am sorry.
I let you down.
I failed
To make you whole, and
I apologise.

Was there a suppressed anger in Peck towards a God who has failed Peck, rather than the other way around?

Whatever one thinks about the Lord apologising to Peck, there was little evidence most of the time of Peck apologising to Kathy. She recalled that 'sometimes I felt it was a real conflict between us because there were times on the ship I wanted to go to church, and he wanted to have communion, two of us, in the suite. I went to the two services on the ship, the Catholic and the non-denominational one.' When she'd tell him later he'd be upset. She'd counter, '"Well, we had our communion, but Scotty, it was not authentic. There was no connection to God, it was your way of using God to give me a lecture about, 'God, I'm going to talk to Kathy when we get to the Falkland Islands about this or that.' That's not a prayer. That's not communion, community." I said I needed something. He could certainly talk the talk and convince many people. And I know how much he loved God, and how much he cared. [But he had this] fear of even that love, I mean fear to let God's love in. I mean if he could let any love in he could let God's love in. Not to experience God's love is sad. I don't know whether it was his adult arrogance that he couldn't let God love him. But I think it had to do more with his childhood. I think it was all back to that.'

Nonetheless, she said, 'for the last two and a half weeks of his life he was wonderful to me. Finally we were loving each other like the man I came to love. He was being very sweet. But up to that point he was a little monster.' The end was very close, the coma was not continual but during the periods he emerged from it his thought patterns were generally disconnected and erratic. At one point he was telling Kathy about the wings, all sorts of fluttering wings he could see and hear.

The days dwindled down to the final three. On Thursday (22 September 2005), she said, he was vomiting, desperate and gasping for air. 'He grabbed me and said, "Honey Bunny, don't let me die. I'm afraid, help me, help me." So you know, we got him calmed down.' On the Friday Dr Clark wanted to increase his morphine but the final decision was not to. That same morning, as the nurses were busying around, said Kathy, one of them mentioned about something being 'over there', and Peck burst into the Second World War song, 'Over there, over there . . .'

On Saturday morning he was being cleaned up, the nurses were with him, and he said, 'Good morning.' One person present was George Moskoff from California. Moskoff, on his own initiative, had offered to assist Peck on some of his non-writing projects. Moskoff, plus Peck's friend Phil Mirvin, and Kathy were in his room. Gail and Valerie had visited him that morning. Phil suggested to Kathy they go for a walk. They did and George remained with Peck. Later, when it was time for the nursing shift to change, Kathy went back upstairs and George went down. Peck's eyes were closed, Kathy said, 'He was breathing quietly, sleeping inside a semi-drug-induced comatose thing. The nurses were counting pills between shifts, and I was with Scotty alone. I was telling him about the light on the trees. I was telling him what a light he had been to me and to so many people. I was telling him it wasn't always the best of times but I forgave him for all his shit. And I apologised for any shit I gave him. I was talking about South America and the fun times we had over twenty-one years, and thanking him for all that. And I told him I loved him very much. I just wanted to say a prayer. I'd been saying things like, you know, made-up prayers, "Dear God, please save Scotty," kind of thing. And then I said the Lord's Prayer. And as I said Amen, he died and left. He absolutely died when I said Amen. He sighed, and then I looked at him, and I looked around the room, and looked at him again, and I said, "Oh my gosh, my darling, be with God, and thank you." And at that point it was a perfect death. It was his final gift to me and my final gift to him. It couldn't have been better.'

Later, as Dr Clark told those attending the memorial service, 'doctors do sometimes make the worst patients and Scotty refused a medication I knew would have eased his suffering, consequently he suffered more than he needed too, and consequently that was painful to watch. He resisted Kathy's efforts to care for him even though she'd become expert in his care, at this point truly his twenty-four/seven guardian angel. With only ten days remaining in his life a remarkable transformation occurred, for reasons I do not understand. Literally overnight, from one day to next, that lifelong deep-seated need for control vanished completely. I'd never seen anything quite like it. He literally surrendered his care, and I believe his whole being to Kathy. Just a few days later, on a bright, sunlit Indian summer day, he died peacefully in her arms. At peace. At long last.'

Christopher Peck, in his summing up, surmised that his father wasn't a Jekyll and Hyde character 'because Jekyll split himself into vice and virtue, but Scotty's virtue was really a sham. His narcissism left him a very lonely person, and his saintliness (which I found creepier than his cruelty) was a plea for love. I don't think he loved because he enjoyed loving others; he loved in order to be loved back.'

There was a family burial service at the little church in Quaker Hill, the church closest to where Judge Peck and Elizabeth Peck had their final country home, and where they are buried. Scott had much earlier bought a plot there, though the cemetery is now 'closed' – there is no room for further grave sites. Peck was cremated. His nephew, the Rev. David Peck, already en route to the United States' West Coast for meetings, was routed through New York City on his return in order to see his uncle and Kathy. Peck died 'the day before I left [England],' said David, 'so instead of a sick visit I took his funeral at Quaker Hill. I think it significant that in a liturgy, in a remarkable act of ecumenical generosity, a Congregational church that did not use fermented wine allowed me to celebrate a requiem Eucharist and preach. I used the propers [prayer and psalms] from the Sanctorale in the American Episcopal Church Book of Common Prayer for "a teacher of the faith". For me this was the public contribution of his life and faith which, despite the many failings of his private life, were those the Church could and should celebrate.'

The Rev. Stephen Bauman gave the eulogy. 'Not long before he died, Kathy, Melissa [Bauman] and I, and a few others, were able to carry him out into his garden that he loved so very much. It was an absolutely beautiful day. Bright sun, startlingly white clouds, flowers in bloom, the air buzzing with life. We shared a Eucharist, the main event in Scotty's religious life. It was near perfect, I thought. We were completely alert. The moments were teeming with life and death and the mystery that holds them both as with a tender caress. Not many days are like that, of course. But that day was at least as true as any other. And the truth of it spoke of the grace that binds all things together, the good, the bad and the ugly. In this wondrous redemptive grace lies our hope. I think Scotty clung to that. I think that was the essence of his spiritual awakening.'

Present in the little Quaker Hill church were a handful of family members: Kathy; Lily, two of Lily and Scott's children, Belinda – with her husband and children – and Christopher. Nephew David (the Rev. Peck), his sisters, Heather and Lisa, attended, with their mother, Greg (for MacGregor). There was an additional group of close friends. The press announcement of M. Scott Peck's death stated Lily and Scott had only two children. No names were mentioned. The second daughter, Julia, was omitted. Kathy and Gail had awkwardly discussed whether or not Julia should be included in the announcement. The uncertainty, said Kathy, lay in the fact that Julia had much earlier ordered Gail not to make email contact or keep her apprised of details of her father's activities, and, to Gail's eyes, had seemingly long-since detached herself from the family. Julia was not mentioned in Peck's will. All three women in the final New Preston household could agree, to quote Kathy, that 'Scotty was truly in a lot of pain about his family.'

What remains remarkable about Peck's closing months is not Peck's often outrageous behaviour, but the candour with which Kathy, Gail and Valerie (and, on the sidelines, Christopher) could still address their relationships with Peck in a detached yet supportive manner. Peck had never been easy to live with. The Parkinson's disease anger and anguish, exacerbated by the cancer and the knowledge he'd returned home from the Mayo Clinic to die, brought to the surface a nastiness difficult to contend with. Yet the three women were able to display love for Peck, each in her own way, despite a disunited front. They were able to talk of his failings while keeping his strengths in perspective. They understood his fury as the Parkinson's disease further and further deprived him of control. Their quite similar remarks reveal why they were prepared to be candid for this book, even critical of him – because they believed in him, and the worth of his work.

At the 12 November memorial service in Christ Church on New York's Park Avenue, the printed announcement stated, 'Dr Peck is survived by . . . his daughter Belinda . . . his son Christopher.' The Rev. Peck included Julia in the public prayers for the family. There had been no general invitation to the memorial service, those who came heard by word of mouth. About one hundred people were present in the church where Peck's parents had worshipped. There were readings and reminiscences by Peck's friends and Kathy. All present were invited to approach the Eucharistic table. Closing prayers preceded the robust 'Once to Every Man and Nation' that marched the service to its conclusion. There was a reception following, downstairs. People lingered for hours and then, finally, tenderly, possibly permanently, parted to return home, or to their hotels before flying out to California, Georgia, Tennessee and elsewhere the following day. (Lily later moved to Massachusetts where, son Christopher could report, 'Mother is in fine health. Her old house was very remote from anything fun, or even an airport or train for a quick escape.')

Peck, who had fought with his father, was buried from his father's church and his ashes interred in a plot close to his parents. Was this all the family he had left?

The bulk of Peck's approximately $4.5 million estate (not including the house) was divided between Belinda and Christopher. Kathy received, she said, the house and 'a small sum of money'. (A local realtor said the house in Bliss Hollow would fetch 'around $1.5 million, somewhere in there.') Kathy said Gail, one of the two executors, received 'about $300,000.' Months later, Gail, asked if she had been fairly dealt with by Peck in his will, replied, 'less so than her, I'll tell you. You know, for less than a year's work that [the Peck house] is not bad, regardless of how she wanted to cry and wear his robes. I think he was excessively generous in his pre-nup, but I don't think she coerced him, I wouldn't want that to come across. I don't want this to be about Kathy and me. It was a doomed situation, it really was, looking back at it. He tweaked it all along. And in the end she has succeeded in erasing me from him.'

Apparently there were legal confusions left behind as well. 'Peck,' said Gail, 'had X amount of attorneys, and one didn't know what the other one did and it was confusing. It was Scotty. We all miss him and kind of shake our heads and go, "Oh, how typical." Gail said she'd 'given it some thought, and what comes back to me is that Scotty was the focal point of our problems, our disagreements and everything else, and was also the focal point for us at the end. I think we did try hard to do what was best for him at the end. Kathy and I knew Scotty was a major part of the problem and we both were terribly sucked into it. But towards the end we rose above it to give him what he wanted, and honour what he wanted.' In an emailed reply (27 September 2006) three days after Scotty's death, Gail wrote, 'There definitely is a void, coming to work today was terrible. To know he is no longer in the house is terribly sad. There has been no man in my past, present and God, I hope not the future, that could infuriate me more, make me cry more, make me want to strangle him more, or create such devotion to him and loyalty. I will miss him terribly. Sooo, here's to your book about him. May it make people think and know him better (all parts of him).' In a closing email that followed, Gail said she did not want the final months of Peck's life depicted merely as a conflict between her and Kathy.

She'd served Peck for eighteen-and-a-half years, she said, and many people were aware of the important role she'd played during that period. She obviously felt deeply that Kathy had 'erased' her from Scotty's life.

Valerie maintained her simultaneously involved yet detached perspective on the household and on Peck. She said she and Gail had 'always been very protective of Scotty and Lily. Very protective. I would not trash him, but I will be truthful. There's a whole big difference. I miss him every day.'

Kathy also reflected on her openness in discussing Peck's strengths and shortcomings. She concluded, 'I'm much more honest than Scotty was. I'm not going to lie. I don't want anything I say to be used critically against him, but I don't mind it being used honestly. Scotty was such a paradox,' she said. 'On the one hand I feel terribly sad and upset that we didn't have more time. On the other, incredible gratitude we had the time that we had. It's such a mixed feeling: a wedding day, filled with love and joy, and times when he would steam with anger, and give me such a steely stare.' She said, 'I remember the sound of his breath as he slept, and it's hard for me to go to bed and realise he's gone, the way he felt in my arms, and yet what solace he brought as well as the pain. For every dark moment a moment of such brilliance it was overwhelming. I try to remember the man that he was – not the one I would like to build out of fantasies and "if onlys" and things to comfort me. I find more and more as the days go by the balm of forgiveness kind of washes over the cracks in my heart.'

Kathy said that after Peck's death she stayed for a time in Florida with friends, and while there attended the King Tut exhibit. There is a quote from Howard Carter, who discovered Tutankhamen's tomb, that she felt was apt for Peck: *The mystery of his life still eludes us. The shadows move but the dark is never quite dispersed.*

Asked if she was going to unpack her boxes now, Kathy replied, 'I can't unpack. I've got to leave because I can't afford to keep the house.' Months later she thought she might remain, if she could afford its upkeep. She was still plumbing the deeper reaches of the relationship, she said. 'I've read a book that describes Scotty's condition perfectly, *Controlling People*, by Patricia Evans. It has helped me understand Scotty,' she said, 'and has been a major relief. I understand him, and my reaction to him, and to Gail. Their pathologies were a perfect match. I've joined a grief group,' she added, 'a lot of women in the same place. It's been very helpful. It brings up so many questions: is it better to have loved? But it's interesting how grief just waits in ambush, like Cato (Burt Kwouk) in *The Pink Panther*. Valentine's Day was difficult. I remember and smile. What a paradox.'

In the spring of 2006 at the house on Bliss Road, letters still arrived addressed to 'Dr M. Scott Peck'. There are 'letters every day from people who don't know that he is dead,' Kathy said, 'thanking him for the incredible contribution he made to their lives. And I must say that every day there is some insight into myself that he has also made possible. I think the thing that has moved me so much is that Scotty lives on through the things he's written and done; he has affected our lives, and I think that sometimes there's something – a quality or action in my own life – that makes me smile and think, that's a part of him living in me. He lives on in the people who have read or known him.'

His nephew, Father David, was well aware of the remarkable aspects of Scott Peck's accomplishments. Scotty's 'personal life and many family relationships were in such deep disarray I could never begin to fathom him,' he said. 'This personal tragedy, which is not new or unique, meant that tragically he could teach others what he needed to know and do for himself but could not and did not.' Father Peck also said – in the light of the deaths of his grandfather and his own father (David, Scott's brother) – 'There are interesting spiritual and theological and psychological issues here: he who dies last with the most toys wins. Scotty has certainly won among the men of his family. It is human nature and tragedy that even when one reaches this, there is an emptiness; because, of course, it is reconciliation; forgiveness; love, that is missing, and by definition unforthcoming. We are simply left with our appetite for approval and no-one left in the restaurant.'

Peck was that solitary diner.

'I happen to be a Christian,' Peck said, 'because I think that the Christian doctrine, on the whole, approaches reality more closely than other religious doctrines. I said "on the whole" because there are some things other religions do better than Christianity. The little bit of Islamic theology I've read seems to emphasise remembering. The Muslims tend to be better at remembering than we Christians are. But, *on the whole*, I believe Christianity approaches reality a little more closely. I emphasise *approaches*. Reality, like God, is not something we can tie up in a nice little package, put in our briefcases, and possess. Reality, like God, is only something we can *approach, not possess*. We are God's to be possessed by.

'The prevailing Judeo-Christian view of the world is that this is a naturally good world that has somehow been contaminated by evil,' he said. 'My own view – speculation – is that maybe it is the other way around: we live in a naturally evil world that has somehow been mysteriously contaminated by goodness. There is no question that evil is a mystery, but I think the mystery of goodness is an even greater mystery.'

Distrusting people, distrusting love, distrusting himself, he placed – to the extent he was capable – what little fragment of trust remained, in God. And hoped God understood. He'd written what he had to say, and in every book stayed true to his profession of faith. He hoped his readers, too, would understand.

APPENDIX:
PECK AND JONES

'**I**'ve sent you a long, nasty letter,' said Peck, on the telephone. He was in a New Milford, Connecticut hospital bed awaiting gall-bladder surgery. 'I'm still trying to push something on you,' he said. 'That's fine,' I said. 'I'll read it and ignore it, like the others.'

'The anaesthetist just walked in.'

'That's fine, I'll call you back. What? Half an hour?'

'I'd prefer you'd call me back next week, because I'm tired.'

And so it was, but not quite as planned. For by the next week Peck was in the famed research centre, the Mayo Clinic in Rochester, Minnesota. It was not merely gall bladder, it was pancreatic cancer. His kidneys shut down, he was on dialysis. On Sunday, 14 August, when I returned home extremely late from a vacation noted for thunderstorms and delayed flights, there was a voicemail from Kathy Peck at the Mayo Clinic. Scott was not likely to last, and if I wanted to talk to him I should call.

I tried several times the following morning. Finally, just before noon, Kathy answered the telephone. Scott had bounced back. He and I chatted for a brief time. His voice was weak, his spirit wasn't. We joshed and exchanged pleasantries for a few minutes until his voice faded. I reminded him that we'd an agreement that he'd never see the manuscript. What he didn't know, I told him, was that because of his condition – no longer able to read – it had always been my intention to take the book, on publication, to his home and read it to him. 'How parental,' he commented, not critically. I continued, bluntly but essential to the topic, that as he knew he would not live long enough now to know what the book said, once he was back in New Preston from Mayo, I would come to New

Preston and read him the draft Introduction and two chapters. I knew which two chapters I intended, one about his books and one about FCE and his friends commenting on Peck's personality. He was deeply touched that I would do so.

A couple of weeks later I made my way across the flagstone patio, past his SUV with its 'THLOST' licence plate, past the large rounded stone engraved in Roman lettering, 'In Search of', to the side door. Gail was there, Kathy was upstairs with Scotty. Later I saw Valerie. Two nurses were on the upstairs level when I went into Peck. He was on his back in a railed bed. I stood to his left side, took his hand and held it as I said a short Celtic prayer aloud. He winced at several of the words, or phrases, or cadences. I'd sent him a copy of the book it came from when we first began our conversations.

For a period of thirty years I was first editor, then editor-at-large, of the *National Catholic Reporter*. I was editor when the newspaper gave *The Road Less Travelled* its second review. In 2003 I had inter-viewed Peck for an extended essay in the same newspaper on his reactions to living with Parkinson's disease. Those were my personal connections to Scott Peck. As a newspaper editor, I'd always con-tended a story was not complete until the readers were heard from. In that spirit, this book would not be complete without this postscript of what it was Peck wanted in his biography, which differed, no doubt about it, from what I was writing. Call it 'Scotty's Turn'.

Two things intrigued me in the three years occupied by this book, that Evil has become a topic for exploration, journalistic and scientific, and that as I've travelled and popped into bookstores and libraries around the US, I've learned that *The Road Less Travelled* is still being purchased (in small numbers) and borrowed (yes, quite regularly). By asking individuals, I found out *The Road* is still being read for the first time; by a couple who run the local gym; a care-giver going through a bitter divorce. Still being quoted, a columnist in the local weekly wrote not long ago, '"Life is difficult" has become part of the national DNA.' As for evil, Mo Hayder's *The Devil of Nanking* is a 2005 novel that explores the nature of evil, with the principal character agonising over whether ignorance is or is not evil. Psychologist Sue Grand's 2000 *The Reproduction of Evil*, John Conroy's 2001 *Unspeakable Acts, Ordinary People*, all add to that still murmured discussion about evil, individual and by a group.

In June 2002, fifteen months before there was any discussion of a Peck biography, Scotty and I were chatting on the telephone about books. Towards the end of that 2002 conversation, Peck asked if I could confirm for him the given name and birth date of the Rev. Malachi Martin. I said I could, and did so through a friend, Desmond Fisher, in Ireland. Many months later, when this biography was under way, Peck said he was dedicating *Glimpses of the Devil* to Martin. I told him he'd fallen for Martin as a father figure. When *Glimpses* appeared, Peck answered that 'father figure' charge in the book itself, then doubled the thrust by including me in the acknowledgements. I told him he doth protest too much.

It was the first of his thrusts and my parries. The paradoxical M. Scott Peck both did and did not want a biography written about him, and both did and did not want me to write it. He tried hard, unsuccessfully, to make it a collaborative effort. We had several serious areas of disagreement, and he never actually ceased trying to influence how I'd say what I might say. He was mightily offended, his pride wounded, by my reaction to his 2003 CD that featured his song *Free Will.* He asked my opinion. I said it wasn't the sort of music I listened to, but it sounded like a cross between 'stained-glass blue grass and Tom Lehrer'. (Lehrer, a Harvard mathematics professor, gained musical prominence in the 1960s for songs with lyrics of amusing irony, such as *Poisoning Pigeons in the Park.*) When exasperated with me, Peck would occasionally resurface his discontent. I was guilty of *lèse majesté.*

During our hours of interviews we were generally cordial conversationalists; he was sometimes delighted with the questions, even if they were tough, yet on occasion would chide, goad, and say the question indicated I failed to understand him. I would always reply that such was the risk of cooperating with a biographer. As he did with most people he met, Peck felt he had something to teach me. I made it clear I had no wish to become the student. I remained a detached observer and listener, and resisted his blandishments – and occasional barrage of lengthy letters – to be more than that. He only rarely bristled or brooded during our hours of conversations.

It was when I'd suggest that in his admission of infidelities or admission of failure as a father he showed little evidence of remorse that he truly went on the defensive. Later, on the telephone and in person, he would periodically return to that observation and attempt to develop his comments further, usually more in self-exculpation than explanation. Knowing his life was not unblemished, he'd remark one doesn't have to be a saint to be a prophet.

Finally, he felt I had thoroughly misunderstood his relationship with God and his role as a Christian prophet and pilgrim. And in that long, nasty letter he let it all pour out. It hadn't been the first time.

But let him speak for himself in excerpts from a small selection of his letters and emails to me. About the book (29 September 2003): 'I am excited and intrigued about your suggestions of writing my biography. I recognise that you are talking about something other than a fully authorised biography but do not consider this to be a barrier to our continuing to work together, although before becoming totally committed I would like to have more discussions with you as to precisely what an unauthorised biography might mean.' (I told him it meant he would not see any drafts or the final manuscript prior to publication.) 'Hot dog! It looks as if it's going to be a go, and I'm as excited as a child [2 October 2003]. You are inked into my calendar for 18–19 December. I had fantasised the possibility that one of my children would approach you in a desire to be heard. Should that happen with any of my children, it is their responsibility and not yours. Not seeing your early or final drafts doesn't bother me because I think I will have an idea of the tone of book for the reasons you state.

'I can't find it at the moment but I recall you saying something about me being compelled to talk about God. There is great truth to that and considerable untruth. I do tend to talk about God a great deal for a number of reasons of which the greatest is that, as I ended my poem, God is the name of the game. However, I suspect that when we are together you may be surprised by how little I talk about God.' He'd earlier said, 'In order to do justice to your subject in writing about me you may well have to write about God on a deeper and more self-involved level than any biographer has ever to my knowledge done before.'

He did not like my noting, early on in our conversations, that he was always talking about his father, and said I was using it as a journalist's 'hook' for the book – 'I do talk an extraordinary amount about my father but that doesn't mean I have a neurosis about him.'

'I expect/imagine/suspect there will be plenty of ambiguity [23 December 2003]. I believe I told you I had consulted about our relationship with one of those younger men to whom I used to be a mentor, and he told me I had to grapple with you over Tom Lehrer etc. Well, about two to three days ago he wrote: "I have no doubt you will satisfy your need to communicate your experience. Arthur will follow you into the domain of God's communication with you. I suppose if you expect everyone to understand that God has a personal relationship with him or her, you will be hesitant or perhaps confusing. But there will be those who understand that the Divine longs for conversation with us all. I think it is up to the reader to decide if you have been crazy or blessed. I think that is the Way of all spiritual writing." Sounds right to me. What think thou? I sure hope you don't find my words meddling. They are largely meant to be supportive of what you wrote.'

On this occasion, I replied in kind (23 December 2003). 'Nor do I find your words meddling. I'm too strong a character and too long a writer. If you weren't an equally strong character I wouldn't be interested in doing a book on you. We both know going in that this will never be the book you would have written about yourself – for we've both been written about enough to know that. But if it's a ripping good tale about one man's life on the God quest, the joys and sorrow and mistakes, the attempts to bring God into the life of others, it'll do nicely, thank you. If the readers identify their life experience in elements of your life, or in the holes in your life; if they see God in their lives through God in your life, I suspect the project will have succeeded despite us both.'

He wrote (7 January 2004), 'I am busy at the moment [he was courting Kathy by phone and working on *Glimpses*] but will begin contemplating the answers to your questions about what my conscious was in regards to the seventies and eighties. [He spoke a lot about the sixties.] I am starting to feel uneasy again that we have so quickly drifted away from my personal experiences of God intervening in my life and will want to talk with you when we call about how to best deal with my unease.'

'Reflecting on our talk yesterday [3 February 2004] about me not taking time off to be a good father, etc. I was being a bit one-sided. I am a responsibilityholic. Throw some responsibility out in the middle of a group and I'm likely to dive for it while others sit there. This also means that I tend to take on lots of guilt that I probably shouldn't.'

'I am an evangelist for many things [3 March 2004] including Jesus and Christianity. But above all else, although distinctly related

to the two, I believe I am an evangelist for (or is it of?) 1. the Truth
and 2. the concept of life as a pilgrimage. In that order. Can you
believe such brevity and conciseness?'

'Sorry to have dumped on you the way I did last evening [15
August 2004]. Most of it you didn't deserve (I hope). That was
twenty-five-plus pent-up years of resentment. The question for my
therapy and perhaps for the book is why I haven't done it before.
But I'm grateful to you because I had to start with someone
somewhere. It is a compliment to you that you apparently felt safe
to me. What popped me off was my awareness of how defensive I
felt after our Friday afternoon session, how old that defensiveness
was and how inappropriate it was. Ergo, high time I went on the
offence. It was not a polished offensive and I apologise to you for
that. I guess that my biography strikes me as a matter of such
consequence because it seems to me a potential opportunity to offer
the public a glimpse of the hand of God at work.'

'But either you or the biography process do disconcert me [24
April 2005]. Am I trying to write YOUR biography of me? In this
instance, yes. But it is not that I want you to depict me as saintly.'
Peck wanted this to be a book about Christianity as he saw it. I
wanted it to be a book about Peck as I, through others – and his own
words – saw him.

He continued that he regularly failed to be on his guard when
dealing with the media, and referred to the visit of Andrew Billen of
The Times of London. 'I determined that when the reporter arrived I
would ask him why *The Times* was the least bit interested in my new
book (*Glimpses of the Devil*) or in a piece about me, and would
enquire whether he was freelancing it and whether the story was his
own proposal and why. Yet all this utterly slips my mind when he
arrives – even after he informs me he is an atheist. Instead I just
blab on as if he were my best friend. What an asshole I am! I can't
even blame the forgetfulness of Parkinson's since I've been guilty of
this rather stupid "innocence" many times in years long past.

'In writing to Carl [Brandt Junior] you described yourself as
writing my "unauthorised biography, albeit with my cooperation
thus far." I appreciated the accuracy of that designation.' [Brandt, of
Brandt and Brandt literary agency in New York, was Peck's Exeter
school peer, the literary agent who sold the manuscript of what
became *The Road Less Travelled*. I'd written to Carl Brandt requesting
an interview. Nothing came of the request.] Continued Peck, 'But let

me use this as an opportunity, before it is too late, to suggest once again that we (yes, we) could write the biography "out of community". When I first proposed this I don't think I explained it adequately.' [His fresh explanation altered nothing.]

Finally the 'long, nasty letter', a missive of almost 4,000 words that arrived in three batches. Main points included his dismay about my Tom Lehrer remark, and my question regarding some of his liaisons. It was also his strongest plea for a collaborative biography. He indirectly accused me of having an adversarial attitude towards him, of asking others about his marriage, and intending a book that tended towards sensationalism. He repeated an earlier charge that three people I'd interviewed 'opined that you "were certainly doing me no favour", that the book "would not be a complimentary one", or that you "did not comprehend what I was about". They advised I should stay clear of you. I have not taken their advice because I like you and sort of trust you. Yet there are reasons I cannot discount their advice. In particular there have been a number of occasions when we have been totally out of synch.

'Far more relevant has been what seems to be an extraordinary blind spot you have about the "inner life". For the average person who is not given to self reflection I would call it an area of ignorance. For an extremely well educated writer who was long editor in chief of an influential Roman Catholic magazine to seemingly not know what a contemplative is or a mystic and then to seemingly have no understanding of the Holy Spirit, one is virtually compelled to diagnose not a tiny blind spot but a gigantic one.' [When I reminded him of his high praise, in writing, for, *Facing Fear with Faith*, which I'd co-written with Dolores Leckey, a volume not short of mystics, contemplatives and poets, he remembered and apologised. He wrote, poignantly (8 July 2004), 'I'm sorry my memory was so faint about *Facing Fear with Faith*. I hope you will understand that I not only have great trouble reading but am still overloaded and rapidly lose track of everything here. I hope to God by the end of this month I will have crashed through the tapes of the finish line and into retirement. I'm not sure whether it's been a mad hundred-yard dash or a marathon. I thought what you read to me about my being non-denominational was understanding and an elegant apologia and clear explanation of the dimensions of my ever enlarging faith. I wonder if it would be interesting for us to talk about why I talk so much?'

I did not pry into his married life. Any comments on it essentially arise voluntarily from others in the three closing chapters. I did early on ask many interviewees about their impression of Lily, for they would be my only guide to her character. Even at the memorial service, when I introduced myself to Lily and two of their children for the first time, I assured them I was simply letting them know who I was and was not asking for an interview. Whenever I was in Peck's home, he and whoever was present knew, because I made it clear each time I entered, that anything I heard in casual conversation was not part of the book, that if I wanted information I'd formally ask with a tape recorder running.

One of his Peck's written communications of length was a list of his 'significant contributions'. It is a list significant because once more it illustrates, even just weeks before his death, how acute his mental faculties remained when he was focused. It is a valuable summary, severely edited to present it here:

- *The Road Less Travelled* did, I believe, break dramatically with traditional, Freudian-oriented psychiatric thought in that I proposed that most psychological disorders are disorders of consciousness of the conscious mind, not the unconscious.
- I have repeatedly taught that most psychological disorders are 'thinking disorders'. For example, narcissists are people who cannot think about others; obsessive/compulsives have great difficulty in thinking about the big picture; passive dependent people cannot think for themselves, etc.
- Until I wrote 'The Healthiness of Depression' (in *The Road*), depression was thought of solely as a bad thing and was not seen as a somewhat graceful signal of there being something wrong which we needed to work on. Indeed, I believe there is evidence for a depression centre in the brain, depression serves a life-saving function just as anger does.
- I am the first to have been explicit about ways in which I actually used religious concepts in the course of psycho-therapy (*The Road* and other books).
- I believe I was the first to suggest that Evil should be considered a disease and should have a specific place in the diagnostic manual of psychiatrists.
- I do not know if there has been any other sociological analysis of group evil other than *Little Brown Brother*, written

a century ago about the Philippine-American War, but I think my sociological analysis of My Lai, if not totally original, is generally considered to be the best such analysis around.

- For generations we have been locked into 'nature vs nuture'. No-one else has suggested it is more complicated, that it is obviously 'nurture and nature and God'.
- Although fiction writers offer innumerable examples of the death of romantic love in human relationships, to my knowledge I was the first psychiatrist ever to specify it was a norm.
- I am struck by what a seminal work *The Road Less Travelled* was.

He prepared his list to impress on me the range of his achievements. In so doing, he finally acknowledged the brilliance of his first book. He'd avoided acknowledging its full worth because he resented the fact more attention had not been paid to many of his subsequent books. At last he was at peace with what he'd accomplished in *The Road*.

Then came my final visit, to read the Introduction and two chapters to him. He was physically brave. He'd said he would hold off the morphine derivatives in order to be at his most clear-headed when I read to him and asked him questions. He insisted, for part of the first day, and with extreme physical difficulty, on leaving his bed, being wheelchaired to the electric stairs, and, once downstairs, being interviewed in the sunroom as before. He could not sustain that for long and instead was assisted to a day bed.

I read him the Introduction. He listened, commented, asked questions for clarification, or would have me repeat a sentence. He occasionally made a demurring sound, at times expressed approval. That done, and to get the worst over first – most of my first questions were factual checks from earlier conversations – I asked him about his children coming to see him at the clinic. His defensive answers were indicative of the pain he felt at having alienated them all. Later, upstairs, after reading him a chapter, he again had comments and questions. We had a brisk discussion. It changed nothing.

Peck lay there, propped up on his bank of pillows in the sunlit room, tubes keeping him in bodily balance, nurses occasionally coming in and out, Kathy and others occasionally stopping by to listen to parts of the reading. I asked him, given all that he had written about death, given his advice to Christians to accept they still would be afraid, and given his own reliance on God, what was it like, now, facing death. He replied, 'It's like waiting for the postman [he didn't say "mailman"].' I said, 'That's it? That's all you feel?' And he said, 'Yes, waiting for the postman to come.'

The following morning I read him a chapter replete with many comments about him from FCE colleagues and friends. At times others were in the room, listening, other times not. He was alert, would stop me, make a comment, ask a question. Once the reading was done, I had a couple of questions. We were alone when I went around to his left side and took his hand. As on my arrival, I prayed aloud, softly. He closed his eyes.

> We bow our heads
> In the eye of the God who created us
> In the eye of the Son who purchased us
> In the eye of the Spirit who cleansed us
> In friendship and affection.
> Through Thine own anointed one, O God,
> Bestow upon us fullness in our need
> Love toward God
> The affection of God
> The smile of God
> The wisdom of God
> The grace of God
> The fear of God
> And the will of God
> To do on the world of the Three
> As the angels and saints do in Heaven;
> Each shade and light,
> Each day and night,
> Each time in kindness,
> Give Thou us Thy Spirit.

I squeezed his hand, said, 'Goodbye, Scotty, God bless.' He kept his eyes squeezed tightly closed; applied pressure to my hand, said nothing. I left.

FURTHER READING

Books by M. Scott Peck, MD

The Road Less Traveled: a New Psychology of Love, Traditional Values and Spiritual Growth (Simon & Schuster, New York, 1978)

People of the Lie: the Hope for Healing Human Evil (Simon & Schuster, New York, 1983)

What Return Can I Make: Dimensions of the Christian Experience (Simon & Schuster, New York, 1985), with Carmelite Sister Marilyn von Waldner's music and Patricia Kay's artwork. Reissued in 1999 as *Gifts for the Journey.*

The Different Drum: Community-Making and Peace (Simon & Schuster, New York, 1987)

A Bed by the Window: A Novel of Mystery and Redemption (Bantam Books, New York, 1990)

The Friendly Snowflake: a Fable of Love, Faith and Family (Turner Publishing, Nashville, Tennessee, 1992)

Further Along the Road Less Travel: the Unending Journey Toward Spiritual Growth (Touchstone, Simon & Schuster, New York, 1993)

Meditations from the Road (Simon & Schuster, New York, 1993)

A World Waiting to Be Born: Civility Rediscovered (Doubleday, New York, 1993)

In Search of Stones: A Pilgrimage of Faith, Reason, and Discovery (Hyperion, New York, 1995)

In Heaven as on Earth: a Vision of the Afterlife (Hyperion, New York, 1996)

Denial of the Soul: Spiritual and Medical Perspectives on Euthanasia and Mortality (Harmony Books, New York, 1997)

The Road Less Traveled and Beyond: Spiritual Growth in an Age of Anxiety (Simon & Schuster, New York, 1997)

Golf and the Spirit: Lessons for the Journey (Three Rivers Press, New York, 1999)

Glimpses of the Devil: a Psychiatrist's Personal Accounts of Possession, Exorcism and Redemption (Free Press, Simon & Schuster, New York, 2005)

Additional Suggestions

Behanna, Gertrude (aka 'Elizabeth Burns'), *The Late Liz: the Autobiography of an Ex-Pagan* (Hawthorne Books, New York, 1957)

Banks, Coleman (trans.), *The Essential Rumi* (Castle Books, Edison, N.J., 1995)

Kaminer, Wendy, *I'm Dysfunctional, You're Dysfunctional: the Recovery Movement and Other Self-Help Fashions* (Addison-Wesley, New York, 1992)

Lisagore, Nancy and Frank Lipsius, *A Law Unto Itself: the Untold Story of the Law Firm Sullivan & Cromwell* (William Morrow, New York, 1988)

Manchester, William, *The Arms of Krupp: 1587-1968* (Little Brown, New York, 1968)

Marquand, John P., *The Late George Apley*, (Groset and Dunlap, New York, 1937)

INDEX

ABOUT THE AUTHOR

British-born author and journalist Arthur Jones was educated at Ruskin College, Oxford and has reported from more than 30 different countries in his career. He has served as an international correspondent for the *Financial Times* and worked as a broadcaster for Irish and Australian radio. He was editor of the *National Catholic Reporter* and a former New York associate editor and European bureau chief of *Forbes* magazine. The author of 10 books, Arthur Jones is married and lives in My Lady's Manor ('Lord Baltmore's Guifte, 1713'), Maryland.